# The Housing Grants, Construction and Regeneration Act 1996

AUSTRALIA
LBC Information Services
Brisbane ● Sydney ● Melbourne ● Perth


CANADA
Carswell
Ottawa ● Toronto ● Calgary ● Montreal ● Vancouver


AGENTS:
Steimatzky's Agency Ltd., Tel Aviv;
N. M. Tripathi (Private) Ltd., Bombay;
Eastern Law House (Private) Ltd., Calcutta;
M.P.P. House, Bangalore;
Universal Book Traders, Delhi;
Aditya Books, Delhi;
MacMillan Shuppan KK, Tokyo;
Pakistan Law House, Karachi

# The Housing Grants, Construction and Regeneration Act 1996

with annotations by

## Andrew Arden Q.C.
(LL.B)

and

## Caroline Hunter
(B.A., Barrister, Lecturer in Law, University of Nottingham)

with specialist contributions from

## Charles Gardner
(Partner at Reynolds Porter Chamberlain)

and

## Rudi Klein
(Specialist Engineering Contractors' Group).

LONDON
SWEET & MAXWELL
1996

Published in 1996 by
Sweet & Maxwell Limited of
100 Avenue Road
London NW3 3PF
Typeset by MFK Information Services Ltd,
Hitchin, Herts
Printed and bound in Great Britain by
Butler & Tanner Ltd, Frome and London

A CIP catalogue record for this book is available
from The British Library

ISBN 0–421–58480 7

# CONTENTS

# Preface to 1996 Housing Acts

Since 1979, housing law has undergone a revolution. The principal changes were, first, the introduction of security of tenure, right to buy and other "tenants' charter" provisions of the Housing Act 1980, as extended by the Housing and Building Control Act 1984, and secondly the substitution of assured protection for Rent Act protection in the private sector by the Housing Act 1988, and—in the same Act—the transfer to assured protection from secure for the tenants of registered housing associations, as well as measures for transferring stock from public to private ownership.

Other changes included the introduction of a new housing subsidy system in the 1980 Act, replaced by the Local Government and Housing Act 1989 at the same time as the introduction of the ring-fenced Housing Revenue Account (itself backed by new local government capital finance controls of general application), the "shorthold" concept in the private sector, initially as an exemption from Rent Act protection (1980) Act, subsequently from assured protection (1989 Act), and the growth of rights for long leaseholders (Landlord and Tenant Act 1987, Leasehold Reform, Housing and Urban Renewal Act 1993). Along the way, in 1985 the Housing Acts were consolidated, housing association funding was re-shaped by the 1988 Act, and grant aid for unfit and unsatisfactory housing—as it had evolved between 1964 and 1974—was reformed by the 1989 Act.

The two 1996 Acts touch most of these—and a number of other—areas. In broad outline, Pt. I of the Housing Act 1996 re-casts the so-called "quasi-public sector" from (principally) registered housing associations into a body of registered social landlords (designed to encourage local housing companies, but including existing registered associations). Part II strengthens the existing law on Houses in Multiple Occupation. Part III governs the private sector: its Chaps. I and III extend the rights of long leaseholders, by reference back to both the 1987 and the 1993 Acts (and to the Leasehold Reform Act 1967); Chap. II changes the emphasis of assured protection to make shortholds the presumptive norm (which accords with practice in the fully private sector, but alters it where landlords are registered associated). Part IV is concerned with housing benefit (and is of minor effect).

Part V represents a new direction in public housing, under the general heading of "Conduct of Tenants". Chapter I creates the "introductory" (originally, probationary) tenancy, as an adoptive exemption from full security, and is not dissimilar in kind from shorthold in that it permits the recovery of possession without any need for specific grounds. Chapter II extensively broadens the traditional "nuisance and annoyance" ground so as to include activity on and around estates and to make it easier to use, and introduces a new ground to enable possession to be recovered when one partner has left the home on account of the violence of the other. (Analogous changes are made to assured protection.) Chapter III facilitates injunctive relief, also designed to tackle anti-social behaviour on and around public sector estates.

Parts VI and VII should be read together. Part VI introduces a national allocation regime, designed (a) to eliminate access to public housing by categories of immigrant, and (b) to prevent the dominance of allocation to the homeless. Part VII restates the law of homelessness, with a number of changes, including (i) the exclusion of categories of immigrant, and (ii) the reduction of rights from the allocation of a permanent (or indefinite) home to accommodation which will be of limited duration (pending allocation under Pt. VI. Ironically, intervening case-law means that this may have served to have increased rather than, as intended, to have reduced the rights of the homeless).

Part I of the Housing Grants, Construction and Regeneration Act 1996 is designed to eliminate—in all but a small, residual category—entitlement to mandatory grant-aid; in addition, it introduces the "deferred action notice" to slow down the use of the unfitness and disrepair provisions of the Housing Act 1985. Part II comprises a statutory re-writing of construction law; Pt. III introduces the Architects' Registration Council in place of a number of boards and committees under the Architects (Registration) Act 1931; and, Pt. IV puts on a statutory basis the Single Regeneration Budget, which in recent years had come to replace such schemes as Estate Action and City Challenge. It also provides for relocation grants which may become available where clearance area action is taken under the Housing Act 1985.

Because the changes contained in these two Acts reflect such a wide range of housing policies, each Part has its own—in some cases extensive—Introduction (though both sets of annotations share this Preface). The above is a cursory identification of principal issues; readers' attention is invited to the individual Part Introductions for more (and more accurate) detail. We would like to take this opportunity, however, to express our thanks to a number of people who have helped, directly or indirectly, in the preparation of these annotations.

Our colleagues at Arden Chambers have commonly found themselves dragged into impromptu debate on the meaning of one or another clause (unusually at an extremely inconvenient time) and, in particular, Christopher Baker and Jonathan Manning made substantive contributions in relation to Pt. VII of the Housing Act. The Current Law team at Sweet & Maxwell provided swift and efficient support. We could not produce material (especially of such bulk) and keep abreast of the (large number of) changes as the Bills passed through Parliament, without the technical aid with which Sweet & Maxwell provides us over the range of our publications for them (including the Housing Encyclopedia and the Housing Law Reports).

Finally, we pay tribute to Emma (aged 4), and Thomas (aged 7) and Sophie (aged 4), who could probably have made more sense of the material than we have done and to whom it—and much else—is dedicated.

The law was stated as at July 31, 1996, although it was possible to add some subsequent cases, and we have scheduled at p. xxv the commencement orders which were available by proof-stage.

Andrew Arden Q.C.                        Caroline Hunter
Arden Chambers,                          Nottingham University
59 Fleet Street,                         and
London, EC4Y 1JU.                        Arden Chambers.

September 30, 1996.

# TABLE OF CASES

References are to the Introduction or the General Note to the specified section, Part or Schedule.

# Table of Cases

# Table of Cases

# Table of Cases

# Table of Cases

## Table of Cases

# TABLE OF STATUTES

**References are to the Introduction or the General Note to the specified section, Part or Schedule.**

# Table of Statutes

# TABLE OF STATUTORY INSTRUMENTS

**References are to the Introduction of the General Note to the specified section, Part or Schedule.**

# TABLE OF SECTIONS IN FORCE

**The following provisions of the Housing Grants, Construction and Regeneration Act 1996 have been brought into force by commencement orders up to and including S.I. 1996 No. 2352 (C.61) or by sections of the Act:**

| Provision | Date of Commencement | S.I. |
|---|---|---|
| ss.2, 3 (partially) | 11.09.96 | 1996 No. 2352 |
| s.7 (partially) | 11.09.96 | 1996 No. 2352 |
| s.12 (partially) | 11.09.96 | 1996 No. 2352 |
| s.17 (partially) | 11.09.96 | 1996 No. 2352 |
| s.19 (partially) | 11.09.96 | 1996 No. 2352 |
| s.25 (partially) | 11.09.96 | 1996 No. 2352 |
| s.27 (partially) | 11.09.96 | 1996 No. 2352 |
| s.30 (partially) | 11.09.96 | 1996 No. 2352 |
| s.33 (partially) | 11.09.96 | 1996 No. 2352 |
| ss.44–47 (partially) | 11.09.96 | 1996 No. 2352 |
| ss.51, 52 (partially) | 11.09.96 | 1996 No. 2352 |
| s.61 (partially) | 11.09.96 | 1996 No. 2352 |
| ss.63, 64 (partially) | 11.09.96 | 1996 No. 2352 |
| ss.67, 68 (partially) | 11.09.96 | 1996 No. 2352 |
| s.74 | 11.09.96 | 1996 No. 2352 |
| s.76 (partially) | 11.09.96 | 1996 No. 2352 |
| s.79 | 11.09.96 | 1996 No. 2352 |
| s.85 (partially) | 11.09.96 | 1996 No. 2352 |
| s.86 | 11.09.96 | 1996 No. 2352 |
| s.87 (partially) | 11.09.96 | 1996 No. 2352 |
| s.89 | 11.09.96 | 1996 No. 2352 |
| s.92 (partially) | 11.09.96 | 1996 No. 2352 |
| s.94 | 11.09.96 | 1996 No. 2352 |
| ss.101, 102 (partially) | 11.09.96 | 1996 No. 2352 |
| ss.104–106 (partially) | 11.09.96 | 1996 No. 2352 |
| s.108 (partially) | 11.09.96 | 1996 No. 2352 |
| s.114 (partially) | 11.09.96 | 1996 No. 2352 |
| s.125 (partially) | 01.10.96 | 1996 No. 2352 |
| ss.126–130 | 24.09.96 | s.150(2) |
| ss.131–135 (partially) | 11.09.96 | 1996 No. 2352 |
| ss.139, 140 (partially) | 11.09.96 | 1996 No. 2352 |
| s.141 | 24.09.96 | s.150(2) |
| s.142 | 24.09.96 | s.150(2) |
| ss.143–145 | 24.09.96 | s.150(2) |
| s.146 | 24.07.96 | s.150(1) |
| s.147 (partially) | 24.09.96 | s.150(2) |
| ss.148–151 | 24.07.96 | s.150(1) |
| Pt. III of Sched. 3 | 24.09.96 | s.150(2) |

# HOUSING GRANTS, CONSTRUCTION AND REGENERATION ACT 1996*

(1996 c. 53)

ARRANGEMENT OF SECTIONS

PART I

GRANTS, &C. FOR RENEWAL OF PRIVATE SECTOR HOUSING

CHAPTER I

THE MAIN GRANTS

---

*Annotations by Andrew Arden Q.C., LL.B., Caroline Hunter, B.A., Barrister, Lecturer in Law, University of Nottingham, Charles Gardner, Partner at Reynolds Porter Chamberlain, Rudi Klein of the Specialist Engineering Contractors' Group.

### Chapter II

#### Group repair schemes

PART III

ARCHITECTS

*The Architects Registration Board*

PART IV

GRANTS &C. FOR REGENERATION, DEVELOPMENT AND RELOCATION

*Financial assistance for regeneration and development*

PART V

MISCELLANEOUS AND GENERAL PROVISIONS

*Miscellaneous provisions*

An Act to make provision for grants and other assistance for housing purposes and about action in relation to unfit housing; to amend the law relating to construction contracts and architects; to provide grants and other assistance for regeneration and development and in connection with clearance areas; to amend the provisions relating to home energy efficiency schemes; to make provision in connection with the dissolution of urban development corporations, housing action trusts and the Commission for the New Towns; and for connected purposes.                [24th July 1996]

PARLIAMENTARY DEBATES
   *Hansard*, H.L. Vol. 568, col. 1558; Vol. 569, cols. 976, 1004, 1459; Vol. 570, cols. 1576, 1650, 1836, 1905; Vol. 571, cols. 11, 37, 87, 795, 856, 901, 971, 1419; Vol. 574, col. 1316. H.C. Vol. 277, col. 45; Vol. 281, col. 21.

INTRODUCTION
   This Act makes provision, *inter alia*, with regard to grants for renewal of private sector housing, including group repair schemes and home repair assistance and deferred action notices. The Act also makes provision as regards construction contracts, entitling a party to such a contract to payment by instalments, stage payments or other periodic payments for any work under the contract, except in certain circumstances. The Act also amends the law relating to architects.

## PART I

### GRANTS, &C. FOR RENEWAL OF PRIVATE SECTOR HOUSING

INTRODUCTION AND GENERAL NOTE
   The principal purpose of this Part is to downgrade grant assistance for housing which is unfit or otherwise in need of works, from mandatory (so far as it has been such) to discretionary aid. Mandatory grants for property falling below a defined standard of acceptability have been available since the House Purchase and Housing Act 1959 (c. 33); the principal structure of grant-aid as it has been known over recent years was introduced by the Housing Act 1974 (c. 44), subsequently consolidated into the Housing Act 1985 (c. 68), and then replaced by Pt. VIII of the Local Government and Housing Act 1989 (c. 42), the latter of which introduced "means-testing". Under that Act, grants for works to prevent or remedy unfitness for human habitation or serious disrepair, were—broadly—mandatory. Under this Act, the only mandatory grants will be "disabled facilities grants" (see s.24).
   The problem is one of money. *The Future of Private Housing Renewal Programmes, A Consultation Document* issued by the D.O.E. in June 1993, foreshadowed the change: "For 1994/95 onwards, expenditure is projected to grow above planned provision ... It is clear that this will

give rise to unsustainable financial pressure ... The domination of mandatory grants has contributed to a number of unintended consequences. It has become increasingly difficult for authorities to act strategically and, where appropriate, on an area basis ... The current system of mandatory grants, requiring authorities to deal with valid applications within 6 months, tends to encourage pepper-potting of assistance whether or not this is the most appropriate course. The build up of financial pressures exacerbates this effect" (paras. 3.3, 3.4).

The White Paper, *Our Future Homes*, June 1995, Cm. 2901, which preceded both this Act and its sister legislation, the Housing Act 1996 (c. 52), considered grant-aid in its Chapter Two, on Promoting Sustainable Home Ownership. Describing us as a "nation of home improvers", it states that since 1990, almost 350,000 house renovation, disabled facilities and minor works assistance grants had been given, totalling more than £1 billion (p.16). None the less, "Further change is needed. Some authorities have been unable to meet the demand for mandatory renovation grants and disabled facilities grants within their available budgets. The case for help to private owners needs to be considered alongside other local housing priorities ... The present grant provisions give local authorities little scope for making the best use of resources. In many areas a strategic approach—which aims at the renewal of a whole area or which focuses on special problems—is likely to be more cost-effective than meeting individual needs as they arise" (p.17).

Accordingly, renovation grants for owner occupied property would become discretionary, while assistance for landlords—which would likewise only be discretionary—would be confined to renewal areas (under the Local Government and Housing Act 1989). This was developed in the linked Explanatory Paper, *The Future of Private Housing Renewal Programmes*, June 1995: "Although only a small minority of privately owned homes are both unfit and owned by people who cannot afford essential repairs, the problem can only be tackled over a period of years. Both cost and logistics preclude the immediate repair of all unfit houses" (para. 2.2). "... The present right to mandatory renovation grants has created unrealistic expectations. The demand for grants has greatly exceeded the resources available for the purpose at a time of general expenditure constraint..." (para. 2.3, or "the lion's share of resources", *per* Minister of State, Department of the Environment (Earl Ferrers), *Hansard* (H.L.), Second Reading, February 20, 1996, col. 981). In substance, the future is to lie with strategic activity, developed in authorities' Housing Investment Programmes (para. 2.5).

Landlords were to meet costs as an overhead of the business, although discretionary grants in renewal areas were to be available so as not to frustrate local authority policies (para. 3.2): these additional restrictions have not, however, (yet) moved forward into legislation (see *Hansard* (H.L.), Second Reading, February 20, 1996, col. 981, and see the reserve power in s.31, below). All grants were still to be means-tested or otherwise to have regard to applicants' resources (para. 3.3). Transitional provisions would preserve the right to mandatory grants under the 1989 Act which were not decided before commencement of this Part: see now s.102, below. The Explanatory Paper added:

"Local authorities will need to consider the implications of the changes to those who have made enquiries about the availability of grant but have not submitted formal applications. In particular authorities will wish to consider what steps they should take to ensure that those enquirers having a reasonable expectation of a mandatory grant are fully aware of the proposal" (para. 3.6).

This last conceals direct reference to one of the means to which authorities without sufficient resources were obliged to resort, waiting lists for application forms. Once an application under the 1989 Act was made, it had to be determined within six months; many authorities, however, were reported to have maintained a waiting-list for application forms, to prevent time beginning to run. (This attracted particular attention in Birmingham during 1995, but that authority was far from the only authority to rely on patience, and/or ignorance, in order to meet what the government had come to accept was a burden that authorities simply could not meet. The legality of maintaining waiting lists was never tested in court, perhaps reflecting a growing awareness of their dubious standing and a preference for quiet concession over dramatic defeat.)

Local authorities also exercise functions in relation to unfitness under the Housing Act 1985 (c. 68), which requires them to take one of three courses of action in relation to a property that is unfit for human habitation as defined in s.604 of that Act (as amended by the 1989 Act): to require it to be repaired, or to close it to human habitation, or to cause it to be demolished. Where repairs were required, an owner could seek a mandatory grant:

"With the abolition of mandatory grants ... [l]ocal authorities will ... be given an additional 'deferred action' option under which they may decide that, while there is unfitness that requires repair, dealing with it is not essential or does not have priority. ... The authority will also be required to review its decision after 12 months" (para. 6.2; see now Chapter IV, below).

One other aspect of grant-aid to which attention has been paid and may be drawn is the changes designed to "reduce the opportunities for abuse. Grant is primarily intended to help people remain in their own homes. To further this objective only people who have both owned and lived in a property for three years will normally qualify for grant" (paras. 8.1, 8.2), although this would not apply in renewal areas, or for disabled facilities grants, or the home repairs grants introduced by Chap. III, below (but which are expected to be confined to an amount of £2,000 in any one year, and £4,000 in any three year period: see para. 5.3, and s.36, below). The claw-back provisions have likewise been tightened to prevent "windfall gain from grant assistance" (para. 8.3), and to encourage enforcement local authorities will have to repay subsidy to the D.O.E. "where grant has been or *could have been* recovered" (para. 8.4, emphasis added).

Relocation grants, designed to "help to keep local communities together by assisting people" (*Hansard* (H.L.), Second Reading, February 20, 1996, Minister of State, Department of the Environment (Earl Ferrers), col. 982, see also *The Future of Private Housing Renewal Programmes*, s.7), are governed by Pt. IV of this Act.

The length of this Act, and in particular of this Part (*cf.* the 1989 Act, Pt. VIII, which was only 38 sections long) reflects what appears to be a new approach to drafting legislation, with two key aspects: first, provisions are generally broken down into smaller, more digestible sections; secondly, "because it has been drafted largely to include and to restate previous legislation rather than simply to amend it. It therefore avoids the maddening consequence of having to read the Bill and having constantly to refer in cross-reference to existing statutes" (*Hansard* (H.L.), Second Reading, February 20, 1996, col. 977, Minister of State, Department of the Environment (Earl Ferrers)).

**Note**

Although, therefore there is much that is familiar, if not identical, to earlier grant law, and although as such it is certain that some if not many of the earlier subordinate instruments filling out much of the detail of how this Part will operate in practice will be restated under this Part, the temptation to use such materials—and guidance under the previous law—in explanation or elaboration of this Part has been resisted, as (until the new details are available) these notes will quickly be not merely out of date in that respect but actively tend to mislead (and, in the *interregnum*, may subsequently prove guilty of having raised false expectations). With very few exceptions (where earlier guidance or instrument is the only practicable way to explain an otherwise elliptical statutory expression), these notes (as those in the Housing Act 1996) are accordingly confined to the policy statements or publications already available, and the statutory provisions themselves.

CHAPTER I

THE MAIN GRANTS

*Introductory*

## Grants for improvements and repairs, &c.

**1.**—(1) Grants are available from local housing authorities in accordance with this Chapter towards the cost of works required for—

    (a) the improvement or repair of dwellings, houses in multiple occupation or the common parts of buildings containing one or more flats,

    (b) the provision of dwellings or houses in multiple occupation by the conversion of a house or other building, and

    (c) the provision of facilities for disabled persons in dwellings and in the common parts of buildings containing one or more flats.

(2) A grant relating to—

    (a) the improvement or repair of a dwelling, or

    (b) the provision of dwellings by the conversion of a house or other building,

is referred to as a "renovation grant".

(3) A grant relating to the improvement or repair of the common parts of a building is referred to as a "common parts grant".

(4) A grant for the provision of facilities for a disabled person—

    (a) in a dwelling, or

    (b) in the common parts of a building containing one or more flats, is referred to as a "disabled facilities grant".

(5) A grant for—
(a)  the improvement or repair of a house in multiple occupation, or
(b)  the provision of a house in multiple occupation by the conversion of a house or other building,

is referred to as an "HMO grant".

(6) In the following provisions of this Chapter the expression "grant", without more, means any of these types of grant.

DEFINITIONS
"common parts": s.58.
"disabled persons": s.100.
"dwelling": s.101.
"flat": s.58.
"house in multiple occupation": s.101.
"improvement": s.101.
"local housing authority": s.101.

GENERAL NOTE
This Part introduces a new system of grant-aid for private housing to replace that contained in the Local Government and Housing Act 1989, Pt. VIII. Applications under the 1989 Act not approved before this Part comes into force are governed by s.102, below.

Under the Housing Act 1985, Pt. XV, which was replaced by the 1989 Act, Pt. VIII, there were five main grants: the *improvement* grant, for the conversion of premises into dwellings, or for "major" works of improvement; the *intermediate* grant for the improvement of dwellings lacking standard amenities; the *repairs* grant, for works of repair or replacement not associated with conversion, major improvement or the provision of standard amenities; the *special* grant for works to a house in multiple occupation; and the *common parts* grant for the repair or improvement of common parts of a building containing one or more flats.

The 1989 Act replaced these five with four new principal grants: a *renovation* grant for the improvement or repair of a dwelling, or provision of dwellings by conversion; a *common parts* grant for the improvement or repair of the common parts of a building; a *disabled facilities* grant for the provision of facilities for a disabled person; and *HMO* grant for the improvement or repair of a house in multiple occupation ("HMO") or for the provision of an HMO by conversion. The 1989 Act, s.131, introduced what was effectively a fifth grant—for minor works, including thermal insulation, to a dwelling.

This Act retains the four principal grants available under the 1989 Act, and replaces the minor works grant with a new category of "home repair assistance" under Chap. III, below. Reduction of number of grants was not the purpose, so much as reduction in their status from mandatory to discretionary: see Introduction to Pt. I, above.

*Local housing authorities*
These are district councils, London borough councils, the Common Council of the City of London, Welsh county councils or county borough councils and the Council of the Isles of Scilly, and those unitary authorities on which housing has devolved under the Local Government Act 1992 (c. 19): see s.1 of the Housing Act 1985.

*Improvement or Repair*
Although there has been much case-law in recent years on the distinction between improvement and repair, as the expression used in this Act is inclusive of both, nothing turns on that distinction in this context. Indeed, as "improvement" includes alteration and enlargement (s.101), there is (as there long has been in this area) no room for substantive argument: on the face of it, any works that are not mere routine maintenance would qualify, even, *e.g.* major works of planned maintenance that in their own right can also be considered repairs and even improvement—*cf. R. v. Hackney L.B.C., ex p. Secretary of State for the Environment* (1989) 88 L.G.R. 96, Q.B.D.

Rather than case-law, therefore, what governs the phrase are the purposes and other provisions of the legislation (see, *e.g.* ss.4 [more than 10 years old], 12 [purposes for which grant may be given, including compliance with s.189 or s.190 of the Housing Act 1985, unfitness or disrepair notice, insulation and heating, internal arrangement, means of escape from fire], 45 [recalculation or withholding of grant because not completed to satisfaction of authority]), and the explicit directions as to work excluded from grant by the Secretary of State under s.5, and as to construction standards and otherwise required by the Secretary of State under s.12(1)(g)–(i).

*Conversion*

In *R. v. Bristol City Council, ex p. Naqvi* (1994) 26 H.L.R. 640, Q.B.D., the applicant owned a shop with a flat above. In November 1991, planning permission was granted for change of use of the ground floor from shop to residential use, and to combine it with the flat to make one dwelling. Although it was held in that case that the true nature of the scheme was one for the provision of a dwelling by conversion (see below, s.4), it was also noted that works of improvement or repair can include the conversion of some accommodation provided that the dwelling as a whole still retained its identity and that the overall nature of the proposal remained one of improvement and repair.

Although the section refers to the provision of dwelling*s* (in the plural), this means one or more dwellings: see s.12(2), below.

*Dwelling*

Dwelling is defined by s.101 as "a building or part of a building occupied or intended to be occupied as a separate dwelling, together with any yard, garden, outhouses and appurtenances belonging to it or usually enjoyed with it". The dwelling, to be "separate", must contain all the facilities for normal living activity, *e.g.* a kitchen (see, *e.g. Neale v. Del Soto* [1945] K.B. 144, C.A.; *Winters v. Dance* [1949] L.J.R. 165, C.A.), although not necessarily its own bathroom/lavatory (see, *e.g. Cole v. Harris* [1945] K.B. H.L.; *Marsh v. Cooper* [1969] 1 W.L.R. 803, C.A.). The latter could, however, be amongst the services or amenities specified by the Secretary of State under s.12(1)(h), below.

*Appurtenances.* This extended definition dates back to the Artizans' and Labourers' Dwellings Act 1868 (c. 130), and has been maintained since (see, *e.g.* Housing of the Working Classes Act 1890 (c. 70), s.29, Housing Act 1925 (c. 14), s.135, Housing Act 1936 (c. 51), s.188, Housing Act 1957 (c. 56), s.189, Housing Act 1985 (c. 68), s.56). In *Trim v. Sturminster R.D.C.* [1938] 2 K.B. 508, under the 1936 Act, 10 acres of grassland were let together with a cottage. On the question whether they were appurtenant to the cottage, it was held that the expression "appurtenances" meant only such matters as outhouses, yards and gardens, but not the land itself: how much of the land could be included in this definition depended on the facts, but would certainly be less than the whole of the 10 acres that had been thus let.

In *Clymo v. Shell-Mex & B.P.* (1963) 10 R.R.C. 85, C.A., under the Rating and Valuation Act 1925 (c. 90), it was held that open land surrounded by depot buildings was appurtenant to the buildings, on the basis that had there been a conveyance or demise the land would have passed without any need specifically to mention it. In *Methuen-Cambell v. Walters* [1979] Q.B. 525, under the Leasehold Reform Act 1967 (c. 88), it was held that land cannot ordinarily be appurtenant to land, although the ordinary and strict meaning of the word appurtenant could yield to a wider meaning if the context so requires.

In *Hansford v. Jago* [1921] 1 Ch. 322, a right of way was held to come within the word appurtenance. In *Sovmots Investments v. Secretary of State for the Environment* [1979] A.C. 144, H.L., however, it was held that appurtenances could not include rights of way and other ancillary rights not yet defined or in some cases even in existence (though specifically over-turned by the Local Government (Miscellaneous Provisions) Act 1976 (c. 57), s.13, so far as concerns compulsory purchase by local authorities). In *R. v. Lambeth L.B.C., ex p. Clayhope* at first instance ((1986) 18 H.L.R. 541), it was held that the common parts and the roof of a block of flats were not appurtenant to each and every flat (this was not considered in the Court of Appeal—above—as it did not arise in the light of the finding that the flats were not houses).

In *F.F.F. Estates v. Hackney L.B.C.* [1981] Q.B. 503, 3 H.L.R. 107, C.A., however, the court, considering the meaning of dwelling in connection with improvement notices under Pt. VII of the Housing Act 1985, said that the case-law on rights passing on a conveyance was not of "any real help".

*Common Parts*

This includes, by s.58, "the structure and exterior of the building and common facilities provided, whether in the building or elsewhere, for persons who include the occupiers of one or more dwellings in the building". The facilities do not, accordingly, have to be exclusive to occupiers of the dwellings.

The words "structure and exterior" have been held to include the partition wall between a house and the adjoining house (*Green v. Eales* (1841) 2 Q.B. 225), windows (*Quick v. Taff Ely B.C.* [1986] Q.B. 809, C.A., see also *Ball v. Plummer, The Times,* June 17, 1879, and *Boswell v. Crucible Steel Co* [1925] 1 K.B. 119, but *cf. Holiday Fellowship v. Hereford* [1959] 1 W.L.R. 221), and essential means of access to a house (*Brown v. Liverpool Corporation* [1969] 3 All E.R.

1345; 13 H.L.R. 1, C.A.), although not a back yard (*Hopwood v. Cannock Chase D.C.* [1975] 1 W.L.R. 373, 13 H.L.R. 31, C.A., and *King v. South Northamptonshire D.C.* (1991) 24 H.L.R. 284, C.A.). The latter (or its equivalent, *e.g.* common gardens, car-parks) will, however, be brought in by the reference to facilities "whether in the building or elsewhere".

A roof will invariably form a part of the structure and exterior, and, thus, the common parts, even if it may also be considered a part of the top floor flat, and/or if the tenant of the top floor flat has liability for its maintenance: consider *Douglas-Scott v. Scorgie* [1984] 1 W.L.R. 716, 13 H.L.R. 97, C.A.

In the context of reduction of rateable value under the Housing Act 1974 (c. 44), Sched. 8, for the purposes of the Leasehold Reform Act 1967 (c. 88), the Court of Appeal adopted a wide view of what was meant by structural:

"It is something appertaining to the fabric of the building so as to be part of the complete whole. A house is a complete unity. Structure implies concern with the constituent or material parts of that unity. That involves more than the load bearing elements, such as walls, roof and foundations. Rather it is that which pertains to basic fabric and parts, as distinguished from decoration and fittings" (*Pearlman v. Keepers & Governors of Harrow School* [1979] 1 Q.B. 56, C.A.).

*House in Multiple Occupation*

House in multiple occupation—or HMO—is defined by s.100 applying the definition to be found in Pt. VII of the Local Government and Housing Act 1989, which in turn (s.101) incorporates the definition to be found in the Housing Act 1985, Pt. XI, *save* that it excludes those parts of the HMO occupied as a separate dwelling by persons forming a single household. A house in multiple occupation is (1985 Act, s.345, as amended by the 1989 Act, Sched. 9, para. 44) "a house which is occupied by persons who do not form a single household", defining "house" to include "any part of a building which (a) apart from this subsection would not be regarded as a house; and (b) was originally constructed or subsequently adapted for occupation by a single household".

The definition therefore has three elements: "house", "occupied" and "by persons who do not form a single household".

*House.* The extended definition statutorily incorporates the decisions in *R. v. London Borough of Southwark, ex p. Lewis Levy* (1983) 8 H.L.R. 1; *R. v. Camden L.B.C., ex p. Rowton (Camden Town)* (1983) 10 H.L.R. 28, in which the term "house" was held—for the purposes of HMO legislation—to apply to a hostel or building used for multiple-occupation or as a lodging-house. Similarly, a large house operating as a holiday home for children has been held to be a house: *Reed v. Hastings Corporation* [1964] L.G.R. 588. In that case Lord Harman said " ... 'house' means what it obviously is, namely, a place fitted and used and adapted for human habitation". The decision was followed in *R. v. Hackney L.B.C., ex p. Evenbray* (1987) 19 H.L.R. 557, where it was held that a part of a hotel occupied by homeless families was a house, since it was a building constructed and used for human habitation.

*Occupied.* In order to show that the house is occupied it is not necessary to show any particular legal arrangement: *Minford Properties v. Hammersmith L.B.C.* (1978) 247 E.G. 561. The word broadly means "lived in": *Silbers v. Southwark L.B.C.* (1977) 76 L.G.R. 421. This is wide enough to cover a bed and breakfast hotel occupied by homeless families placed there by local authorities in pursuance of their duties to the homeless under Pt. III of the 1985 Act or Pt. VII of the Housing Act 1996 (c. 52): *Thrasyvoulou v. Hackney L.B.C.* (1986) 18 H.L.R. 370.

*Single household.* There is no statutory definition of single household. It has been said that "both the expression 'household' and membership of it is a question of fact and degree, there being no certain indicia the presence or absence of which is by itself conclusive..." (*per* Lord Hailsham, *Simmons v. Pizzey* [1979] A.C. 37, H.L.). In that case, some 75 women were in occupation of a women's refuge. None of the occupants intended to live there indefinitely. No occupant had any special part of the house to herself, so that there was no concept of separate households. Rather, the women organised the business of the house collectively, eating and undertaking the arrangements of the house together. It was held that this could not, however, amount to occupation as a single household.

More recently, in *Barnes v. Sheffield City Council* (1995) 27 H.L.R. 719, the Court of Appeal considered whether a group of students living in a shared house were a single household. The Court said that although it would be wrong to suggest that there was a litmus test which could be applied to the question whether there were separate households, the following factors were helpful indicators:

(a) whether the persons living in the house came to it as a single group or whether they were independently recruited;

(b) what facilities were shared;

(c) whether the occupiers were responsible for the whole house or just their particular rooms;

(d) whether individual tenants were able to, or did, lock other occupiers out of their rooms;

(e) whose responsibility it was to recruit new occupiers when individuals left;

(f) who allocated rooms;

(g) the size of the property;

(h) how stable the group composition was;

(i) whether the mode of living was communal.

The decision of the county court judge that the house was not an HMO because the group of students occupying it were a single household, was upheld.

See also *Silbers v. Southwark L.B.C.*, above; *cf. Hackney L.B.C. v. Ezedinma* [1981] 3 All E.R. 438.

*Disabled Persons*

This is defined in s.100 and means a person whose sight, hearing or speech is substantially impaired, who has a mental disorder or impairment of any kind, or which is physically substantially disabled by illness, injury, impairment present since birth, or otherwise: s.100(1).

Persons aged 18 or more are taken to be disabled if registered under s.29 of the National Assistance Act 1948 (c. 29), or if a person for whom welfare arrangements *have* been made under that section, or for whom such arrangements *might be* made (in the opinion of the social services authority): s.100(2).

Persons under 18 are taken to be disabled if registered under the Children Act 1989 (c. 41), Sched. 2, para. 2, or if the social services authority consider them to be a disabled child within the 1989 Act, Pt. III: s.100(3).

The social services authority are the authority having responsibility under the Local Authority Social Services Act 1970 (c. 42), which means a London borough council or the Common Council of the City of London or the Council of the Isles of Scilly, in England, in the area of a unitary authority that authority, and otherwise, in a metropolitan county the district council, and in a non-metropolitan county the county council and in Wales the county or county borough: Local Government Acts 1972 (c. 70) and 1992 (c. 19); 1970 Act, s.1 (as amended)—s.100(4).

## Applications for grants

**2.**—(1) No grant shall be paid unless an application for it is made to the local housing authority in accordance with the provisions of this Chapter and is approved by them.

(2) An application for a grant shall be in writing and shall specify the premises to which it relates and contain—

(a) particulars of the works in respect of which the grant is sought (in this Chapter referred to as the "relevant works");

(b) unless the local housing authority otherwise direct in any particular case, at least two estimates from different contractors of the cost of carrying out the relevant works;

(c) particulars of any preliminary or ancillary services and charges in respect of the cost of which the grant is also sought; and

(d) such other particulars as may be prescribed.

(3) In this Chapter "preliminary or ancillary services and charges", in relation to an application for a grant, means services and charges which—

(a) relate to the application and the preparation for and the carrying out of works, and

(b) are specified for the purposes of this subsection by order of the Secretary of State.

(4) The Secretary of State may by regulations prescribe a form of application for a grant and an application for a grant to which any such regulations apply is not validly made unless it is in the prescribed form.

DEFINITIONS

"grant": s.1(6).

"local housing authority": s.101.

GENERAL NOTE

All applications for all categories of grant must be made to the local housing authority in writing and must contain:

(i) particulars of the works for which the grant is sought (the relevant works);

(ii) two estimates from different contractors of the costs of carrying out the works (the authority may dispense with this requirement for a particular case);

(iii) particulars of any preliminary or ancillary services and charges, if a grant is sought for these costs;

(iv) other prescribed particulars.

Only those charges and services as specified by the Secretary of State which relate to the application and the preparation and carrying out of works may be claimed for (subs. (3)).

The Secretary of State has reserved the power to prescribe the use of a particular application form: subs. (4). Without the exercise of such power, the authority cannot impose their own requirements (as under the 1985 Act, although many authorities have nonetheless claimed the right to treat as invalid applications not received on their own forms. The point is not academic, as levels of grant-aid may be affected by whether an application has been "made" or not).

## *Preliminary conditions*

## Ineligible applicants

**3.**—(1) No grant is payable under this Chapter unless the applicant is aged 18 or over on the date of the application.

In the case of a joint application, any applicant under the age of 18 years on the date of the application shall be left out of account.

(2) No grant is payable under this Chapter if the person who would otherwise qualify as the applicant for the grant is—

(a) a local authority;

(b) a new town corporation;

(c) an urban development corporation;

(d) a housing action trust;

(e) the Development Board for Rural Wales;

(f) a health authority, special health authority or NHS trust;

(g) a police authority established under section 3 of the Police Act 1964;

(h) a joint authority established by Part IV of the Local Government Act 1985;

(i) a residuary body established by Part VII of that Act; or

(j) an authority established under section 10(1) of that Act (waste disposal).

(3) No grant is payable under this Chapter if the applicant is of a description excluded from entitlement to grant aid by regulations made by the Secretary of State.

(4) Regulations under subsection (3) may proceed wholly or in part by reference to the provisions relating to entitlement to housing benefit, or any other form of assistance, as they have effect from time to time.

DEFINITIONS

"grant": s.1(6).

"housing action trust": s.101.

"local authority": s.101.

"new town corporation": s.101.

"urban development corporation": s.101.

GENERAL NOTE

There are three categories of person who may not apply for a grant:

(i) *Persons under 18.* If there is a joint application, and one of the applicants is a minor, *i.e.* under 18 (see the Family Law Reform Act 1969 (c. 46), s.12), he or she is to be disregarded. The exclusion of persons under 18 is not effected by the requirements for legal interest to be found in ss.8, 9, below, on the basis that a minor cannot hold a legal estate in land (Law of Property Act 1925 (c. 20), s.1(6)), as a person under 18 can enjoy rights in equity, and can propose to become an owner on achievement of majority. Indeed, a conveyance to a minor of a legal estate takes effect as a contract to convey the estate or interest to him on his majority (*ibid.*, s.19(1)). Likewise, a conveyance to two persons, one of whom is a minor, takes effect as a conveyance to the adult, on trust for himself and the minor (*ibid.*, s.19(2)).

In addition, it must be considered unlikely that a mentally handicapped person could apply (even for a disabled facilities grant), unless he can understand the implications of the application, and his responsibilities thereunder: *cf. R. v. Oldham M.B.C., ex p. Garlick; R. v. Bexley L.B.C., ex p. Bentum; R. v. Tower Hamlets L.B.C., ex p. Begum* [1993] A.C. 509, 25 H.L.R. 319, H.L., under Pt. III of the Housing Act 1985 (homelessness), in which it was held that there was only a duty to offer accommodation to those applicants who could decide whether or not to accept, not including persons so disabled that they have neither the capacity themselves to apply nor to authorise an agent on their behalf. There must be the capacity to understand and respond to the offer, and to undertake its responsibilities; whether or not a person so qualifies is a matter for the authority.

(ii) *Public bodies.* The list of public bodies excluded from the grant system is not confined to housing authorities, but includes authorities with a wider remit which are likely to hold housing, and some bodies (see subparas. (f)–(h)) which have inherited specific responsibilities from local authorities, and either with them acquired some extent of housing stock, or have acquired stock on their own part incidental to their principal functions, either for employees, or else when exercising compulsory purchase powers.

"local authority" means a county, district or London borough council, the Common Council of the City of London, a Welsh county council or county borough, or the council of the Isles of Scilly (see s.101 and the Housing Act 1985, s.4);

"new town corporation" means a development corporation of the Commission for New Towns (see s.101 and the Housing Act 1985, s.4);

"urban development corporation" means an urban development corporation established under Pt. XVI of the Local Government, Planning and Land Act 1980 (c. 65) (see s.101 and the Housing Act 1985, s.4); and,

"housing action trust" means a housing action trust established under Pt. III of the Housing Act 1988.

(iii) *Prescribed applicants.* The Secretary of State has reserved power to add to the class of person who may not apply, including by relying on regulations governing housing benefit or other welfare assistance as they may be amended from time to time. What is in mind here is the exclusion of immigrants with limited leave to remain who are disqualified from recourse to public funds (*Hansard* (H.C.), Report, July 8, 1996, col. 35, Parliamentary Under-Secretary-for State for the Environment (Mr Clappison)).

## The age of the property

**4.**—(1) A local housing authority shall not entertain an application for a grant in respect of premises provided (by construction or conversion) less than ten years before the date of the application, unless—

(a) the application is for a disabled facilities grant, or

(b) the application is for an HMO grant in respect of a house in multiple occupation provided by conversion.

(2) The Secretary of State may by order amend subsection (1) so as to substitute another period for that specified.

DEFINITIONS
"disabled facilities grant": s.1.
"HMO grant": s.1.
"local housing authority": s.101.

GENERAL NOTE
In broad terms, grants are not intended for new properties. However, HMOs provided by conversion form "a special case" (*Hansard* (H.C.), Report, July 8, 1996, col. 21, Parliamentary Under-Secretary of State for the Environment (Mr Clappison)). Likewise, application for a disabled facilities grant may be justified regardless of the age of the property. Other grants, however, may not be awarded unless premises are provided—by construction or conversion—at least 10 years before application, although the Secretary of State may prescribe a different period.

In *R. v. Bristol City Council, ex p. Naqvi* (1994) 26 H.L.R. 640, Q.B.D., the applicant owned a shop with a flat above. In November 1991, planning permission was granted for change of use of the ground floor from shop to residential use, and to combine it with the flat to make one dwelling. Application for grant was refused on the basis that the dwelling (that would be produced) had been provided for less than 10 years and did not fulfil the pre-condition in the analogous provisions of the 1989 Act (s.103).

The application failed on the provisions of the 1989 Act distinguishing mandatory and discretionary grants. It was held, however, that the scheme was one for the provision of a dwelling by conversion, so that the 10-year rule applied to the *building* out of which the dwelling was to be provided, not the dwelling itself (see also notes to s.1, above).

### Excluded descriptions of works

**5.**—(1) No grant is payable in respect of works of a description excluded from grant aid under this Chapter by regulations made by the Secretary of State.

(2) Regulations may be made with respect to local housing authorities generally or to a particular local housing authority and may be made with respect to particular areas.

(3) Regulations may specify descriptions of works for which grant aid is not to be available without the Secretary of State's consent, which may be given—

(a)  to local housing authorities generally or to a particular local housing authority,

(b)  with respect to particular areas, or

(c)  with respect to applications generally or to a particular description of application.

DEFINITIONS
"local housing authority": s.101.

GENERAL NOTE
This section allows the Secretary of State to override local policies by excluding categories of work nationally or locally from the availability of grant-aid. So far as the power is without any procedural preconditions, it is exercisable subject only to the conventional constraints of public law: see also notes to s.13, below.

It may be thought, however, that the general duty of fairness would require *some* (however informal) extent of consultation if the Secretary of State were to plan to use this power in relation to an authority whose policies would be affected by it: the courts are willing to supplement statutory procedures where it is necessary to do so in order to ensure the achievement of fairness (*Wiseman v. Boreman* [1971] A.C. 297, H.L.; *R. v. Hull Prison Visitors, ex p. St. Germain* [1979] 1 W.L.R. 1401; *Lloyd v. McMahon* [1987] A.C. 625, see also most recently *R. v. R.B. Kensington & Chelsea, ex p. Grillo* (1995) 28 H.L.R. 94, C.A., on the duty—or want of duty—to give reasons [see below, notes to s.34], which is itself imported by the requirement of fairness [see, *e.g. R. v. Higher Education Funding Council, ex p. Institute of Dental Surgery* [1994] 1 W.L.R. 242]. See also *R. v. Bristol C.C., ex p. Bailey* (1994) 27 H.L.R. 307, Q.B.D., on the want of duty to give reasons for the refusal of a grant: see s.34, below).

### Defective dwellings

**6.**—(1) No grant is payable if—

(a)  the dwelling, house or building is or forms part of a building of a class designated under section 528 or 559 of the Housing Act 1985 (defective dwellings),

(b)  the applicant is eligible for assistance under Part XVI of that Act in respect of a defective dwelling which is or forms part of the dwelling, house or building concerned, and

(c)  the relevant works are, within the meaning of that Part, works required to reinstate that defective dwelling.

(2) If the local housing authority consider that the relevant works include works for which assistance is available under Part XVI of the Housing Act 1985 (assistance for owners of defective housing), they shall treat the application as if the relevant works did not include those works.

DEFINITIONS
"dwelling": s.101.
"local housing authority": s.101.
"relevant works": s.2.

GENERAL NOTE

Part XVI of the Housing Act 1985 contains provisions initially enacted in the Housing Defects Act 1984 (c. 50), which are concerned with system-built housing which has, by reason of construction or design, proved defective to the point that some of it has at times—and, sometimes, merely in some areas—become unsaleable. Pt. XVI contains a framework for assistance by way of *either* reinstatement grant, *or* repurchase, available in respect of those properties designated for the purpose by the Secretary of State (1985 Act, s.528), or within a local (discretionary) designation (1985 Act, s.559). The form of assistance is chosen by the authority, with a presumption in favour of reinstatement (if the property is likely to provide satisfactory housing for a period of 30 years and it is likely that a would-be buyer could obtain a mortgage), having regard to cost of works and value of property once repaired: the 1985 Act, s.538.

This section means that the provisions of Pt. XVI and of this Act are mutually exclusive so far as concerns the works the subject of the application for grant (see s.2(2), above): if relevant works (within the Act) *are* works required to reinstate the defective dwelling (within the 1985 Act, Pt. XVI), no grant is available (subs. (1)); if they merely *include* reinstatement works, then those works are automatically excluded from the grant application (subs. (2)).

## *Renovation grants*

## Renovation grants: owner's applications and tenant's applications

**7.**—(1) A local housing authority shall not entertain an application for a renovation grant unless they are satisfied—

(a) that the applicant has, or proposes to acquire, an owner's interest in every parcel of land on which the relevant works are to be carried out, or

(b) in the case of an application other than a conversion application, that the applicant is a qualifying tenant of the dwelling (alone or jointly with others) but does not have, or propose to acquire, an owner's interest in the dwelling.

(2) References in this Chapter to an "owner's application" or a "tenant's application", in relation to a renovation grant, shall be construed accordingly.

(3) In accordance with directions given by the Secretary of State, a local housing authority may treat the condition in subsection (1)(a) as met by a person who has, or proposes to acquire, an owner's interest in only part of the land concerned.

(4) References in this Chapter to "a qualifying owner's interest", in relation to an application for a renovation grant, are to an owner's interest meeting the condition in subsection (1)(a) or treated by virtue of subsection (3) as meeting that condition.

(5) In this Chapter a "qualifying tenant", in relation to an application for a renovation grant, means a person who (alone or jointly with others) is a tenant of the premises to which the application relates—

(a) who is required by the terms of his tenancy to carry out the relevant works and whose tenancy is not of a description excluded from this subsection by order of the Secretary of State, or

(b) whose tenancy is of a description specified for the purposes of this subsection by order of the Secretary of State.

(6) In subsection (5) "tenant" includes a person having a licence to occupy the premises concerned which satisfies such conditions as may be specified by order of the Secretary of State.

References in this Chapter to tenants and other expressions relating to tenancies, in the context of a tenant's application for a renovation grant, shall be construed accordingly.

DEFINITIONS

"common parts": s.58.
"conversion application": s.58.

"dwelling": s.101.
"house in multiple occupation": s.101.
"local housing authority": s.101.
"owner's interest": s.101.
"relevant works": s.2.
"renovation grant": s.1.
"tenancy": s.101.

GENERAL NOTE
An applicant for a renovation grant, accordingly, either for improvement or repair, or else for the provision of dwellings by conversion (s.2(2), above), must either already have—or be intending to have—an appropriate interest in the property, unless the application falls within the exemption in s.95 (applications relating to certain church lands and applications made by charities).
There are two classes of application: owner's applications and tenant's applications.

*Owner's application.* An owner has to have—or be proposing to acquire—an owner's interest in every parcel of land on which the relevant works are to be carried out: subs. (1)(a). This may, however, be reduced to an interest in only part, on a direction from the Secretary of State: subs. (3). "Owner's interest" means a freehold interest, or a leasehold interest with at least five years unexpired, which the applicant holds solely or jointly: s.101, below. Where the application is from a prospective owner, approval of the grant must await acquisition of the relevant interest: s.13(3).
"Land" includes "buildings and other structures, land covered by water, any estate, interest, easement, servitude or right in or over land": Interpretation Act 1978 (c. 30), Sched. 1.

*Tenant's application.* Tenants may only apply for a renovation grant if it is *not* a "conversion grant", which means an application for a grant within s.2(2)(b), *i.e.* the provision of a dwelling by conversion, see s.58, below. The tenant must not have or be proposing to acquire an owner's interest in the dwelling or parts to which work is to be carried out (subs. (1)(b)). The tenancy may be sole or joint, and one only of the joint tenants may apply (*ibid.*).
"Tenancy" includes sub-tenancy, and an agreement for a tenancy or sub-tenancy: s.101. This means a legally enforceable contract. All contracts entered into since September 27, 1989, for the sale or other disposition of land—therefore, including grant of lease—must have been made in writing, and by including all of the terms in one document (or, where contracts are exchanged, in each of them): Law of Property (Miscellaneous Provisions) Act 1989 (c. 34), s.2. The terms need not be set out in the document, however: they can be incorporated by cross-reference to another document. The document must be signed by or on behalf of each of the parties, save in the case of exchange, where each document must be signed by at least one: *ibid.*, s.2(3).
These requirements do not apply to leases within s.54(2) of the Law of Property Act 1925 (*ibid.*, s.2(5)(a)), which means "the creation by parol of leases taking effect in possession for a term not exceeding three years ... at the best rent which can be reasonably obtained without taking a fine", which includes a periodic tenancy). It was *formerly* the case that a contract for a tenancy had to be in writing, even if the grant itself would not require to be in writing: Law of Property Act 1925, s.40 (and see *Botting v. Martin* (1808) Camp. 317; *Crago v. Julian* [1992] 1 W.L.R. 372, C.A.). Section 40 was, however, replaced by s.2 of the 1989 Act (*ibid.*, s.2(8)).
A tenant's application must also fall within one of the following categories:
(i) the tenant is required under the terms of his tenancy to carry out the relevant works, and the tenancy is not of a class disqualified by the Secretary of State. It is unlikely that tenants under short leases (those with five or more years remaining will have an owner's interest, see s.101) will have any obligation to repair or improve. In all leases of less than seven years, the Landlord and Tenant Act 1985, s.11, imposes a repairing obligation on the landlord as to the structure and exterior of the dwelling and services (though this may be contracted out with leave of the county court, under the Landlord and Tenant Act 1985, s.12); or
(ii) the tenancy is one of a type specified by the Secretary of State.
A tenant's application also requires a certificate of intended letting (unless the authority decides that it is unreasonable to require it) from the tenant's landlord: see s.9(3).
It is not only tenants who may apply, but also licensees provided the licence satisfies specified conditions: subs. (6). As to the distinction between tenancy and licence, see generally *Street v. Mountford* [1985] A.C. 809, 17 H.L.R. 402, H.L.; *Eastleigh B.C. v. Walsh* [1985] 1 W.L.R. 525, 17 H.L.R. 392, H.L.; *A.G. Securities v. Vaughan* [1990] 1 A.C. 417, (1989) 21 H.L.R. 79, H.L. In short, where residential accommodation is granted for a term at a rent with exclusive possession, the grantor providing neither attendance nor services, the legal consequence will normally be the creation of a tenancy.

In *Burrows v. Brent L.B.C.* (1995) 27 H.L.R. 748, C.A., a *post*-possession order agreement for the tenant to remain on terms (including payment off the arrears) was held to have created a new agreement, which was either tenancy or licence. However, in *Greenwich L.B.C. v. Regan* (1996) 28 H.L.R. 469, C.A., the court, distinguishing *Burrows*, held that it was a question of fact in every case whether what had taken place was the variation of an existing relationship, or the creation of a new tenancy or licence; where the variation was of payment off arrears, it was likely to be referable to the court's powers to modify a suspended order (and, thus, to a modification of the relationship).

The mere acceptance of use and occupation charges does not create a licence (not even if a rent rebate is awarded): *Westminster C.C. v. Basson* (1990) 23 H.L.R. 225, C.A. However, a distinction must be drawn between a case where an occupier seeks to take advantage of bureaucratic incompetence in order to build up an argument in favour of authorised occupation amounting to a licence, and a case such as *Tower Hamlets L.B.C. v. Ayinde* (1994) 26 H.L.R. 631, C.A., where the occupation was wholly above board, numerous requests were made for the transfer of a tenancy into the occupier's name, and payment was being made, which could only lead to one conclusion, that a tenancy had been created. See also *Vaughan-Armatrading v. Sarsah* (1995) 27 H.L.R. 631, C.A.

*Subs. (1)*
The test is the subjective one, which prohibits approval unless the authority "are satisfied" as to the conditions: see General Note to s.13, below, as to the powers of the court to intervene.

### Renovation grants: certificates required in case of owner's application

**8.**—(1) A local housing authority shall not entertain an owner's application for a renovation grant unless it is accompanied by an owner-occupation certificate or a certificate of intended letting in respect of the dwelling to which the application relates or, in the case of a conversion application, in respect of each of the dwellings to be provided.

(2) An "owner-occupation certificate" certifies that the applicant—
(a) has or proposes to acquire a qualifying owner's interest, and
(b) intends that throughout the grant condition period he or a member of his family will live in the dwelling as his (or that member's) only or main residence.

(3) A "certificate of intended letting" certifies that the applicant—
(a) has or proposes to acquire a qualifying owner's interest, and
(b) intends that throughout the grant condition period the dwelling will be let or available for letting as a residence (and not for a holiday) to a person who is not connected with the owner for the time being of the dwelling.

In paragraph (b) "letting" does not include a letting on a long tenancy.

(4) In subsection (3) references to letting include the grant of a licence to occupy premises.

References in this Chapter to tenants and other expressions relating to tenancies, in the context of a certificate of intended letting, shall be construed accordingly.

(5) Where section 10 applies (prior qualifying period in certain cases) a local housing authority shall not entertain an owner's application for a renovation grant unless it is also accompanied by a certificate specifying how the requirements of that section are met.

DEFINITIONS
"conversion application": s.58.
"dwelling": s.101.
"grant condition period": s.44.
"local housing authority": s.101.
"long tenancy": s.101.
"member of family": s.97.
"owner's interest": s.101.
"qualifying owner's interest": s.7.
"renovation grant": s.1.

GENERAL NOTE

This section sets out the "occupation" preconditions to consideration of applications for a renovation grant by an owner. Unless these preconditions are fulfilled, no grant may be entertained. See also ss.9, 10, below.

Apart from certifying the current interest of the applicant in the property, the certificates are concerned with future intentions at the time of the application, and may be distinguished from conditions as to future occupation, and breach of such conditions, see ss.48 and 49. Under the corresponding former provisions of the 1989 Act, this meant that non-compliance with the intentions set out in this section did not also *necessarily* amount to breach of conditions as set out in those sections or entitle the authority to recover on disposal: the grant conditions have now, however, largely been harmonised with the certificates in order to prevent abuse (see Introduction to Pt. I, above): see ss.48, 49, below.

Where the application is a conversion application, the preconditions have to be fulfilled in respect of each of the dwellings to be provided: subs. (1). The occupation preconditions are not applicable to applications in respect of certain church lands and applications made by charities: s.95, below.

There are two categories of application, and accompanying conditions:

(i) Owner-occupation certificate, together (where the requirement is not excluded by s.10(3)) with proof of prior qualification; *or*

(ii) Certificate of intended letting.

*Owner-occupation certificate.* This certifies that the applicant has or that he proposes to acquire a qualifying owner's interest (as defined by ss.7(4) and 101) in the dwelling and that he or a member of his family intends to occupy the dwelling within the building as his only or main residence for at least 12 months from the certified date: subs. (1). There are accordingly two sub-criteria:

(a) Only or main residence. The phrase "only or main residence" is to be found in the Leasehold Reform Act 1967, s.1(2), where it has been held that a tenant who occupies part but sublets the remainder of his home qualifies: *Harris v. Swick Securities* [1969] 1 W.L.R. 1604, C.A. In *Poland v. Cadogan* [1980] 3 All E.R. 544, C.A. it was held that while long absence may not prevent residential occupation, a long absence abroad with the premises sublet may indicate a lack of intention to occupy, sufficient to defeat the meaning in that Act. In *Powell v. Radford* (1970) 21 P. & C.R. 99, C.A., a claim under the 1967 Act by a husband and wife each to be occupying a different house as the main home was upheld, although considered unusual. Because of the different nature of the rights, these decisions, too, must be treated with caution, and can be distinguished by the statutory context.

Under the Housing Acts 1985 and 1988, the phrase used is "only or principal home". This probably bears no different meaning. In *Crawley B.C. v. Sawyer* (1988) 20 H.L.R. 98, C.A., it was expressly held that there was no material difference between this phrase and occupation as a residence under the Rent Acts, as that phrase had been interpreted, although this must be treated with some caution as many of the cases under the Rent Acts were concerned with people who had two homes, and the substantive issue was whether—in the light of the second home—the first was still in use as "a" home: see *Bevington v. Crawford* (1974) 232 E.G. 191, C.A.; *Gofor Investments v. Roberts* (1975) 119 Sol. Jo. 320, C.A.; see also *Langford Property Co. v. Tureman* [1949] 1 K.B. 29, C.A., and *Beck v. Scholtz* [1953] 1 Q.B. 570, C.A., for two cases usefully illustrating where the line is drawn.

Under the Housing Act 1985, it is clear that occupation must be as an "only or principal home", but subject to this *caveat* occupation—as a home or as a residence—under the two codes of security of tenure (Housing Act and Rent Act) has the same general meaning ("a substantial degree of regular personal occupation ... of an essentially residential nature": *Herbert v. Byrne* [1946] 1 W.L.R. 519, C.A.).

Accordingly, it is not necessary to show actual or continuous physical occupation of the home, so long as the property is still in use as a home, to demonstrate which it will usually be necessary to show some physical or tangible signs of continued such use, coupled with an intention to resume physical occupation (see *Brown v. Brash* [1948] 2 K.B. 247, C.A.): see, *e.g.*, *Roland House Gardens v. Cravitz* (1974) 29 P. & C.R. 432, C.A.; *Hampstead Way Investments v. Lewis-Weare* [1985] 1 W.L.R. 164, 17 H.L.R. 152, H.L.; *Brickfield Properties v. Hughes* (1980) 20 H.L.R. 108, C.A. Absence in hospital will not affect residence: *Tomkins v. Rowley* [1949] E.G.D. 314, C.A.

In *Sawyer* (above), the tenant left his secure tenancy to live with his girlfriend. The gas and electricity to the premises the subject of the secure tenancy were subsequently cut off and the following year he informed the local authority that he was living with his girlfriend and that they intended to purchase her home. The authority instituted possession proceedings but by the time of the hearing, the tenant and his girlfriend had separated and he was again living at the premises. He gave evidence that he had not abandoned the premises and had every intention of returning to them and the judge found that they were at all times his principal home, a decision upheld by the Court of Appeal.

See also *Regalian Securities v. Scheuer* (1982) 5 H.L.R. 48, C.A., and *Richards v. Green* (1984) 11 H.L.R. 1, C.A. A tenancy may go in and out of security, depending on whether the occupation requirement is fulfilled (see, *e.g. Hussey v. Camden L.B.C.* (1994) 27 H.L.R. 5, C.A.). If the reason for the finding of non-occupation is subletting or parting with possession of the whole of the premises, however, then under Housing Act 1985, s.93 security will be lost and cannot be recovered. A distinction must be drawn, however, between subletting and a mere sharing arrangement where one of the occupiers alone holds the tenancy, and another lives or shares the property with him, from which the normal or natural inference will be that the sharer is no more than a lodger or licensee of the tenant: see *Monmouth B.C. v. Marlog* (1994) 27 H.L.R. 30, C.A.

(b) Member of the family. See notes to s.98, below.

*Certificate of Intended Letting.* This certifies that the applicant has, or intends to acquire, a qualifying owner's interest (as defined by ss.7(4) and 101) *and* intends that throughout the period of the grant condition the dwelling will be let—or available for letting—as a residence, for a period of not less than five years on a tenancy, which is *not* a long tenancy, to someone other than a member of his family. There are two elements to which attention may be drawn:

(a) "Long tenancy" has the meaning given it by Housing Act 1985, s.115, *i.e.* a tenancy granted for a fixed term exceeding 21 years, a tenancy for a term fixed by law under a grant with a covenant or obligation for perpetual renewal, except a tenancy by sub-demise from a tenancy which is not itself a long tenancy, and any tenancy granted in pursuance of the right to buy under Pt. V of the 1985 Act. A tenancy determinable by notice after death is expressly not a long lease, unless the lease constitutes a shared ownership tenancy: 1985 Act, s.115(2).

(b) "Holiday" is not a defined expression. There has been a number of cases on whether or not premises are let for the purposes of a holiday, which arose under the exemption from security of tenure conferred by the Rent Act 1977 (c. 42), s.9. A second alleged holiday letting must be a dubious entity, and any knowledge that the owner acquires during the first letting will be admissible as to the purpose of the second: *R. v. Rent Officer for Camden L.B.C., ex p. Plant* (1981) 7 H.L.R. 17, Q.B.D. A person believed by the owner to be on holiday, but not actually so, would probably not contravene the intention (or, as it translates into breach, see s.49, below), for the purpose would remain holiday whatever the tenant's own plans: *Buchmann v. May* [1978] 2 All E.R. 993, 7 H.L.R. 1, C.A.

To prove want of intention, or a breach, it would be necessary to show that the owner knew—actually or constructively, *e.g.* through an agent—that the tenant was not on holiday: *ex p. Plant.* A working holiday may well be a holiday for this purpose: *Buchmann*; see also *McHale v. Daneham* (1979) 249 E.G. 969, C. C.

*Subs. (4)*
As to licences, see notes to s.7, above.

*Subs. (5)*
See notes to s.10, below.

## Renovation grants: certificates required in case of tenant's application

**9.**—(1) A local housing authority shall not entertain a tenant's application for a renovation grant unless it is accompanied by a tenant's certificate.

(2) A "tenant's certificate" certifies—

(a) that the applicant is a qualifying tenant of the dwelling, and

(b) that he or a member of his family intends to live in the dwelling as his (or that member's) only or main residence.

(3) Except where the authority consider it unreasonable in the circumstances to require such a certificate, they shall not entertain a tenant's application for a renovation grant unless it is also accompanied by a certificate of intended letting (see section 8(3)) by the person who at the time of the application is the landlord under the tenancy.

(4) Where section 10 applies (prior qualifying period in certain cases) a local housing authority shall not entertain a tenant's application for a reno-

vation grant unless it is also accompanied by a certificate specifying how the requirements of that section are met.

GENERAL NOTE
  This section governs the preconditions when the application for a renovation grant is by a tenant. Such a renovation grant application cannot be a conversion application: see s.7(1)(b). The tenant's certificate must certify (i) that the tenant is a qualifying tenant (as to which, see s.7(5), above), and (ii) that the tenant or a member of his family (as to which, see notes to s.98, below) intends to live in the dwelling as his only or main residence (as to which, also see notes to s.8, above): subs. (2). A tenant must also present a certificate of intended letting (again, see notes to s.8, above) from his landlord, unless the authority consider it unreasonable to require one: subs. (3).

*Subs. (3)*
  The test is whether the authority consider it unreasonable to require a certificate: see General Note to s.13, below, as to the powers of the court to intervene.

*Subs. (4)*
  See notes to s.10, below.

## Renovation grants: prior qualifying period

   **10.**—(1) Subject to subsection (3), a local housing authority shall not entertain an application to which this section applies unless they are satisfied—
   (a) that the ownership or tenancy condition (see section 11) was met throughout the qualifying period, and
   (b) in the case of an application accompanied by an owner-occupation certificate or a tenant's certificate, that the applicant lived in the dwelling as his only or main residence throughout that period.
   In the case of a joint application it is sufficient if those conditions are met by any of the applicants.
   (2) The qualifying period for the purposes of this section is the period of three years, or such other period as may be specified by order of the Secretary of State, ending with the date of the application.
   (3) A local housing authority may dispense with compliance with either or both of the conditions in subsection (1), and may do so either generally or in relation to particular cases or descriptions of case.
   (4) Subject to subsection (5), this section applies to every application for a renovation grant, other than—
   (a) a conversion application,
   (b) an application in respect of a dwelling in a renewal area,
   (c) an application in respect of works to provide means of escape in case of fire or other fire precautions, or
   (d) an application of any other description excepted from this section by order of the Secretary of State.
   (5) This section does not apply to a landlord's application unless the Secretary of State by order so provides, which he may do with respect to all landlord's applications or any description of landlord's application.
   Any such order may provide that this section applies to a landlord's application notwithstanding that it is of a kind mentioned in paragraphs (a) to (d) of subsection (4).

(6) A "landlord's application" for a renovation grant means an owner's application which is accompanied by a certificate of intended letting.

A conversion application for the provision of two or more dwellings shall not be treated as a landlord's application if any of the certificates accompanying the application is an owner-occupation certificate.

DEFINITIONS

"local housing authority": s.101.
"owner-occupation certificate": s.8.
"renewal area": s.101.
"tenant's certificate": s.9.

GENERAL NOTE

The purpose of this section is to prevent "carpet-bagging". That is to say, people moving into accommodation—*e.g.* in the area of an authority which is presently in funds for the award of discretionary grants—in order to renovate with the assistance of grant-aid, and sell as soon as the period for the application of grant conditions has expired (see ss.44, 45, 48 and 49). See also Introduction to Pt. I, above. Accordingly, an applicant (or if more than one of them, at least one of them) is now required to satisfy the authority:

(i) that "the ownership or tenancy condition" was met, throughout a qualifying period of three years (or such other period as may be specified by the Secretary of State: subs. (2)), ending with the date of the application, and

(ii) *save* in the case of an owner's application accompanied by a certificate of intended letting (as to which, see s.8, above), which is known as a landlord's application (see subs. (5)), that the applicant—be he owner or tenant—has lived in the dwelling the subject of the application throughout that period, as his only or main residence (as to which, see notes to s.8, above).

Accordingly, and on the face of it, *all* applicants must show that they have enjoyed the relevant interest for the qualifying period, while those who are applying in respect of their own homes must *also* show residence over that period. This will permit authorities to adopt policies, *e.g.* preferring owner-occupiers or tenants, without correspondingly encouraging abuse, *e.g.* "to help speculative purchasers increase their profits on the sale of the property or to enable an applicant to move up market by buying an unfit property and then improving it with the benefit of a renovation grant" (*Hansard* (H.L.), Committee (First Day), March 26, 1996, col. 1609, Minister of State, Department of the Environment (Earl Ferrers)).

The authority may, however, disapply the condition in its entirety: subs. (3). Further, the requirement so far as it applies to a landlord's application is inapplicable unless and until the Secretary of State brings it back into play: see subs. (4).

The ownership or tenancy condition is, essentially, no more than that the owner or tenant has had the qualifying owner's or qualifying tenant's interest (see s.7) for the qualifying period, but this is subject to provisions which "deem" compliance, *i.e.* inheritance, age and ill-health, domestic breakdown: see s.11, below.

There are five categories of application which are in practice exempt from the requirements:

(a) application for a renovation grant to provide dwellings by conversion (see s.2(2)(b)), treating an application for conversion any one dwelling of which it is intended that the landlord shall occupy as *not* being a conversion application for this purpose (subs. (5)), so that the requirements will continue to apply in the normal way;

(b) application in respect of a dwelling in a renewal area, meaning an area of unsatisfactory living conditions declared by the authority under Pt. VII of the Local Government and Housing Act 1989, replacing the housing action and general improvement area policies of the Housing Act 1985;

(c) application in respect of works to provide means of escape in case of fire, or other fire precautions;

(d) applications within a description specified for this purpose by the Secretary of State; and

(e) "landlord's applications" (unless the Secretary of State orders that all or some such applications should be brought within the requirement).

A landlord's application is an owner's application accompanied by a certificate of letting, *i.e.* the same category of applicant as is identified by subs. (1)(b); the effect is to disapply subs. (1)(a)—ownership throughout the qualifying period—unless and until it is re-applied by order.

*Subs. (1)*

The test is the subjective one, which prohibits approval unless the authority "are satisfied" as to the conditions: see General Note to s.13, below, as to the powers of the court to intervene.

## Prior qualifying period: the ownership or tenancy condition

**11.**—(1) The "ownership or tenancy condition" for the purposes of section 10 is that the applicant had a qualifying owner's interest in, or was a qualifying tenant of, the dwelling.

That condition shall be treated as having been met in the following circumstances.

(2) Where the applicant took his owner's interest or became a qualifying tenant under the will or on the intestacy of a member of his family, the ownership or tenancy condition shall be treated as having been met—

    (a)  during any period when the deceased both held a qualifying owner's interest in or was a qualifying tenant of the dwelling and lived in the dwelling as his only or main residence, and

    (b)  if immediately before his death the deceased both—

        (i) held such an interest or was such a tenant, and

        (ii) lived in the dwelling as his only or main residence,

during any period not exceeding one year when his personal representatives, or the Public Trustee under section 9 of the Administration of Estates Act 1925, held such an interest or was such a tenant.

(3) The local housing authority may treat a person as continuing to meet the residence requirement in subsection (2)(a) or (b)(ii) for up to a year after he has, by reason of age or infirmity—

    (a)  gone to live with and be cared for by a member of his family, or

    (b)  gone to live in a hospital, hospice, sheltered housing, residential care home or similar institution.

(4) Where the applicant took his owner's interest or became a qualifying tenant by virtue of a disposal made by a member of his family, and the authority are satisfied—

    (a)  that the person making the disposal was elderly or infirm, and

    (b)  that he made the disposal with the intention of—

        (i) going to live with and be cared for by a member of his family, or

        (ii) going to live in a hospital, hospice, sheltered housing, residential care home or similar institution as his only or main residence,

the ownership or tenancy condition shall be treated as having been met during any period ending on the date of the disposal when the person making the disposal held a qualifying owner's interest in or was a qualifying tenant of the dwelling.

(5) Where the applicant took his owner's interest or became a qualifying tenant by virtue of a disposal made by his spouse, and the authority are satisfied that the disposal was made as a result of arrangements in relation to divorce, judicial separation or declaration of nullity of marriage, the ownership or tenancy condition shall be treated as having been met during any period ending on the date of the disposal when the spouse held a qualifying owner's interest in or was a qualifying tenant of the dwelling.

(6) The references in subsection (5) to the spouse of the applicant—

    (a)  in the case of divorce, include his former spouse, and

    (b)  in the case of a declaration of nullity, shall be construed as references to the other party to the marriage.

DEFINITIONS
  "dwelling": s.101.
  "member of family": s.98.
  "qualifying owner's interest": s.7.
  "qualifying tenant": s.7.

GENERAL NOTE
  The purpose of this section is to create certain exceptions to the otherwise rigid requirement that the qualifying interest (owner's or tenant's—see s.7, above) has been held by the applicant

for three years before the application (see s.10(1)). This section requires the authority to treat it as fulfilled in the following cases.

(i) *Inheritance.* The interest—ownership or tenancy—will be treated as having been held if the applicant took it under the will or on the intestacy of a member of his family (as to which, see notes to s.98, below), for such period as the deceased held that interest and occupied the property as his only or principal residence (as to which, also see notes to s.8, above), *together with* (assuming the deceased so qualified immediately before his death) a period of up to one year when the interest was held by person representatives or the Public Trustee, *i.e.* if so qualifying at death, the period can be extended for a year while probate is undertaken (subs. (2)), disregarding (at the authority's discretion—see notes to s.13, below) a period of a year during which the deceased had gone to live with a member of his family (not necessarily the applicant) or else had moved into a hospital, residential care home or the like, by reason of age or infirmity (subs. (3)).

Accordingly, on inheritance there is not only taken into account the deceased's former occupation, but also a period of up to a year after death—for probate—and a period of up to a year before death—for ill health.

(ii) *Age and health disposals.* The authority are also obliged to treat the qualifying interest—ownership or tenancy—as having been held for the three year period if the applicant took it from a member of his family (as to which, see notes to s.98, below) because the person from whom he took it was elderly or infirm, and disposed of his interest in it either to go and be cared for by a member of the family (not necessarily the applicant), or else had moved into a hospital, residential care home or the like, to live in it as his only or principal residence (as to which, also see notes to s.8) (subs. (4)).

"Residential care home" has a technical meaning for the purposes of the Registered Homes Act 1984 (c. 23): "any establishment which provides or is intended to provide, whether for reward or not, residential accommodation with both board and personal care for persons in need of personal care by reason of old age, disablement, past or present dependence on alcohol or drugs, or past or present mental disordered"—s.1. This definition is not imported into this Act, and the expression "or similar institution" means that it is unnecessary to rely on it, although it is undoubtedly such establishments which, *inter alia*, are in mind.

(iii) *Domestic breakdown.* Subsection (5) is designed to cater for transfers of interest—ownership or tenancy—whether by the court or by agreement, which are related to divorce, judicial separation or nullity, without loss of the right to apply for grant (without a new period of qualification).

## Renovation grants: purposes for which grant may be given

**12.**—(1) The purposes for which an application for a renovation grant, other than a conversion application, may be approved are the following—

(a) to comply with a notice under section 189 of the Housing Act 1985 (repair notice in respect of unfit premises) or otherwise to render the dwelling fit for human habitation;

(b) to comply with a notice under section 190 of that Act (repair notice in respect of premises not unfit but in need of substantial repair) or otherwise to put the dwelling in reasonable repair;

(c) to provide adequate thermal insulation;

(d) to provide adequate facilities for space heating;

(e) to provide satisfactory internal arrangements;

(f) to provide means of escape in case of fire or other fire precautions, not being precautions required under or by virtue of any enactment (whenever passed);

(g) to ensure that the dwelling complies with such requirements with respect to construction or physical condition as may be specified by the Secretary of State;

(h) to ensure that there is compliance with such requirements with respect to the provision or condition of services and amenities to or within the dwelling as are so specified;

(i) any other purpose for the time being specified for the purposes of this section by order of the Secretary of State.

(2) The purpose for which a conversion application may be approved is to provide one or more dwellings by the conversion of a house or other building.

(3) If in the opinion of the authority the relevant works are more or less extensive than is necessary to achieve any of the purposes set out in subsection (1) or (2), they may, with the consent of the applicant, treat the application as varied so that the relevant works are limited to or, as the case may be, include such works as seem to the authority to be necessary for that purpose.

(4) The reference in paragraph (f) of subsection (1) to precautions required under or by virtue of an enactment does not include precautions required to comply with a notice under section 352 of the Housing Act 1985 (notice requiring execution of works to render house in multiple occupation fit for number of occupants) so far as it relates to premises which are not part of a house in multiple occupation for the purposes of this Part.

(5) In exercise of the powers conferred by paragraphs (g) and (h) of subsection (1) the Secretary of State may specify requirements generally or for particular cases, and may specify different requirements for different areas.

DEFINITIONS
　"conversion application": s.58.
　"dwelling": s.101.
　"reasonable repair": s.96.
　"renovation grant": s.1.

GENERAL NOTE
This section comprises a major part of the concept of the renovation grant, by identifying those purposes for which (alone) the application may (see s.13, below) be approved. They are as follows:

(i) *Housing Act notices.* Notices may be served under the Housing Act 1985, s.189, to carry out works to remedy unfitness (as defined *ibid.*, s.604—see below, s.97), or s.190 to put into reasonable repair (as defined in s.96, below) property which, though not unfit, requires substantial repairs or is in such a state of disrepair as to interfere materially with the personal comfort of an occupying tenant (see further, note below);

(ii) *Heat and energy.* To provide thermal insulation, and to provide adequate facilities for space heating—the two will commonly be related;

(iii) *Internal arrangement.* Internal arrangement probably means such matters as narrow, steep or winding staircases, want of handrails, inadequate landings, ill-defined changes in floor level, one bedroom entered only through another (see Ministry of Housing and Local Government Circular 68/69, App., para. 23). It used to be one of the key *indicia* of unfitness, under the Housing Act 1985, s.604 (and back to 1954), for the purposes of local authority action, and it remains one of the criteria under the Landlord and Tenant Act 1985, s.10, but the Local Government and Housing Act 1989, Sched. 9, para. 83, substituted a new s.604 in the 1985 Act (see notes to s.98, below), from which internal arrangement was omitted. It remains a purpose of renovation, however.

(iv) *Fire precautions.* Renovation grants are available for fire escapes and other precautions, *not* including those required under or by statute, *e.g.* not including those required under Building Acts and/or Regulations over the years, nor those required by a local authority in relation to a house in multiple occupation under the Housing Act 1985, s.352, *cf.* below, s.17. There is, however, one category of fire precaution which will qualify, by subs. (4): that is, precautions which are required to comply with a notice under the 1985 Act, s.352, so far—and only so far—as they relate to premises which are *not* part of an HMO, *i.e.* fire precaution works in self-contained units within houses in multiple occupation", (*Hansard* (H.C.), May 21, 1996, Standing Committee F, Third Sitting, col. 110, Parliamentary Under-Secretary of State for the Environment (Mr Clappison)).

(v) *Secretary of State's requirements.* The Secretary of State has power to prescribe construction standards, or requirements as to physical conditions, and with respect to the provision or condition of services and amenities to or in the dwelling.

(vi) *Secretary of State's added purposes.* The Secretary of State likewise has power to prescribe further purposes.

*Housing Act 1985 Notices*
*Section 189.* (as amended—see words in single square brackets—by the Housing Act 1988, Sched. 15, para. 1, and—see words in double square brackets—by the Local Government and Housing Act 1989, Sched. 9, para. 1):

"(1) [Subject to subsection (1A)] where the local housing authority are satisfied that a [dwelling house] [[or house in multiple occupation]] is unfit for human habitation, they shall serve a repair notice on the person having control of the [dwelling-house] [[or house in multiple occupation if they are satisfied, in accordance with section 604A, that serving a notice under this subsection is the most satisfactory course of action.]].

...

"(2) A repair notice under this section shall—
(a) require the person on whom it is served to execute the works specified in the notice [[(which may be works of repair or improvement or both)]] [and to begin those works not later than such reasonable date, being not earlier than the [[twenty-eighth day after the notice is served]] as is specified in the notice and to complete those works within such reasonable time as is so specified, and]
(b) state that in the opinion of the authority the works specified in the notice will render the [dwelling-house] [[or, as the case may be, house in multiple occupation]] fit for human habitation."

For the meaning of unfitness, see notes to s.97, below. For the persons who may be served, see notes to s.82, below.

*Section 190.* (as amended—see words in single square brackets—by the Housing Act 1988, Sched. 15, para. 2, and—see words in double square brackets—by the Local Government and Housing Act 1989, Sched. 9, para. 2):
"(1) [[Subject to subsection (1BB)]] where the local authority—
(a) are satisfied that a [dwelling-house] [[or house in multiple occupation]] is in such a state of disrepair that, although not unfit for human habitation, substantial repairs are necessary to bring it up to a reasonable standard, having regard to its age, character and locality, or
(b) are satisfied [whether] on a representation made by an occupying tenant [or otherwise] that a [dwelling-house] [[or house in multiple occupation]] is in such a state of disrepair that, although not unfit for human habitation, its condition is such as to interfere materially with the personal comfort of the occupying tenant [[or, in the case of a house in multiple occupation, the persons occupying it (whether as tenants or licensees)]],
they may serve a repair notice on the person having control of the [dwelling-house] [[or house in multiple occupation]].

...

"(2) A repair notice under this section shall require the person on whom it is served, [to execute the works specified in the notice, not being works of internal decorative repair, and—
(a) to begin those works not later than such reasonable date, being not earlier than the [[twenty-eight day after the notice is served]] as is specified in the notice; and
(b) to complete those works within such reasonable time as is so specified].

As to "age, character and locality", see notes to s.96, below. For the persons who may be served, see notes to s.82, below.

*Appeals.* There are provisions for appeal against both classes of notice: see also 1985 Act, s.191. See also s.83, below.

*Most satisfactory course of action.* This is not statutorily defined, but by 1985 Act, s.604A, the Secretary of State has power to issue guidance to which the authority are bound to have regard. Authorities are not bound to follow the guidance blindly; and they may depart from its provisions so long as they have first had regard to them—*De Falco, Silvestri v. Crawley B.C.* [1980] Q.B. 460, C.A., *Miller v. Wandsworth L.B.C.*, *The Times*, March 19, 1980, *Lambert v. Ealing L.B.C.* [1982] 1 W.L.R. 550, 2 H.L.R. 58, C.A. As Parliament has required authorities to have regard to it, however, deviation may amount to a *prima facie* case that it has not been taken into account, sufficient at least (in practice) to call for an explanation from the authority: *cf. Padfield v. Minister of Agriculture, Fisheries & Food* [1968] A.C. 997, H.L. The Act is, of course, the governing instrument and if there is a conflict between a provision of the Act and of the guidance, the Act takes precedence: *R. v. Waveney D.C., ex p. Bowers* [1983] Q.B. 238, 4 H.L.R. 118, C.A.

The current guidance under s.604A is to be found in DOE Circular [6]/90, Local Government and Housing Act 1989, Area Renewal, Unfitness, Slum Clearance and Enforcement Action, Annex F. This guidance is to be treated as guidance on the most satisfactory course of action under this Act: s.98(2), below.

*Subs. (3)*
With the consent of an applicant, the authority can treat an application for works which are more extensive than needed to achieve any of the statutory purposes of a renovation grant as reduced to those which are so necessary, alternatively to increase the works the subject of an application which would otherwise not achieve the purposes: without such consent and corre-

sponding variation, the application will not be one which the authority enjoy power to approve—see s.13(2), below.

## Renovation grants: approval of application

**13.**—(1) The local housing authority may approve an application for a renovation grant if they think fit, subject to the following provisions.

(2) The authority shall not approve an application for a renovation grant unless they are satisfied that the works are necessary for one or more of the purposes set out in section 12(1) or (2).

(3) Where an authority entertain an owner's application for a renovation grant made by a person who proposes to acquire a qualifying owner's interest, they shall not approve the application until they are satisfied that he has done so.

(4) An authority proposing to approve an application for a renovation grant shall consider whether the premises to which it relates are fit for human habitation.

(5) If it appears to the authority that the premises are not fit for human habitation, they shall not approve the application unless they are satisfied—

(a) that on completion of the relevant works, together with any other works proposed to be carried out, the premises will be fit for human habitation,

(b) that there are satisfactory financial and other arrangements for carrying out those works, and

(c) that the carrying out of the works is the most satisfactory course of action.

(6) In considering whether to approve an application for a renovation grant the authority shall have regard to the expected life of the building (taking account, where appropriate, of the effect of carrying out the works).

DEFINITIONS
"fit for human habitation": s.97.
"local housing authority": s.101.
"owner's application": s.101.
"qualifying owner's interest": s.7.
"relevant works": s.2.
"renovation grant": s.1.

GENERAL NOTE
This the last of the series of the sections creating an entitlement to apply for, and a discretion to approve, renovation grants; it contains the residual limitations:
(i) *Purposes*. The authority cannot approve the grant unless the works are needed for one or more of the s.12 purposes;
(ii) *Owner's interest*. Application may be made by a person planning to acquire an owner's interest (see s.7(1)), but may not be approved until it has been acquired;
(iii) *Fitness for human habitation*. No grant may be approved unless on completion of the works the subject of the application (the relevant works—see s.2) together with other works which may be proposed, *i.e.* unaided (for a variation under s.12(3) would vary what comprised the relevant works themselves), the property will be fit for human habitation (as to which, see notes to s.97, below), and that there are satisfactory financial arrangements and other arrangements (*e.g.* temporary rehousing of tenants) for carrying out the works, and that carrying out the works is "the most satisfactory course of action" (also see notes to s.97, below).
In addition, the authority are obliged to "have regard to" the expected life of the building after the works have been done: subs. (6).
The amount of the grant is governed by ss.30, 31, 33, below.

*Discretion and public law*
*Introduction*. Although it was a major part of the purpose of this Act (see Introduction to Pt. I, above) that grant-aid should be reduced from mandatory status to discretionary, there is no such thing as a "pure" discretion; all decisions of public bodies are ultimately reviewable by the

courts, usually by judicial review, under R.S.C. Ord. 53, in the Crown Office list of the High Court, if their decision-making procedures are defective, so that the decision that follows will be considered *ultra vires*.

*Literature.* Judicial review, and the corresponding principles of administrative law, is a growth area of legal activity and has generated both a substantial body of case-law, and of legal literature. New editions of the two leading text-books in the area have both recently been issued: *Administrative Law*, Wade & Forsyth, 7th. ed. (1994), and *Judicial Review of Administrative Action*, de Smith, Woolf & Jowell, 5th. ed. (1995). Recourse may also usefully be had to *Judicial Remedies in Public Law*, Lewis (1992), and, for the increasing reliance on E.C. law, its companion volume, *Remedies and the Enforcement of European Community Law*, Lewis (1996). Introductory texts are to be found in *Judicial Review Proceedings*, Manning (1995), and *Judicial Review: Law and Procedure*, 2nd ed., Gordon (1996).

*Ultra Vires.* What the principles invariably involve is that authorities should always approach their decisions in a lawful manner. If it can be shown that a public body such as a local authority have approached their decision unlawfully, the decision will be void and the courts will not give effect to it. A decision improperly reached is *ultra vires, i.e.* outside the authority's powers, and without effect in law, whether it is because on the face of the statute there was no authority to engage in the action at all, or because the statute has been misconstrued, or because the authority have misapplied the statute in another sense, *e.g.* by failing to use the powers to implement the purpose of the statute, or by reaching a decision under the statute by reference to something which is irrelevant, or in ignorance of something which is relevant, to the way the power under the statute is intended to be operated (see, most recently, *Crédit Suisse v. Allerdale M.B.C., Crédit Suisse v. Waltham Forest L.B.C., The Times,* May 20, 1996, C.A.).

*Wednesbury.* It is always important to bear in mind that the court does not act as an appeal tribunal from the authority's decision; instead, it is undertaking an investigation into the way in which the decision has been reached: *Associated Provincial Picture Houses v. Wednesbury Corporation* [1948] 1 K.B. 223, C.A. Lord Greene M.R. said:

"What, then, is the power of the courts? They can only interfere with an act of executive authority if it be shown that the authority has contravened the law. It is for those who assert that the local authority has contravened the law to establish that proposition ... It is not to be assumed *prima facie* that responsible bodies like the local authority in this case will exceed their powers; but the court, whenever it is alleged that the local authority have contravened the law, must not substitute itself for that authority ... When an executive discretion is entrusted by Parliament to a body such as the local authority in this case, what appears to be an exercise of that discretion can only be challenged in the courts in a strictly limited class of case. ... When discretion of this kind is granted the law recognises certain principles upon which that discretion must be exercised, but within the four corners of those principles the discretion ... is an absolute one and cannot be questioned in any court of law. What then are those principles? They are well understood. They are principles which the court looks to in considering any question of discretion of this kind. The exercise of such a discretion must be a real exercise of the discretion. If, in the statute conferring the discretion, there is to be found expressly or by implication matters which the authority exercising the discretion ought to have regard to, then in exercising the discretion it must have regard to those matters. Conversely, if the nature of the subject-matter and the general interpretation of the Act make it clear that certain matters would not be germane to the matter in question, the authority must disregard those irrelevant collateral matters" (p.228).

"There have been in the cases expressions used relating to the sort of things that authorities must not do ... I am not sure myself whether the permissible grounds of attack cannot be defined under a single head. ... Bad faith, dishonesty—those of course, stand by themselves—unreasonableness, attention given to extraneous circumstances, disregard of public policy and things like that have all been referred to, according to the facts of individual cases, as being matters which are relevant to the question. If they cannot all be confined under one head, they at any rate ... overlap to a very great extent. For instance, we have heard in this case a great deal about the meaning of the word 'unreasonable'.

"It is true the discretion must be exercised reasonably. Now what does that mean? ... It has frequently been used and is frequently used as a general description of the things that must not be done. ... A person entrusted with a discretion must ... direct himself properly in law. He must call his own attention to the matters which he is bound to consider. He must exclude from his consideration matters which are irrelevant to what he has to consider. If he does not obey those rules, he may truly be said, and often is said, to be acting 'unreasonably'. Similarly, there may be something so absurd that no sensible person could ever dream that it lay within the powers of the authority. Warrington L. J. in *Short v. Poole Corporation* [1926] Ch. 66 gave the example of the red-haired teacher, dismissed because she had red hair. That is unreasonable in one sense. In another sense it is taking into consideration extraneous matters. It is so unreasonable that it might almost be described as being done in bad faith; and, in fact, all these things run into one another ..." (p.229).

"It is true to say that, if a decision on a competent matter is so unreasonable that no reasonable authority could ever have come to it, then the courts can interfere... But to prove a case of that kind would require something overwhelming ... [The] proposition that the decision of the local authority can be upset if it is proved to be unreasonable, really meant that it must be proved to be unreasonable in the sense that the court considers it to be a decision that no reasonable body could have come to. It is not what the court considers unreasonable, a different thing altogether... The effect of the legislation is not to set up the court as an arbiter of the correctness of one view over another. It is the local authority that are set in that position and, provided they act, as they have acted, within the four corners of their jurisdiction, this court ... cannot interfere ..." (pp.230–231).

"The court is entitled to investigate the action of the local authority with a view to seeing whether they have taken into account matters which they ought not to take into account, or, conversely, have refused to take into account or neglected to take into account matters which they ought to take into account. Once that question is answered in favour of the local authority, it may still be possible to say that, although the local authority have kept within the four corners of the matters which they ought to consider, they have nevertheless come to a conclusion so unreasonable that no reasonable authority could ever have come to it. In such a case, again, I think the court can interfere. The power of the court to interfere in each case is not as an appellate authority to override a decision of the local authority, but as a judicial authority which is concerned, and concerned only, to see whether the local authority have contravened the law by acting in excess of the powers which Parliament has confided in them" (pp.233–234).

*Modern Re-classification.* The principles of administrative law may be expressed, and classified, in a number of different ways. In *Council of Civil Service Unions v. Minister for the Civil Service* [1985] 1 A.C. 374, H.L., Lord Diplock re-classified them under three headings: "illegality", "irrationality" and "procedural impropriety".

"By 'illegality' as a ground of judicial review I mean that the decision-maker must understand correctly the law that regulates his decision-making power and must give effect to it. Whether he has or not is par excellence a justiciable question to be decided, in the event of dispute, by those persons, the judges, by whom the judicial power of the state is exercisable.

"By 'irrationality' I mean what can by now be succinctly referred to as 'Wednesbury unreasonableness'... It applies to a decision which is so outrageous in its defiance of logic or of accepted moral standards that no sensible person who had applied his mind to the question to be decided could have arrived at it. Whether a decision falls within this category is a question that judges by their training and experience should be well equipped to answer, or else there would be something badly wrong with our judicial system... 'Irrationality' by now can stand upon its own feet as an accepted ground on which a decision may be attacked by judicial review. I have described the third head as 'procedural impropriety' rather than failure to observe basic rules of natural justice or failure to act with procedural fairness towards the person who will be affected by the decision. This is because susceptibility to judicial review under this head covers also failure by an administrative tribunal to observe procedural rules that are expressly laid down in the legislative instrument by which its jurisdiction is conferred, even where such failure does not involve any denial of natural justice ...".

This statement has been described as "a valuable, and already 'classical'" statement (though, again, "certainly not exhaustive" (*per* Lord Scarman in *Nottinghamshire County Council v. Secretary of State for the Environment* [1986] 1 A.C. 240, H.L. at p.249).

It may be noted that in *C.C.S.U.* Lord Diplock raised—but did not answer—the question whether or not the principle of "proportionality" might yet be imported into domestic administrative law from Europe (at p.410), although it is considered (see *R. v. Secretary of State for the Home Department, ex p. Brind* [1991] 1 A.C. 696, H.L.) that it does not enjoy any standing independently of conventional unreasonableness. Proportionality is the doctrine that there has to be a reasonable relationship between the governmental (including local) action under review, and its purpose in a given context.

*Practical classification.* In practice, the principles tend to overlap with one another. They may be considered under one or more of the following sub-headings:

(i) A statutory authority must take into account all the relevant factors before making their decision, and must disregard the irrelevant: *Wednesbury*. See also *Bristol District Council v. Clark* [1975] 1 W.L.R. 1443, C.A. It is sufficient to void a decision on the basis that an irrelevant factor has been taken into account if the factor is significant, or potentially of influence, meaning that if it had not been taken into account, the decision may have been different: see also *Hanks v. Ministry of Housing and Local Government* [1963] 1 Q.B. 999, *R. v. Lewisham L.B.C., ex p. Shell (UK)* [1988] 1 All E.R. 938, C.A.

(ii) The decision must be based on the facts; a decision totally at variance with the facts or for which there is no factual basis cannot be sustained:

"If a judgment requires, before it can be made, the existence of some facts, then although the evaluation of those facts is for the Secretary of State alone, the courts must enquire whether those facts exist, and have been taken into account, whether the judgment has been made on a proper self-direction as to those facts, whether the judgment has not been made on other facts which ought not to have been taken into account ..." (*per* Lord Wilberforce, *Secretary of State for Education and Science v. Metropolitan Borough of Tameside* [1977] A.C. 1014, H.L., at p.1047).

(iii) The authority must not act in bad faith or dishonestly: *Wednesbury*.

(iv) The authority must direct themselves properly in law, so that a decision based on a misunderstanding or misapplication of the law will not have been reached properly: *ibid*. This is the point in *Wednesbury* that is restated as "illegality" in *C.C.S.U.* See also *Anisminic v. Foreign Compensation Commission* [1969] 2 A.C. 147, H.L.

(v) The authority must act so as to promote, and not to defeat, the objects or policy of the Act in question: *Padfield v. Minister of Agriculture, Fisheries & Food* [1968] A.C. 997, H.L.; see also *Meade v. Haringey L.B.C.* [1979] 1 W.L.R. 1, C.A. Powers conferred for public purposes must be used in a way that Parliament can be presumed to have intended: *R. v. Tower Hamlets L.B.C., ex p. Chetnick Developments* [1988] A.C. 858, H.L.

(vi) The decision must not be one to which no reasonable authority could have come: this is conclusive evidence that the decision is improper: *Wednesbury*; see also *C.C.S.U.* and *Nottinghamshire*.

(vii) The authority must reach their own decision on each individual case; they must not fetter their discretion by approaching a decision with a predetermined policy as to how they will deal with any case falling within a particular class. The leading case on this is now probably *British Oxygen Co. v. Minister of Technology* [1971] A.C. 610, H.L. See also *R. v. Secretary of State for the Environment, ex p. Brent L.B.C.* [1982] Q.B. 593.

While a public authority can adopt a policy or limiting rule in order to guide the future exercise of their discretion if they think good administration requires it, they must consider its application individually in every case where it is sought to make an exception: *Stringer v. Minister of Housing and Local Government* [1970] 1 W.L.R. 1281, C.A.; *Cummings v. Birkenhead Corporation* [1972] Ch. 12, C.A.; *Elliott v. Brighton B.C.* (1981) 79 L.G.R. 506, C.A. *British Oxygen* was adopted and applied by the House of Lords in *In Re Betts* [1983] 2 A.C. 613, 10 H.L.R. 97, H.L. Even the "guideline" approach was disapproved by Templeman L.J. in *Att.-Gen., ex rel. Tilley v. Wandsworth L.B.C.* [1981] 1 W.L.R. 854, C.A., but the other two judges expressly reserved their positions on this and, of course, *British Oxygen* is the superior authority. See further note, below, on Policies.

(viii) It is the authority who are entrusted with the decision-making power and must make the decision. They cannot avoid their duties by adopting the decision of another body: *Lavender & Sons v. Minister of Housing and Local Government* [1970] 1 W.L.R. 1231. See also *R. v. Bolsover District Council and the Rent Officer for the Derbyshire Registration Area, ex p. East Midlands Development, and Denis Rye* (1995) 28 H.L.R. 329, Q.B.D., where the authority could not lawfully delegate to a rent officer their function of determining a notional increase in rental value (for grant aid purposes: see s.31, below), even though statutorily entitled to take his advice into account. (However, in the absence of any evidence to contradict the basis on which a rent officer had proceeded, it was considered unrealistic to expect them to adopt any other figure.)

(ix) As the full authority are *prima facie* entrusted with the decision-making power, the full authority must reach the decision unless they have, as they are empowered to do under Local Government Act 1972, s.101, delegated this power to a sub-committee or to an officer. It is they who must execute it: it cannot be transferred to another (even by the court), see *Gardner v. London Chatham and Dover Railway (No. 1)* (1867) L.R. 2 Ch. App. 201; *Marshall v. South Staffordshire Tramways* [1895] 2 Ch. 36 and, most recently, *Parker v. Camden L.B.C.* [1986] 1 Ch. 162, C.A.

There can be no delegation to a single member, as there cannot be a committee or sub-committee of one: *R. v. Secretary of State for the Environment, ex p. Hillingdon L.B.C.* [1986] 1 W.L.R. 807, C.A. (However, there can be delegation to an officer, to be exercised in consultation with a member, so long as the member does not play the dominant role to the extent that the officer cannot be said to have reached the decision himself: *R. v. Port Talbot B.C., ex p. Jones* [1988] 2 All E.R. 207, Q.B.D.). There can be no delegation to a person or body outside the authority, even a company formed by the authority: *Crédit Suisse v. Allerdale M.B.C., Crédit Suisse v. Waltham Forest L.B.C., The Times,* May 20, 1996, C.A.

(x) In all cases, an authority must act fairly, or in accordance with natural justice: *Re HK* [1967] 2 Q.B. 617, C.A.; see also *Sevenoaks D.C. v. Emmott* (1979) 39 P. & C.R. 404, C.A. The extent of this duty will depend upon circumstances, and the nature of the decision.

*Variations on a theme.* These propositions or principles are all, by and large, variations upon a theme. In *R. v. Greater London Council, ex p. Bromley L.B.C.* [1983] 1 A.C. 768, H.L., the arguments in the House of Lords were described as different ways of saying the same thing. Lack of natural justice or administrative fairness will usually mean that a public body have also failed to take something relevant into account, *i.e.* the views of the person affected, and what they might have told the authority. Similarly, the policy of an Act is a relevant consideration, and so also are the correct meaning of the law, and the correct facts. Bad faith or dishonesty would indicate consideration of irrelevant matters. Improper delegation, and the application of policy where an individual decision is required, both amount to a failure to consider the question (in the particular case) at all, which necessarily means that there has been a failure to take all that is relevant into account. (See also *Wednesbury*, above.)

*Burden of proof.* Whenever the decision of a public body is challenged on these principles, the burden of proof lies upon the person seeking to show that the decision is void: *Wednesbury, Cannock Chase D.C. v. Kelly* [1978] 1 W.L.R. 1, C.A. The allegations must be both substantiated, and particularised: *ibid.* For example, it is never enough to say simply that the applicant is a homeless person and in priority need, because this would not be enough to raise the inference of a duty: the duty arises only when the authority are satisfied, or have reason to believe, or consider that the fact or state of affairs is as it is claimed to be. It must be alleged that they have refused or failed to reach a decision, or that such decision as has been reached must be treated by the courts as void, for want of compliance with specified principles, and the factual basis for this allegation must be set out.

*Policies*

It is the application of "policies" which is most likely to lead authorities into error. On the one hand, the very purpose of the legislation is to liberate authorities' discretion to select and target their own renewal policies (see Introduction to Pt. I, above); on the other, it is trite public law that a policy cannot be applied so rigidly that no exceptions are made, or so that each individual case—or, in context, renovation grant application—is not decided on its own merits. See the cases cited above, para. (vii).

In *R. v. Bristol C.C., ex p. Bailey* (1994) 27 H.L.R. 307, Q.B.D., the authority declined to pay a discretionary renovation grant on the basis that it was the policy of the authority only to pay such grants where properties were unfit. This decision could be, and was, appealed to the authority's Housing (Special Purposes) Sub-committee, which confirmed the refusal in "all the circumstances relevant to this case", which was later explained by the authority's solicitor as meaning that the committee considered that officers had correctly determined that the property was not unfit. This was challenged as constituting a fetter on the authority's discretion to award renovation grants, even when there was no unfitness. The authority gave evidence that they had made realistic provision for discretionary grants in appropriate cases. It was held that they were entitled to formulate a policy for the allocation of grants, and that they had not fettered their discretion to depart from it.

In *R. v. Sunderland C.C., ex p. Redezeus* (1994) 27 H.L.R. 477, Q.B.D., however, the authority's "policy" was to award grant at a lower level than provided for by statute, so that, even though there was a clause permitting higher levels in exceptional cases, the policy could not stand as it was outside their statutory powers.

*Expected life.* The authority are bound to "have regard to" the expected life of the property. See note on *Most Satisfactory Course of Action* in notes to s.12, above. The requirement does not and cannot bind the authority to a particular result. So long as the authority have regard to the expected life, they may decide to issue a grant notwithstanding the limited period that will be added, and alternatively would err in law if they declined all grants that did not produce a certain, minimum further life (although they could adopt such a guideline, provided on occasion it would be possible to depart from it).

### Common parts grants

## Common parts grants: occupation of flats by occupying tenants

**14.**—(1) A local housing authority shall not entertain an application for a common parts grant unless they are satisfied that at the date of the application at least the required proportion of the flats in the building concerned is occupied by occupying tenants.

(2) In this Chapter an "occupying tenant", in relation to a flat in a building, means a person who has in relation to the flat (alone or jointly with others)—

(a) a tenancy to which section 1 of the Landlord and Tenant Act 1954 or Schedule 10 to the Local Government and Housing Act 1989 applies (long tenancies at low rents),

(b) an assured tenancy, a protected tenancy, a secure tenancy or a statutory tenancy,

(c) a protected occupancy under the Rent (Agriculture) Act 1976 or an assured agricultural occupancy within the meaning of Part I of the Housing Act 1988, or

(d) a tenancy or licence which satisfies such conditions as may be specified by order of the Secretary of State,

and who occupies the flat as his only or main residence.

References in this Chapter to other expressions relating to tenancies, in the context of an application for a common parts grant, shall be construed accordingly.

(3) The "required proportion" mentioned in subsection (1) is three-quarters or such other proportion as may be—

(a) specified for the purposes of this section by an order of the Secretary of State, or

(b) approved by him, in relation to a particular case or description of case, on application made by the local housing authority concerned.

DEFINITIONS
"common parts grant": s.1.
"flat": s.58.
"local housing authority": s.101.

GENERAL NOTE
This section sets out the first of the conditions which must be satisfied in the case of a common parts grant. See also ss.15, 16, below.

The authority must be satisfied that, at the date of the application, the required proportion (*i.e.* 75 per cent or such other proportion as is prescribed by the Secretary of State: subs. (3)) of the flats in the building are occupied by "occupying tenants": subs. (1).

An occupying tenant is one who:
(i) has one of the interests set out in para. (a) to (d) of subs. (2); and
(ii) who occupies the flat as his only or main residence: see notes to s.8, above.

*Long tenancy at low rent.* On what would be the termination of long tenancies at a low rent which were granted before the commencement of the Housing Act 1988 (January 15, 1989), there is provision under s.1 of the Landlord and Tenant Act 1954 for the lease to continue contractually, until determined in accordance with Pt. I of the 1954 Act, following which the tenancy will become a statutory tenancy under the Rent Act 1977 (see further, note below). Under the Local Government and Housing Act 1989, s.186 and Sched. 10, analogous provision is made for the treatment of long tenancies at a low rent in substance to become assured tenancies under the Housing Act 1988 (which means that they will subsist contractually until a court orders possession: see further, note below). Transitional provisions serve to substitute the latter regime for some long leases which would otherwise have fallen within the former (1989 Act, s.186(3)).

In each case, the protection is available to long leaseholders at low rents, whose tenancies would have been within the principal security Act but for the low rent (see notes below): 1954 Act, s.2; 1989 Act, s.186 and Sched. 10, para. 1. For each purpose, long lease means a tenancy granted for a term certain of more than 21 years: 1954 Act, s.2(4); 1989 Act, Sched. 10, para. 2(3). Time runs from the date of the grant, not from the date of commencement of the lease: *Roberts v. Church Commissioners for England* [1972] 1 Q.B. 278, C.A. (decided under the Leasehold Reform Act 1967). "Low rent" is defined, prior to April 1, 1990, by reference to rateable values, and subsequently by reference under the 1954 Act to fixed amounts and by reference under the 1989 Act to the premium paid as against the term granted: 1954 Act, s.2(5), 1989 Act, Sched. 10, para. 1(2A), as amended by the References to Rating (Housing) Regulations 1990 (S.I. 1990 No. 434).

*Assured tenancy.* Since the coming into force of the Housing Act 1988 (January 15, 1989), assured tenancies have been the usual form of letting in the wholly private sector, and by housing associations, replacing (i) Rent Act security for most private tenants, and (ii) Housing Act 1985 security for most housing association tenants (and in each case, Rent Act control of rents). There are exceptions (see the Housing Act 1988, ss.34, 35), but these are confined to (transitional) cases where there is what might be called some "prior element", *e.g.* grants of new tenancies to tenants within the previous regime, in the same or other property.

There is a number of exceptions to status as an assured tenant or assured agricultural occupancy: see Sched. 1 to the Housing Act 1988. Assured *shorthold* tenancies do not, however, form an exception: while there are special provisions which govern them, they are none the less assured tenancies as it were in their own right (see 1988 Act, s.20(1): "... an assured shorthold tenancy is an assured tenancy which..." complies with stated conditions). Accordingly, a letting of an assured shorthold tenancy is a letting of an assured tenancy, and within this section.

Subject to exceptions and transitional provisions, an assured tenancy is one:

(i) granted after the commencement of the Housing Act 1988 (January 15, 1989),

(ii) which is of a dwelling-house (which may be a house or part of a house: Housing Act 1988, s.45),

(iii) let (which means on a tenancy rather than on a licence, see notes to s.7, above),

(iv) as (which imports consideration of the purpose of the letting),

(v) a separate dwelling (see notes to s.1, above),

(vi) under which the tenant is an individual (rather than corporate body)—or if joint tenants, at least one of the tenants is an individual,

(vii) who uses the dwelling as his only or principal home (see notes to s.8, above).

The exceptions, briefly described, are (1988 Act, Sched. 1):

(a) Tenancies entered into before commencement (this exception is omitted when considering whether a long tenancy falls within the continuation provisions of the Local Government and Housing Act 1989, Sched. 10, see note above);

(b) High rateable value lettings;

(c) Low rent tenancies (see also note above on long tenancy);

(d) Business tenancies within the Landlord and Tenant Act 1954, Pt. II;

(e) Licensed premises;

(f) Agricultural land;

(g) Agricultural holdings;

(h) Lettings to students;

(i) Holiday lettings;

(j) Resident landlords;

(k) Crown tenancies; and,

(l) Public sector tenancies (including local authorities, Commission for the New Towns, new town development corporations, Development Board for Rural Wales, urban development corporation, housing action trust—see generally notes to s.3, above).

Assured tenancies cannot be brought to an end by the landlord, except by obtaining an order of the court: 1988 Act, s.5. This abolishes the distinction which had prevailed in the private sector before the 1988 Act of the distinction between contractual, and statutory, tenancies: see next note. Court orders for possession can only be made on certain grounds: *ibid.*, s.7 and Sched. 2.

*Protected and statutory tenancy.* Until the Housing Act 1988 came into force (January 15, 1989), Rent Act protection was the normal form of security of tenure for private sector tenants, and comprised the code of rent control applicable both to private sector tenants and housing association tenants (whose security, however, was governed by the Housing Act 1985). A protected tenant is a tenant within the Rent Act 1977, whose contractual tenancy has not yet been determined. A statutory tenant is a former protected tenant who enjoys the right to remain in occupation conferred by the 1977 Act, s.2. Save under the transitional provisions of the Housing Act 1988, new protected tenancies could not be granted after January 15, 1989.

Subject to exceptions provisions, a protected or statutory tenancy is:

(i) the letting of a dwelling-house (which may be a house or part of a house: the Rent Act 1977, s.1),

(ii) let (which means on a tenancy rather than on a licence, see notes to s.7, above),

(iii) as (which imports consideration of the purpose of the letting),

(iv) a separate dwelling (see notes to s.1, above),

(v) under which security of tenure pursuant to the statutory tenancy is only available to an individual (rather than corporate body),

(vi) who continues to occupy the dwelling as a residence (see notes to s.8, above): the Rent Act 1977, s.2.

The exceptions, briefly described, are:

(a) High rateable value lettings (1977 Act, s.4);

(b) Low rent tenancies (see also note above on long tenancy) (1977 Act, s.5);

(c) Lettings together with other land (as distinct from land let with the dwelling-house) (1977 Act, s.6);

(d) Lettings with board or attendance (1977 Act, s.7);
(e) Lettings to students (1977 Act, s.8);
(f) Holiday lettings (1977 Act, s.9);
(g) Agricultural holdings (1977 Act, s.10);
(h) Licensed premises (1977 Act, s.11);
(i) Resident landlords (1977 Act, s.12);
(j) Crown lettings (1977 Act, s.13);
(k) Public sector lettings (including local authorities, Commission for the New Towns, new town development corporations, Development Board for Rural Wales, urban development corporation, housing action trust—see generally notes to s.3, above) (1977 Act, s.14);
(l) Housing association lettings (1977 Act, s.15);
(m) Housing co-operative lettings (1977 Act, s.16);
(n) Business tenancies within the Landlord and Tenant Act 1954, Pt. II (1977 Act, s.24).

A contractual tenancy within the Rent Act is determined in the normal way; a statutory tenancy is determined by a possession order, which, like the assured tenancy, can only be made on specified grounds (1977 Act, s.98 and Sched. 15).

*Protected and assured occupancy.* In the case of workers in agriculture and forestry, living in tied accommodation, security of tenure was conferred by the Rent (Agriculture) Act 1976 (c. 80), largely to correspond to security of tenure under (what was to become) the Rent Act 1977 (c. 42). Analogous replacement provisions, governing workers in agriculture, were contained in the Housing Act 1988 (c. 50), and similarly confer a code of security corresponding to that available to assured tenants under that Act.

*Secure Tenancy.* This is the regime applicable to—primarily—local authority tenancies. It was formerly also applicable to housing association tenancies, but save under the transitional provisions of the Housing Act 1988, new housing association tenancies could not be granted after January 15, 1989.

A secure tenancy is:
(i) the letting (on a tenancy or on a licence—Housing Act 1985, s.79(3), *cf.* notes to s.7, above),
(ii) of a dwelling-house (which may be a house or part of a house: 1985 Act, s.112),
(iii) by a public sector landlord (meaning local authority, new town corporation, housing action trust, urban development corporation, Development Board for Rural Wales, or a housing co-operative to which the section applied—1985 Act, s.80, see generally notes to s.3, above),
(iv) as (which imports consideration of the purpose of the letting),
(v) a separate dwelling (see notes to s.1, above),
(vi) under which the tenant is an individual (rather than corporate body)—or if joint tenants, at least one of the tenants is an individual,
(vii) who uses the dwelling as his only or principal home (see notes to s.8, above).
The exceptions, briefly described, are (1985 Act, Sched. 1):
(a) Long tenancies (*i.e.* term certain exceeding 21 years—1985 Act, s.115);
(b) Certain categories of accommodation related to employment;
(c) Land acquired for development;
(d) Accommodation for homeless persons;
(e) Temporary accommodation for persons taking up employment, *i.e.* to encourage job mobility;
(f) Private sector, sub-leasing schemes;
(g) Temporary accommodation during works;
(h) Agricultural holdings;
(i) Licensed premises;
(j) Student lettings;
(k) Business tenancies within Landlord and Tenant Act 1954, Pt. II;
(l) Almshouses.
In addition, the Housing Act 1996 introduces a new and optional exception to secure tenancy, which is the "introductory tenancy" which provides for re-possession merely by following a specified procedure, without more, *i.e.* it does not need specific grounds for possession.

Secure tenancies cannot be brought to an end by the landlord, except by obtaining an order of the court: 1985 Act, s.82. Court orders for possession can only be made on certain grounds: *ibid.*, s.84 and Sched. 2.

*Tenancy or licence.* Licensees (see note to s.7, above) may qualify, if within conditions specified by the Secretary of State, as may any other tenant so specified, who is not within the classes identified above.

## Common parts grants: landlord's and tenants' applications

**15.**—(1) A local housing authority shall not entertain an application for a common parts grant unless they are satisfied—

(a) that the applicant has an owner's interest in the building and has a duty or power to carry out the relevant works, or

(b) that the application is made by at least three-quarters of the occupying tenants of the building who under their tenancies have a duty to carry out, or to make a contribution in respect of the carrying out of, some or all of the relevant works.

(2) References in this Chapter to a "landlord's application" and a "tenants' application", in relation to a common parts grant, shall be construed accordingly.

(3) In deciding whether the requirement in subsection (1)(b) is met—

(a) where a tenancy is held by two or more persons jointly, those persons shall be regarded as a single occupying tenant; and

(b) a tenant whose tenancy is of a description specified for the purposes of that paragraph by order of the Secretary of State shall be treated as an occupying tenant falling within that paragraph.

(4) A person who has an owner's interest in the building and who has a duty or power to carry out any of the relevant works may also join in a tenants' application for a common parts grant; and where such a person does join in an application, he is in this Chapter referred to as a "participating landlord".

DEFINITIONS
   "common parts grant": s.1.
   "local housing authority": s.101.
   "occupying tenants": s.14.
   "owner's interest": s.101.
   "relevant works": s.2.

GENERAL NOTE
This is the second of the conditions which must be satisfied in the case of a common parts grant. See also s.14, above, and s.16, below. The second condition is that the application must qualify:
   *either* as an application by someone with (a) an owner's interest (see s.101, see also note to s.7, above), and (b) a duty or power to carry out the works the subject of the application (a landlord's application—subs. (2)),
   *or* as an application made by at least three-quarters of those occupying tenants (see s.14, above), under whose tenancies there is either a duty to carry out some or all of the works the subject of the application, or else an obligation to make a contribution in respect of them (a tenants' application—subs. (2)).

*Landlords.* Whether or not a landlord has a duty or a power to carry out the works the subject of the application will normally be a matter of construing the terms of tenancies and leases and comparing them to the works in question. The meaning of "common parts" has been discussed in the notes to s.1, above: see also s.58, below—"'common parts' in relation to a building, includes the structure and exterior of the building and common facilities provided, whether in the building or elsewhere, for persons who include the occupiers of one or more flats").
   In some cases, the term may be that implied by s.11(1), as extended by s.11(1A), (1B) of the Landlord and Tenant Act 1985, added by the Housing Act 1988, s.116, applicable to leases and tenancies granted after January 15, 1989:
   "(1) In a lease to which this section applies ... there is implied a covenant by the lessor—
      (a) to keep in repair the structure and exterior of the dwelling-house (including drains, gutters and external pipes),
      (b) to keep in repair and proper working order the installations in the dwelling-house (including basins, sinks, baths and sanitary conveniences, but not other fixtures, fittings and appliances for making use of the supply of water, gas or electricity), and
      (c) to keep in repair and proper working order the installations in the dwelling-house for space heating and heating water.

"(1A) If a lease to which this section applies is a lease of a dwelling-house which forms part only of a building, then, subject to subsection (1B), the covenant implied by subsection (1) shall have effect as if—

   (a) the reference in paragraph (a) of that subsection to the dwelling-house included a reference to any part of the building in which the lessor has an estate or interest; and

   (b) any reference in paragraphs (b) and (c) of that subsection to an installation in the dwelling-house included a reference to an installation which, directly or indirectly, serves the dwelling-house and which either:

      (i) forms part of any part of a building in which the lessor has an estate or interest; or

      (ii) is owned by the lessor or under his control.

"(1B) Nothing in subsection (1A) shall be construed as requiring the lessor to carry out any works or repairs unless the disrepair (or failure to maintain in working order) is such as to affect the lessee's enjoyment of the dwelling-house or of any common parts, as defined in section 60(1) of the Landlord and Tenant Act 1987, which the lessee, as such, is entitled to use".

("'Common parts', in relation to any building or part of a building, includes the structure and exterior of that building or part and any common facilities within it": s.60, 1987 Act, *i.e.* it is in the same terms as s.58 of this Act without the extension to facilities provided in another building, which can, however, be within the landlord's repairing obligation under s.11(1A)(b)).

A landlord's duty to carry out works may be implied by the terms of the lease, or by the absence of any express liability, *e.g.* where maintenance of means of access was implied as necessary, as in *Liverpool C.C. v. Irwin* [1977] A.C. 239, H.L., or where the tenant's obligations to maintain the interior would have been meaningless without a corresponding obligation in respect of the exterior on the part of the landlord, as in *Barrett v. Lounova (1982)* (1988) 20 H.L.R. 584, C.A.

Even if the landlord cannot be said to be under a *duty*, if the leases are silent then a landlord will normally be considered to have *power* to carry out works of repair or maintenance, and certainly so if the works in question, even not within his express responsibilities, fall within the terms of what he can recover by way of service charge.

A landlord (within this definition) may also join in with a tenants' application, in which case he is known as a "participating landlord": subs. (4).

*Tenants.* The application must be by three-quarters of the occupying tenants of the building who have a duty to do the works in question, or to contribute to their cost. Note that this quotient is not of the flats as a whole (three-quarters of which must be occupied by occupying tenants under s.14, above), but of the occupying tenants (thus, *prima facie*, three-quarters of three-quarters). Even so, it is only a quotient of three-quarters of those occupying tenants who have a duty to do some or all of the works in question (which could include a roof or windows), or to contribute to their cost (which will be much more common), which must be fulfilled for a tenants' application to be made.

*Subs. (3)*

This makes two ancillary provisions: (a) that a joint tenancy counts as a sole tenancy for the purpose of determining whether the quotient of tenants has been met, and (b) to allow the Secretary of State to prescribe occupying tenants for this purpose, independently of the power to prescribe additional occupying tenants generally under s.14, *i.e.* if he wishes to apply provisions differentially.

## Common parts grants: certificate required to accompany application

**16.**—(1) A local housing authority shall not entertain a landlord's application for a common parts grant unless it is accompanied by a certificate signed by the applicant which—

   (a) specifies the interest of the applicant in the building, and

   (b) certifies that the required proportion of the flats in the building is occupied by occupying tenants.

(2) A local housing authority shall not entertain a tenants' application for a common parts grant unless it is accompanied by a certificate signed by each of the applicants which—

   (a) specifies the interest of each of the applicants in each flat in the building, and

   (b) certifies that the required proportion of the flats in the building is occupied by occupying tenants.

DEFINITIONS
    "common parts grant": s.1.
    "flat": s.58.
    "local housing authority": s.101.

GENERAL NOTE

This is the third of the conditions which must be satisfied in the case of a common parts grant. See also ss.14, 15, above. The third condition is that the application must be accompanied by either a landlord's certificate or a tenants' certificate, the first of which must specify the interest of the applicant in the building, and the second of which must specify the interest of each applicant in their flats, and both of which must certify that the required proportion of flats in the building (above, s.14) is occupied by occupying tenants.

## Common parts grants: purposes for which grant may be given

**17.**—(1) The purposes for which an application for a common parts grant may be approved are—

(a) to comply with a notice under section 189 of the Housing Act 1985 (repair notice in respect of unfit premises) or otherwise to cause the building to meet the requirements in section 604(2) of that Act;

(b) to comply with a notice under section 190 of that Act (repair notice in respect of premises not unfit but in need of substantial repair) or otherwise to put the building in reasonable repair;

(c) to comply with a notice under section 352 of that Act (notice requiring works to render premises fit for the number of occupants) or otherwise to enable the house to meet one or more of the requirements in subsection (1A) of that section;

(d) to provide adequate thermal insulation;

(e) to provide adequate facilities for space heating;

(f) to provide satisfactory internal arrangements;

(g) to provide means of escape in case of fire or other fire precautions, not being precautions required under or by virtue of any enactment (whenever passed);

(h) to ensure that the building complies with such requirements with respect to construction or physical condition as may be specified by the Secretary of State;

(i) to ensure that there is compliance with such requirements with respect to the provision or condition of services and amenities to or within the building as are so specified;

(j) any other purpose for the time being specified for the purposes of this section by order of the Secretary of State.

(2) If in the opinion of the local housing authority the relevant works are more or less extensive than is necessary to achieve any of the purposes set out in subsection (1), they may, with the consent of the applicant, treat the application as varied so that the relevant works are limited to or, as the case may be, include such works as seem to the authority to be necessary for that purpose.

(3) In exercise of the powers conferred by paragraphs (h) and (i) of subsection (1) the Secretary of State may specify requirements generally or for particular cases, and may specify different requirements for different areas.

DEFINITIONS
    "common parts grant": s.1.
    "local housing authority": s.101.

GENERAL NOTE

See notes to s.12, above, to which this is identical in all respects, save
(i) for the omission of reference to conversion grant (see s.12(2)); and,

(ii) for the inclusion as a purpose of the common parts grant of compliance with a notice under s.352 of the Housing Act 1985.

Note that, in addition to these purposes, a disabled facilities grant application may qualify as a common parts application (*n.b. not* "common parts *grant* application"), if it is for works designed to facilitate access to accommodation or facilities: see s.23, below.

*Housing Act 1985, section 352.* This section is concerned with houses in multiple occupation (as to which, see notes to s.1, above). A house in multiple occupation could, however, be the subject of an application for a common parts grant, if the occupancy conditions of s.14 were fulfilled. If not, then it could still be the subject of application for an HMO grant.

Section 352(1) empowers the authority to serve notice—

"where [in the opinion of the authority, a house in multiple occupation fails to meet one or more of the requirements in paragraphs (a) to (e) of subsection (1A) and, having regard to the number of individuals or households or both for the time being accommodated on the premises, by reason of that failure the premises are not reasonably suitable for occupation by those individuals or households.

"(1A) The requirements in respect of a house in multiple occupation referred to in subsection (1) are the following, that is to say,—

(a) there are satisfactory facilities for the storage, preparation and cooking of food including an adequate number of sinks with a satisfactory supply of hot and cold water;

(b) it has an adequate number of suitably located water-closets for the exclusive use of the occupants;

(c) it has, for the exclusive use of the occupants, an adequate number of suitably located fixed baths or showers and wash-hand basins each of which is provided with a satisfactory supply of hot and cold water;

(d) subject to section 365, there are adequate means of escape from fire; and

(e) there are adequate other fire precautions.]

(2) [Subject to subsection (2A)] the notice shall specify the works which in the opinion of the authority are required for rendering the premises reasonably suitable—

(a) for occupation by the individuals or households for the time being accommodated there, or

(b) for a smaller number of individuals or households, or both, which, in the opinion of the authority, the [house] could reasonably accommodate if the works were carried out [but the notice shall not specify any works to any premises outside the house].

[(2A) Where the authority have exercised or propose to exercise their powers under section 368 to secure that part of the house is not used for human habitation, they may specify in the notice such work only as in their opinion is required to meet such of the requirements in subsection (1A) as may be applicable if that part is not so used.]"

(As amended—see words in square brackets—by the Local Government and Housing Act 1989, Sched. 9).

Section 365—so far as here relevant—obliges an authority in certain circumstances to consult with the local fire authority before serving a notice in respect of means of escape from fire and, since amendment, other fire precautions: 1985, s.365(3), as to be amended by the Housing Act 1996, s.75. For the persons who may be served, see notes to s.82, below. There is provision for appeal against a s.352 notice (1985, s.353); see also notes to s.83, below.

The power to include means of escape from fire, and other fire precautions, in a notice under s.352 overrides the limitation in subs. (1)(g), that the provision of means of escape in case of fire, and other fire precautions, are not within the purposes of a grant if they are required under or by virtue of an enactment: if required under s.352, they will be.

## Common parts grants: approval of application

**18.**—(1) The local housing authority may approve an application for a common parts grant if they think fit, subject to the following provisions.

(2) The authority shall not approve an application for a common parts grant unless they are satisfied that the works are necessary for one or more of the purposes set out in section 17(1).

(3) An authority proposing to approve an application for a common parts grant shall consider whether the building to which the application relates meets the requirements mentioned in paragraphs (a) to (e) of section 604(2) of the Housing Act 1985.

(4) If it appears to the authority that the building does not meet those requirements, they shall not approve the application unless they are satisfied—

(a) that on completion of the relevant works, together with any other works proposed to be carried out, the building will meet those requirements,

(b) that there are satisfactory financial and other arrangements for carrying out those works, and

(c) that the carrying out of the works is the most satisfactory course of action.

(5) In considering whether to approve an application for a common parts grant the local housing authority shall have regard to the expected life of the building (taking account, where appropriate, of the effect of carrying out the works).

DEFINITIONS
"common parts grant": s.1.
"local housing authority": s.101.

GENERAL NOTE
See notes to s.13, above, to which this section corresponds save in the following respects: it is the building which must meet the specified fitness criteria of s.604 of the Housing Act 1985, rather than the premises which are intended to achieve fitness. The relevant criteria are structural stability, freedom from serious disrepair, freedom from dampness, adequate provision for ventilation, and an effective system for the draining of foul, waste and surface water. See notes to s.97, below.

The amount of the grant is governed by ss.31–33, below.

*Disabled facilities grants*

**Disabled facilities grants: owner's and tenant's applications**

**19.**—(1) A local housing authority shall not entertain an application for a disabled facilities grant unless they are satisfied—

(a) that the applicant has, or proposes to acquire, an owner's interest in every parcel of land on which the relevant works are to be carried out, or

(b) that the applicant is a tenant (alone or jointly with others)—

(i) in the case of an application in respect of works to a dwelling, of the dwelling, or

(ii) in the case of a common parts application, of a flat in the building,

and, in either case, does not have or propose to acquire such an owner's interest as is mentioned in paragraph (a).

(2) References in this Chapter to an "owner's application" or a "tenant's application", in relation to a disabled facilities grant, shall be construed accordingly.

(3) In accordance with directions given by the Secretary of State, a local housing authority may treat the condition in subsection (1)(a) as met by a person who has, or proposes to acquire, an owner's interest in only part of the land concerned.

(4) In this Chapter, in relation to an application for a disabled facilities grant—

"qualifying owner's interest" means an owner's interest meeting the condition in subsection (1)(a) or treated by virtue of subsection (3) as meeting that condition; and

"qualifying tenant" means a tenant who meets the conditions in subsection (1)(b).

(5) In this Chapter "tenant", in relation to a disabled facilities grant, includes—

(a) a secure tenant, introductory tenant or statutory tenant,

(b) a protected occupier under the Rent (Agriculture) Act 1976 or a person in occupation under an assured agricultural occupancy within the meaning of Part I of the Housing Act 1988,

    (c) an employee (whether full-time or part-time) who occupies the dwelling or flat concerned for the better performance of his duties, and

    (d) a person having a licence to occupy the dwelling or flat concerned which satisfies such conditions as may be specified by order of the Secretary of State;

and other expressions relating to tenancies, in the context of an application for disabled facilities grant, shall be construed accordingly.

DEFINITIONS
"dwelling": s.101.
"disabled facilities grant": s.1.
"flat": s.58.
"local housing authority": s.101.
"owner's interest": s.101.

GENERAL NOTE
This section begins the series which culminates in the sole remaining mandatory grant (see Introduction to Pt. I, above), the disabled facilities grant (see s.24, below). Application may be made by—

    (i) Someone who has, or proposes to acquire, an owner's interest—see notes to s.7, above (an owner's application—subs. (2)); or

    (ii) A tenant (or one of joint tenants) of the dwelling (a tenant's application—subs. (2)); or

    (iii) A tenant (or one of joint tenants) of a flat in a building, where the application is a "common parts application" (to be distinguished from "common parts *grant* application"—see ss.14, *et seq.*, above) (a tenant's application—subs. (2)).

In the case of either category of tenant's application, the tenant must not also have, or propose to acquire, an owner's interest.

In the case of an application based on proposed ownership, the authority will not be able to approve the grant until the interest has been acquired: see s.24(2).

*Subs. (5)*
All tenants are included: the purpose of this subsection is to *extend* the meaning of tenant (see notes to s.7, above) to include occupiers who are deemed to be tenants under other provisions (*e.g.*, licensees who are secure tenants or introductory tenants—see notes to s.14, above) or are put in an analogous position (as with statutory tenants, who have a "personal right" or "right of irremovability" rather than a true tenancy in the sense of being an interest in land—see *Keaves v. Dean* [1924] 1 K.B. 685, *Jessamine Investments v. Schwartz* [1978] Q.B. 264, and protected and assured occupiers—see notes to s.14, above). The Secretary of State has the power to specify further categories of qualifying licence.

Reflecting the desirability of helping the disabled into, or to keep, work, also included here are employees (full or part-time) occupying premises for the better performance of their duties, and who, as such, are likely to be licensees.

The phrase—better performance of duties—is one derived from the case-law distinguishing service tenancy and service occupation. The former creates a true tenancy and refers merely to someone whose landlord and employer is the same: see *Redbank Schools v. Abdullahzadeh* (1995) 28 H.L.R. 431, C.A.

The latter, on the other hand, amounts to no more than a license and refers to someone who needs to occupy accommodation in order to perform his employment duties: see *Smith v. Seghill Overseers* (1875) L.R. 10 Q.B. 422—approved in *Street v. Mountford* [1985] A.C. 809, 17 H.L.R. 402, H.L.; *Hirst v. Sargent* (1967) 65 L.G.R. 127; *Chapman v. Freeman* [1978] 1 W.L.R. 1298; *Royal Philanthropic Society v. County* (1985) 18 H.L.R. 83, C.A.—all adopting or tending towards a test of necessity rather than mere convenience, *cf. Fox v. Dalby* (1874) L.R. 10 C.P. 285 and *Glasgow Corporation v. Johnstone* [1965] A.C. 609, H.L., where it seemed that a slightly more lax or subjective test, on the part of the employer, might suffice.

The cases should be distinguished from those where what is under consideration is a contractual obligation to reside in particular premises, for some other purpose, *e.g.* exclusion from security under the Housing Act 1985, Sched. 1, para. 2, *cf. Hughes v. Greenwich L.B.C.* [1994] 1 A.C. 170, 26 H.L.R. 99, H.L.

## Disabled facilities grants: the disabled occupant

**20.** In this Chapter the "disabled occupant", in relation to an application for disabled facilities grant, means the disabled person for whose benefit it is proposed to carry out any of the relevant works.

DEFINITIONS
  "disabled facilities grant": s.1.
  "disabled person": s.100.

GENERAL NOTE
  The disabled person for whose benefit works are to be undertaken need not be the owner or tenant himself.

## Disabled facilities grants: certificate required in case of owner's application

**21.**—(1) A local housing authority shall not entertain an owner's application for a disabled facilities grant unless it is accompanied by an owner's certificate in respect of the dwelling to which the application relates or, in the case of a common parts application, in respect of each flat in the building occupied or proposed to be occupied by a disabled occupant.

(2) An "owner's certificate", for the purposes of an application for a disabled facilities grant, certifies that the applicant—

(a) has or proposes to acquire a qualifying owner's interest, and

(b) intends that the disabled occupant will live in the dwelling or flat as his only or main residence throughout the grant condition period or for such shorter period as his health and other relevant circumstances permit.

DEFINITIONS
  "disabled facilities grant": s.1.
  "dwelling": s.101.
  "flat": s.58.
  "grant condition period": s.44.
  "local housing authority": s.101.
  "owner's application": s.19.

GENERAL NOTE
  An owner's application must be accompanied by an owner's certificate. If the application is for a dwelling, then it must be in respect of the dwelling; if the application is a common parts application for a disabled facilities grant, then it must be in respect of each flat which is or is proposed to be occupied by a disabled occupier. The certificate must confirm that the applicant has, or proposes to acquire, an owner's certificate; the certificate must also confirm that it is intended that throughout the grant condition period (normally five years—s.44(3), below)—or for such shorter period as health and other relevant circumstances (*e.g.* availability of home care) will permit—the disabled occupant will live in the relevant property as his only or main residence (as to which, see notes to s.8, above).
  This requirement is not applicable to applications in respect of certain church lands and applications made by charities: s.95, below.

## Disabled facilities grants: certificates required in case of tenant's application

**22.**—(1) A local housing authority shall not entertain a tenant's application for a disabled facilities grant unless it is accompanied by a tenant's certificate.

(2) A "tenant's certificate", for the purposes of an application for a disabled facilities grant, certifies—

(a) that the application is a tenant's application, and

(b) that the applicant intends that he (if he is the disabled occupant) or the disabled occupant will live in the dwelling or flat as his only or main residence throughout the grant condition period or for such shorter period as his health and other relevant circumstances permit.

(3) Except where the authority consider it unreasonable in the circumstances to require such a certificate, they shall not entertain a tenant's application for a disabled facilities grant unless it is also accompanied by an

owner's certificate from the person who at the time of the application is the landlord under the tenancy.

<small>DEFINITIONS</small>
"disabled facilities grant": s.1.
"disabled occupant": ss.20, 100.
"dwelling": s.101.
"flat": s.58.
"grant condition period": s.44.
"local housing authority": s.101.
"owner's certificate": s.21.

<small>GENERAL NOTE</small>
This section makes provision corresponding to the last, where the application is a tenant's application, confirming the intended residence of the disabled occupant. An owner's certificate under s.21 is *also* required, unless the authority consider it unreasonable to require it.

This requirement is not applicable to applications in respect of certain church lands and applications made by charities: s.95, below.

## Disabled facilities grants: purposes for which grant must or may be given

**23.**—(1) The purposes for which an application for a disabled facilities grant must be approved, subject to the provisions of this Chapter, are the following—

(a) facilitating access by the disabled occupant to and from the dwelling or the building in which the dwelling or, as the case may be, flat is situated;

(b) making the dwelling or building safe for the disabled occupant and other persons residing with him;

(c) facilitating access by the disabled occupant to a room used or usable as the principal family room;

(d) facilitating access by the disabled occupant to, or providing for the disabled occupant, a room used or usable for sleeping;

(e) facilitating access by the disabled occupant to, or providing for the disabled occupant, a room in which there is a lavatory, or facilitating the use by the disabled occupant of such a facility;

(f) facilitating access by the disabled occupant to, or providing for the disabled occupant, a room in which there is a bath or shower (or both), or facilitating the use by the disabled occupant of such a facility;

(g) facilitating access by the disabled occupant to, or providing for the disabled occupant, a room in which there is a washhand basin, or facilitating the use by the disabled occupant of such a facility;

(h) facilitating the preparation and cooking of food by the disabled occupant;

(i) improving any heating system in the dwelling to meet the needs of the disabled occupant or, if there is no existing heating system in the dwelling or any such system is unsuitable for use by the disabled occupant, providing a heating system suitable to meet his needs;

(j) facilitating the use by the disabled occupant of a source of power, light or heat by altering the position of one or more means of access to or control of that source or by providing additional means of control;

(k) facilitating access and movement by the disabled occupant around the dwelling in order to enable him to care for a person who is normally resident in the dwelling and is in need of such care;

(l) such other purposes as may be specified by order of the Secretary of State.

(2) An application for a disabled facilities grant may be approved, subject to the provisions of this Chapter, for the purpose of making the dwelling or building suitable for the accommodation, welfare or employment of the disabled occupant in any other respect.

(3) If in the opinion of the local housing authority the relevant works are more or less extensive than is necessary to achieve any of the purposes set out in subsection (1) or the purpose mentioned in subsection (2), they may, with the consent of the applicant, treat the application as varied so that the relevant works are limited to or, as the case may be, include such works as seem to the authority to be necessary for that purpose.

DEFINITIONS
"disabled facilities grant": s.1.
"disabled occupant": ss.20, 100.
"dwelling": s.101.
"flat": s.58.
"local housing authority": s.101.

GENERAL NOTE
This section sets out precisely for what purposes a disabled facilities grant *must* be approved (and see s.24(1)(a), below), in terms of facilitating access by the disabled person for whose benefit the works are proposed to the dwelling in question, or a flat in a building, the principal family room, a bedroom, and facilitating access to and use of a lavatory, a room with a hand-basin, a room with a bath and/or shower, a room for cooking, as well as the introduction of a usable (or any) heating system, facilitating switches, sockets and other means of using power, light and heat, and facilitating the access and movement of a disabled person to allow him to care for someone else normally resident in the property and who is in need of care, *i.e.* himself to act as the carer not merely or necessarily the cared for. The Secretary of State may prescribe other purposes.

Subsection (1)(b) is designed "to be sufficiently flexible to give grant to provide a special safe room or rooms for a disabled person who suffers from behavioural difficulties and for those who live with him, and also to provide safety measures for disabled people generally where these are necessary" (*Hansard* (H.L.), Report, April 18, 1996, col. 833, [Government Whip] [Lord Lucas]).

In addition, a disabled facilities grant *may* also be approved in order to make the dwelling or building suitable for the accommodation, welfare *or employment* of the disabled occupant, in any respect additional to the mandatory purposes (see also s.24(1)(b), below).

*Subs. (3)*
See note to s.12(3), above.

### Disabled facilities grants: approval of application

**24.**—(1) The local housing authority—
(a)  shall approve an application for a disabled facilities grant for purposes within section 23(1), and
(b)  may if they think fit approve an application for a disabled facilities grant not for a purpose within that provision but for the purpose specified in section 23(2),
subject to the following provisions.

(2) Where an authority entertain an owner's application for a disabled facilities grant made by a person who proposes to acquire a qualifying owner's interest, they shall not approve the application until they are satisfied that he has done so.

(3) A local housing authority shall not approve an application for a disabled facilities grant unless they are satisfied—
(a)  that the relevant works are necessary and appropriate to meet the needs of the disabled occupant, and
(b)  that it is reasonable and practicable to carry out the relevant works having regard to the age and condition of the dwelling or building.

In considering the matters mentioned in paragraph (a) a local housing authority which is not itself a social services authority shall consult the social services authority.

(4) An authority proposing to approve an application for a disabled facilities grant shall consider—
  (a)  in the case of an application in respect of works to a dwelling, whether the dwelling is fit for human habitation;
  (b)  in the case of a common parts application, whether the building meets the requirements in section 604(2) of the Housing Act 1985,
and the authority shall take that into account in deciding whether it is reasonable and practicable to carry out the relevant works.

(5) A local housing authority shall not approve a common parts application for a disabled facilities grant unless they are satisfied that the applicant has a power or is under a duty to carry out the relevant works.

DEFINITIONS
  "disabled facilities grant": s.1.
  "disabled occupant": ss.20, 100.
  "fit for human habitation": s.97.
  "local housing authority": s.101.
  "owner's application": s.19.
  "relevant works": s.2.
  "social services authority": s.100.

GENERAL NOTE
  This section mirrors the last, dividing disabled facilities grants into two types: mandatory if within s.23(1), and discretionary if within s.23(2). As to the exercise of discretion, and policies, see notes to s.13, above.
  If an owner's application was based on proposed ownership (see s.19, above), the authority cannot approve the grant until the interest has been acquired: subs. (2).
  The authority shall not approve a grant unless satisfied that the works the subject of the application are "necessary and appropriate to meet the needs of the disabled occupant", to assess which, if not themselves a social services authority (as to which, see notes to s.100, below, *i.e.* if the housing authority are a non-unitary, district council in a non-metropolitan county), the authority must consult the social services authority (the non-metropolitan county council): subs. (3). The decision on whether it is reasonable and practicable to carry out the works having regard to age and condition of dwelling or building is, however, one for the housing authority themselves: *ibid.*
  The amount of the grant is governed by ss.30, 31, 33, below.

*Subs. (4)*
  See notes to ss.13 and 18, above, and 97 below. The authority are not, however, prohibited from approving a grant merely because the dwelling will still be unfit, or fail to meet the relevant and corresponding conditions for a building, but are merely required to take it into account.

*Subs. (5)*
  See notes to s.15, above.

## *HMO grants*

### HMO grants: the interest of the applicant in the property

**25.**—(1) A local housing authority shall not entertain an application for an HMO grant unless they are satisfied that the applicant has or proposes to acquire an owner's interest in every parcel of land on which the relevant works are to be carried out.

(2) In accordance with directions given by the Secretary of State, a local housing authority may treat the condition in subsection (1) as fulfilled by a person who has, or proposes to acquire, an owner's interest in only part of the land concerned.

(3) References in this Chapter to "a qualifying owner's interest", in relation to an application for an HMO grant, are to an owner's interest meet-

ing the condition in subsection (1) or treated by virtue of subsection (2) as meeting that condition.

DEFINITIONS
"HMO grant": s.1.
"local housing authority": s.101.
"owner's interest": s.101.
"relevant works": s.2.

GENERAL NOTE
Only owners can apply for an HMO grant. There is a minor discretion available to the authority—acting only in accordance with directions given by the Secretary of State—whereby the overriding requirement of ownership of all the land on which the works the subject of the application are to be carried can be waived if there is ownership of part of that land. An owner's application can be made on the basis of a proposed acquisition of interest, but in that once there can be no approval of the grant until the interest has been acquired: s.28(3).

For HMO purposes (see s.101, below), owner has the same meaning as under Pt. XI of the Housing Act 1985, where it—
"(a) means a person (other than a mortgagee not in possession) who is for the time being entitled to dispose of the fee simple of the premises whether in possession or in reversion, and (b) includes also a person holding or entitled to the rents and profits the premises under a lease having an unexpired term exceeding three years" (1985 Act, s.398(3)).

## HMO grants: certificate required to accompany application

**26.**—(1) A local housing authority shall not entertain an application for an HMO grant unless it is accompanied by a certificate of future occupation.
　(2) A "certificate of future occupation" certifies that the applicant—
　(a)　has or proposes to acquire a qualifying owner's interest in the house, and
　(b)　intends that throughout the grant condition period the house or a part of it (specified in the certificate) will be residentially occupied, or available for residential occupation, under tenancies or licences by persons who are not connected with the owner for the time being of the house.
　In paragraph (b) "residential occupation" does not include occupation for a holiday, and "tenancies" does not include a long tenancy.

DEFINITIONS
"connected with the owner": s.98.
"grant condition period": s.44.
"HMO grant": s.1.
"local housing authority": s.101.
"long tenancy": s.101.
"owner's interest": s.101.
"tenancy": s.101.

GENERAL NOTE
An application for an HMO grant may not be entertained unless it is accompanied by a certificate stating—
　(i) that the applicant has or proposes to acquire an owner's interest in the house in question, and
　(ii) that he intends that throughout the grant condition period (normally five years—see s.44(3), below) the house, or such part of it as may be identified in the certificate, will be "residentially occupied" under tenancies or licences by persons who are "not connected with the owner for the time being of the house".

*Residential occupation.* There is no magic about this phrase, to which the case-law on occupation as a residence or as an only or main or principal home may have some relevance: see notes to s.8, above. The term is introduced here expressly to exclude holiday lettings: also see notes to s.8, above.

*Tenancy or licence.* Excluded from tenancy for this purpose is a long tenancy, which has the meaning given it by the Housing Act 1985, s.115, *i.e.* normally a tenancy granted for a fixed term exceeding 21 years (see notes to s.8, above). Such tenancies will procure a capital payment and as such are more akin to owner-occupation than tenancy popularly so-called.

As to the distinction between tenancy and licence, see notes to s.7, above. The inclusion of premises licensed by the owner will cover those cases where no occupier has been granted exclusive possession of any part of the house, and there is no joint tenancy of the whole of the house, see *A.G. Securities v. Vaughan, Antoniades v. Villiers* [1990] A.C. 417, 21 H.L.R. 79, H.L., distinguishing between a genuine such arrangement and a mere pretense.

*Connected with the owner.* A person is connected with the owner (see notes to s.25, above) if property is held by personal representatives or trustees, and he is someone who is beneficially entitled to an interest in, or to the proceeds of sale of, the property, *i.e.* the requirement to keep an HMO available for letting is not met by a "letting" between trustee and beneficiary.

A person is *also* connected with the owner if he is a member of the owner's family: see s.98, applying s.113 of the Housing Act 1985, to the expression "member of family"; see notes thereto, below.

## HMO grants: purposes for which grant may be given

**27.**—(1) The purposes for which an application for an HMO grant (other than a conversion application) may be approved are—

    (a)  to comply with a notice under section 189 of the Housing Act 1985 (repair notice in respect of unfit premises) or otherwise to render the house fit for human habitation;

    (b)  to comply with a notice under section 190 of that Act (repair notice in respect of premises not unfit but in need of substantial repair) or otherwise to put the building in reasonable repair;

    (c)  to comply with a notice under section 352 of that Act (notice requiring works to render premises fit for the number of occupants) or otherwise to enable the house to meet one or more of the requirements in subsection (1A) of that section;

    (d)  to provide adequate thermal insulation;

    (e)  to provide adequate facilities for space heating;

    (f)  to provide satisfactory internal arrangements;

    (g)  to provide means of escape in case of fire or other fire precautions, not being precautions required under or by virtue of any enactment (whenever passed);

    (h)  to ensure that the house complies with such requirements with respect to construction or physical condition as may be specified by the Secretary of State;

    (i)  to ensure that there is compliance with such requirements with respect to the provision or condition of services and amenities to or within the house as are so specified;

    (j)  any other purpose for the time being specified for the purposes of this section by order of the Secretary of State.

(2) The purpose for which a conversion application may be approved is to provide a house in multiple occupation by the conversion of a house or other building.

(3) If in the opinion of the authority the relevant works are more or less extensive than is necessary to achieve any of the purposes set out in subsection (1) or (2), they may, with the consent of the applicant, treat the application as varied so that the relevant works are limited to or, as the case may be, include such works as seem to the authority to be necessary for that purpose.

(4) In exercise of the powers conferred by paragraphs (h) and (i) of subsection (1) the Secretary of State may specify requirements generally or for particular cases, and may specify different requirements for different areas.

Definitions
   "HMO grant": s.1.
   "house in multiple occupation": s.101.

This section specifies the purposes for which an HMO grant may be approved, and is identical to s.17, above (see also s.12, above), save that it provides in subs. (2) for a conversion HMO grant, *i.e.* for the provision of an HMO by conversion of a house or other building, under s.1(5)(b).

## HMO grants: approval of application

**28.**—(1) The local housing authority may approve an application for an HMO grant if they think fit, subject to the following provisions.

(2) The authority shall not approve an application for an HMO grant unless they are satisfied that the works are necessary for one or more of the purposes set out in section 27(1) or (2).

(3) Where an authority entertain an application for an HMO grant made by a person who proposes to acquire a qualifying owner's interest, they shall not approve the application until they are satisfied that he has done so.

(4) An authority proposing to approve an application for an HMO grant shall consider whether the house to which the application relates is fit for human habitation and meets the requirements in section 352(1A) of the Housing Act 1985.

(5) If it appears to the authority that the house is not fit for human habitation or does not meet those requirements, they shall not approve the application unless they are satisfied—

(a) that on completion of the relevant works, together with any other works proposed to be carried out, the house will be fit for human habitation and meet those requirements,

(b) that there are satisfactory financial and other arrangements for carrying out those works, and

(c) that the carrying out of the works is the most satisfactory course of action.

(6) In considering whether to approve an application for an HMO grant the local housing authority shall have regard to the expected life of the house (taking account, where appropriate, of the effect of carrying out the works).

DEFINITIONS
"fit for human habitation": s.97.
"HMO grant": s.1.
"local housing authority": s.101.
"qualifying owner's interest": s.25.
"relevant works": s.2.

GENERAL NOTE
This section makes provision parallel to that to be found in ss.13, 18, above—see in particular notes to s.13 on the exercise of discretion, and policies. Note, too, that under this section the authority must consider both the requirements in the Housing Act 1985, s.352(1A) (as to which, see notes to s.17, above), as well as fitness for human habitation (see notes to s.97, below).

No approval can be given to an application on the basis of a proposed acquisition of interest, until the interest has been acquired: subs. (3).

The amount of the grant is governed by ss.31, 33, below.

*Restrictions on grant aid*

## Restriction on grants for works already begun

**29.**—(1) Subject as follows, a local housing authority shall not approve an application for a grant if the relevant works have been begun before the application is approved.

(2) Where the relevant works have been begun but have not been completed, the authority may approve the application for a grant if they are satisfied that there were good reasons for beginning the works before the application was approved.

(3) Where an authority decide to approve an application in accordance with subsection (2), they may, with the consent of the applicant, treat the application as varied so that the relevant works do not include any that are completed.

But in determining for the purposes of the application the physical condition of the dwelling, common parts or house or other building concerned, they shall consider the condition of the premises at the date of the application.

(4) Subject as follows, a local housing authority shall not approve an application for a grant if the relevant works have been completed.

(5) Nothing in this section applies to an application for a grant in respect of works necessary—

(a) to render a dwelling fit for human habitation or to comply with a notice under section 189 or 190 of the Housing Act 1985 (repair notices), or

(b) to enable a house in multiple occupation to meet one or more of the requirements in section 352(1A) of that Act (fitness for the number of occupants) or to comply with a notice under that section.

(6) If the local housing authority consider that the relevant works include works in addition to those necessary for the purposes mentioned in subsection (5)(a) or (b), they shall treat the application as an application to which this section applies so far as it relates to those additional works.

DEFINITIONS
"common parts": s.58.
"local housing authority": s.101.
"relevant works": s.2.

GENERAL NOTE
The starting-point of this section seems at odds with what follows. In substance, a local authority *may* approve an application for a grant (but need not do so, even if otherwise mandatory) where the works the subject of the application have been *commenced but not completed* prior to approval, if satisfied that there were good reasons for beginning the works without awaiting approval, *e.g.* urgency (subs. (2)): as to discretion and policy, see notes to s.13, above. They cannot do so if the works have been completed (subs. (4)).

These prohibitions do not apply, however, if the works were necessary to achieve fitness for human habitation or to comply with a notice under the Housing Act 1985, ss.189, 192 (above, notes to s.12), or to enable an HMO to meet the requirements of s.352(1A) or to comply with a notice under that section (above, notes to s.17). Works additional to those necessary for such purposes are treated in accordance with the residual "good reason" discretion (subs. (5)).

One route the authority can take is to decide to vary the works (with the agreement of the applicant) to exclude those which have been begun before approval, *cf.* ss.12(3), 17(2), 23(3) and 27(3): in reaching their decision on a grant, however, the authority are bound to consider the physical condition of the property, under a number of headings (to achieve the stated purposes under ss.12, 17, 23 and 27, to consider fitness and condition after the works under ss.13, 18, 24 and 28, and to consider expected life under ss.13, 18 and 28). In determining "the physical condition" of the dwelling, for the purpose of deciding whether or not to vary the works to exclude those begun before approval, subs. (3) requires the authority to consider the condition of the premises at the date of application, *i.e.* to disregard intervening, pre-approval works; this appears to mean that the authority cannot refuse the grant because what works remain are not, on their own, necessary to the objectives, although would have been so considered when taken with those which have already been executed.

These provisions apply where the authority know about the works prior to approval: where they subsequently discover that works were started before approval, they may refuse to pay the grant, or any further instalment, or reduce the grant or demand repayment: see s.42, below.

## Means testing in case of application by owner-occupier or tenant

**30.**—(1) This section applies—

(a) to an application for a renovation grant which is—

　　(i) an owner's application accompanied by an owner-occupation certificate, or

　　(ii) a tenant's application; and

(b) to any application for a disabled facilities grant.

(2) An owner's application for a renovation grant shall be treated as falling within this section if it is a conversion application for the provision of two or more dwellings and any of the certificates accompanying the application is an owner-occupation certificate.

(3) If in the case of an application for a renovation grant to which this section applies the financial resources of the applicant exceed the applicable amount, the amount of any grant which may be paid shall, in accordance with regulations, be reduced from what it would otherwise have been.

(4) If in the case of an application for a disabled facilities grant the financial resources of any person of a description specified by regulations exceed the applicable amount, the amount of any grant which may be paid shall, in accordance with regulations, be reduced from what it would otherwise have been.

(5) Provision may be made by regulations—

(a) for the determination of the amount which is to be taken to be the financial resources of any person,

(b) for the determination of the applicable amount referred to in subsection (3) or (4), and

(c) as to circumstances in which the financial resources of a person are to be assumed (by reason of his receiving a prescribed benefit or otherwise) not to exceed the applicable amount.

(6) Regulations may, in particular—

(a) make provision for account to be taken of the income, assets, needs and outgoings not only of the person himself but also of his spouse, any person living with him or intending to live with him and any person on whom he is dependent or who is dependent on him;

(b) make provision for amounts specified in or determined under the regulations to be taken into account for particular purposes.

(7) Regulations may apply for the purposes of this section, subject to such modifications as may be prescribed, any other statutory means-testing regime as it has effect from time to time.

(8) Regulations may make provision requiring any information or evidence needed for the determination of any matter under this section to be furnished by such person as may be prescribed.

(9) In this section "regulations" means regulations made by the Secretary of State with the consent of the Treasury.

Definitions
    "conversion application": s.58.
    "disabled facilities grant": s.1.
    "owner's application": s.7.
    "owner occupation certificate": s.8.
    "renovation grant": s.1.
    "tenant's application": s.7.

General Note
This section provides for means-testing applicants for renovation grants who are owner-occupiers or tenants, and applicants for a disabled facilities grant: excluded are landlord's applications, applications for common parts grants, and applications for HMO grants. These are dealt with, by way of the authority's discretion, under s.31, below. Application for a renovation grant to provide *two* or more dwellings by conversion is treated as an owner's application if the applicant provides an owner-occupation certificate in respect of one of them (see s.8, above, *i.e.* intends to live in one of them; *cf.* s.58, below: a conversion grant may be to provide only one dwelling by conversion, but in such a case it would be "either/or" [landlord's application or owner-occupation certificate] without the need for this express provision)—subs. (2).

Means-testing is carried out by comparison of financial resources and applicable amount, according to a formula or method to be dictated by regulations: subs. (3)–(9).

*Amount of grant.* Subject to means-testing, and to grant maxima specified under s.33, below, and having regard to the express discretion in s.31 and to the wording of subss. (3), (4) ("what [the grant] would otherwise have been") and that of s.32(5) ("the grants that would be payable ... under section 33"), it does seem that—even though most grants are discretionary—there is no residual discretion to approve a grant, but at a lower amount: see *R. v. Sunderland C.C., ex p. Redezeus* (1994) 27 H.L.R. 477, Q.B.D.

## Determination of amount of grant in case of landlord's application

**31.**—(1) This section applies to—
 (a) an owner's application for a renovation grant which is accompanied by a certificate of intended letting (not being an application which falls within section 30: see subsection (2) of that section),
 (b) a landlord's application for a common parts grant,
 (c) a landlord's application for a disabled facilities grant, and
 (d) any application for an HMO grant.
 (2) The reference in subsection (1)(c) to a landlord's application for a disabled facilities grant is to an owner's application in respect of works to a dwelling which is or is intended to be let, or to the common parts of a building in which a flat is or is intended to be let.
 (3) The amount of the grant (if any) shall be determined by the local housing authority, having regard to—
 (a) the extent to which the landlord is able to charge a higher rent for the premises because of the works, and
 (b) such other matters as the Secretary of State may direct.
 (4) The authority may, if they think it appropriate, seek and act upon the advice of rent officers as to any matter.
 (5) The Secretary of State may by regulations make provision requiring any information or evidence needed for the determination of any matter under this section to be furnished by such person as may be prescribed.

DEFINITIONS
 "certificate of intended letting": s.8.
 "common parts grant": s.1.
 "disabled facilities grant": s.1.
 "HMO grant": s.1.
 "landlord's application": ss.10, 15.
 "local housing authority": s.101.
 "owner's application": s.7.
 "renovation grant": s.1.
 "statutory tenancy": s.101.

GENERAL NOTE
 This section, in contrast to the last, deals with what are essentially landlord's applications, whether so-called in relation to common parts and disabled facilities (see subs. (1)(b), (c)) or not so called in relation to renovation grant in subs. (1)(a) (yet could have been—see s.10(5)), or necessarily so in relation to an HMO grant. The authority have discretion to determine the amount of the grant, subject (a) to having "regard to" both the possibility of higher rent attributable to the works, and to such matters as the Secretary of State may direct, and (b) as always, the requirements of administrative law (as to which, see notes to s.13, above).
 The phrase "have regard to" has been considered in the notes to s.12, above, in relation to the determination of the most satisfactory course of action in the context of unfitness. Authorities will not be bound to follow the Secretary of State's directions as to matters to be taken into account blindly and will be able to depart from them so long as they have first had regard to them—*De Falco, Silvestri v. Crawley B.C.* [1980] Q.B. 460, C.A.; *Miller v. Wandsworth L.B.C., The Times*, March 19, 1980; *Lambert v. Ealing L.B.C.* [1982] 1 W.L.R. 550, 2 H.L.R. 58, C.A. As Parliament has required authorities to have regard to them, however, deviation may amount to a *prima facie* case that they have not been taken into account, sufficient at least (in practice) to call for an explanation from the authority: *cf. Padfield v. Minister of Agriculture, Fisheries & Food* [1968] A.C. 997, H.L.
 The sort of matters which are likely to be the subject of directions, as under the 1989 Act, include cost of works, capital values and loan charges. In order to determine subsequent levels of rent, the authority may choose to seek and act on the advice of rent officers: subs. (4). The power of the rent officer to undertake this task is to be found in the Housing Act 1988, s.12, as amended by Sched. 1, para. 13, below.

*Subs. (4)*

The authority cannot lawfully delegate to the rent officer their function of determining the notional increase in rental value, even though they may take his advice and, in the absence of any evidence to contradict the basis on which a rent officer has proceeded, it may be unrealistic to expect them to adopt any other figure: *R. v. Bolsover D.C. and the Rent Officer for the Derbyshire Registration Area, ex p. East Midlands Development, and Denis Rye* (1995) 28 H.L.R. 329, Q.B.D.

## Apportionment in case of tenants' application for common parts grant

**32.**—(1) This section applies where a local housing authority approve a tenants' application for a common parts grant.

(2) The local housing authority shall decide how much of the cost of the relevant works is attributable to the applicants ("the attributable cost").

(3) For the purposes of this section the attributable cost is an amount equal to the following proportion of the cost of the relevant works—

(a) if it can be ascertained, the proportion that the aggregate of the respective liabilities of each of the applicants to carry out or contribute to the carrying out of the relevant works bears to the aggregate of all such liabilities on the part of all persons (including the applicants) so liable; or

(b) if the proportion mentioned in paragraph (a) cannot be ascertained, the proportion that the number of applicants bears to the number of persons (including the applicants) liable to carry out or contribute to the carrying out of works to the building.

(4) The local housing authority shall then apportion the attributable cost to each of the applicants—

(a) in a case where the attributable cost is calculated by reference to the proportion mentioned in subsection (3)(a), according to the proportion that his liabilities to carry out or contribute to the carrying out of the relevant works bears to the aggregate of the applicants' liabilities mentioned in that paragraph; or

(b) in a case where the attributable cost is calculated by reference to the proportion mentioned in subsection (3)(b), equally.

(5) The amount of the grant payable shall be the aggregate of the grants that would be payable to each of the applicants under section 30 or, in the case of a participating landlord, under section 31 if each of the applicants was an individual applicant in respect of his portion of the attributable cost.

(6) Where the interest of an occupying tenant is held jointly by two or more persons, those persons shall be regarded as a single person for the purposes of this section.

DEFINITIONS

"common parts grant": s.1.
"local housing authority": s.101.
"relevant works": s.2.

GENERAL NOTE

Where the application is by tenants for a common parts grant, the authority must first establish how much of the cost of the relevant works is attributable to the applicants—"the attributable cost": subs. (2). This is achieved by applying one of two formulae: subs. (3).

If it is ascertainable, then the attributable cost is the aggregate of the individual proportions of the applicants' responsibility, *e.g.* under service charge provisions in a lease, as against the total cost of the relevant works. Thus, if 10 flats and five applicants (each bearing a one-fifth liability), the attributable cost would be 50 per cent; or, if service charges are allocated according to a different formula, such as floor area, four applicants may have liability between them for—say, purely for the sake of example 60 per cent of the service charge (or relevant element of service charges), in which case the attributable cost would be 60 per cent: subs. (3)(a).

If this approach is not workable, then a strictly numerical apportionment is adopted: subs. (3)(b). Thus, seven applicants, 20 contributors to costs, attributable cost 35 per cent.

Once the attributable cost has been ascertained, it is then apportioned to each of the applicants individually, either on the basis of a similar "proportionate" test, or else strictly numerically, depending on which approach has been used in calculating the attributable cost itself: subs. (4). Section 33 is then applied to determine the grant as if each one of the applicants had applied individually for that amount of grant (and, if one of the applicant's is a participating landlord—see notes to s.15, above—section 34 is likewise brought into play on the same basis).

## Power to specify maximum amount of grant

**33.**—(1) The Secretary of State may, if he thinks fit, by order specify a maximum amount or a formula for calculating a maximum amount of grant which a local housing authority may pay in respect of an application for a grant.

(2) An order under this section may make different provision for different types of grant, or for the same type of grant in different circumstances.

(3) In relation to an application for a grant in respect of works for any of the purposes in section 23(1) (mandatory disabled facilities grant), the order may—

(a) provide for a maximum amount of grant to be paid if the application is approved, and

(b) authorise the local housing authority, if they think fit, to pay a further amount in excess of that maximum but subject to such other maximum (if any) as may be specified in or determined in accordance with the order.

(4) An authority may not, except as mentioned in subsection (3), pay an amount of grant in excess of a specified maximum amount.

DEFINITIONS
"disabled facilities grant": s.1.
"local housing authority": s.101.

GENERAL NOTE
Short, central and to the point: the ultimate limit on grants payable is set by the Secretary of State; save as may be permitted in relation to disabled facilities grants under subs. (3), authorities have no discretion to exceed the maxima set—see subs. (4).

*Decision and notification*

## Decision and notification

**34.**—(1) A local housing authority shall by notice in writing notify an applicant for a grant as soon as reasonably practicable, and, in any event, not later than six months after the date of the application concerned, whether the application is approved or refused.

(2) Where an authority decide to approve an application for a grant, they shall determine—

(a) which of the relevant works are eligible for grant (in this Chapter referred to as "the eligible works"),

(b) the amount of the expenses which in their opinion are properly to be incurred in the execution of the eligible works,

(c) the amount of the costs which in their opinion have been properly incurred, or are properly to be incurred, with respect to preliminary or ancillary services and charges, and

(d) the amount of grant they have decided to pay, taking into account all the relevant provisions of this Chapter.

The total of the amounts referred to in paragraphs (b) and (c) is referred to in this Chapter as "the estimated expense".

(3) If the authority notify the applicant under subsection (1) that the application is approved, they shall specify in the notice—

    (a) the eligible works,
    (b) the amounts referred to in subsection (2)(b) and (c), and how those
        amounts have been calculated, and
    (c) the amount of the grant.
    (4) If the authority notify the applicant under subsection (1) that the application is refused, they shall at the same time notify him of the reasons for the refusal.
    (5) If after an application for a grant has been approved the authority are satisfied that owing to circumstances beyond the control of the applicant—
    (a) the eligible works cannot be, or could not have been, carried out on the
        basis of the amount of expenses referred to in subsection (2)(b),
    (b) the amount of the costs which have been or are to be incurred as mentioned in subsection (2)(c) has increased, or
    (c) the eligible works cannot be, or could not have been, carried out without carrying out additional works which could not have been reasonably foreseen at the time the application was made,
the authority may re-determine the estimated expense and the amount of the grant.
    (6) Where an application for a grant is approved, the local housing authority may not impose any condition in relation to the approval or payment of the grant, except—
    (a) as provided by the following provisions of this Chapter, or
    (b) with the consent of the Secretary of State;
and this applies whether the condition purports to operate as a condition, a personal covenant or otherwise.

DEFINITIONS
    "local housing authority": s.101.
    "preliminary or ancillary services and charges": s.2.
    "relevant works": s.2.

GENERAL NOTE
    The authority are bound to issue their decision on an application as soon as reasonably practicable, and in any event within six months, in writing, stating the constituent financial elements of the grant payable (if approved) (subs. (3)), or the reasons for a refusal (subs. (4)). This permits the applicant to challenge *both* a refusal *and* a lower grant than he believes he is entitled to.

*Financial elements.* So far as concerns the constituent financial elements, this means:
    (i) The relevant works (*i.e.* the works the subject of the application—see notes to s.2, above) which are eligible for grant (*i.e.* under ss.12, 17, 23 and 27, having regard to the duty under ss.13, 18, 14 and 28 not to pay grant on more works than are needed to achieve the objectives)—the eligible works (these may later be revised to include added, unforeseeable works arising in circumstances beyond the control of the applicant—see subs. (4));
    (ii) The amount of expenses properly incurred in relation to these eligible works—see notes to s.2, above: the eligible expense (this may later be revised to include added cost arising in circumstances beyond the control of the applicant—see subs. (4));
    (iii) The amount of costs involved in the application and preparing for and carrying out of the works (see notes to s.2, above); and,
    (iv) The amount of grant (which will include means-testing under s.30, landlord's discretionary amounts under s.31, allocation between applicants under s.32 and maxima under s.33).

*Reasons.* "I hold the view that good local authorities already do what the amendments would require, but there is merit in converting good practice into a general rule," (*Hansard* (H.L.), Report, April 18, 1996, col. 858, [Government Whip] [Lord Lucas]).
    There is no general legal duty to give reasons for administrative decision, save although such a duty can on occasion be implied by law "in appropriate circumstances": *R. v. Secretary of State for the Home Department, ex p. Doody* [1994] 1 A.C. 531, H.L. *per* Lord Mustill (see also *R. v. Civil Service Appeal Board, ex p. Cunningham* [1991] 4 All E.R. 310, where there is something in a decision which "cries out for some explanation", and where the absence of any explanation will support the inference that the reasoning is flawed or aberrant).
    In *R. v. Bristol C.C. ex p. Bailey* (1994) 27 H.L.R. 307, Q.B.D., a duty to give reasons for refusing a grant application under the 1989 Act had been expressly disclaimed, although this may have been a more particular than general decision, as there had been an appeal hearing, in

which all facts and matters were put before a sub-committee, and the issue (whether or not property unfit) was a simple one, *i.e.* the reasons were clear. See further *R. v. Higher Education Funding Council, ex p. Institute of Dental Surgery* [1994] 1 W.L.R. 242, Q.B.D., and *R. v. Kensington & Chelsea R.B.C., ex p. Grillo* (1995) 28 H.L.R. 94, C.A. In *R. v. Corporation of the City of London, ex p. Matson, The Times,* October 20, 1995, C.A., fairness and justice required the Court of Aldermen of the City of London to give reasons when deciding not to ratify the election of an alderman.

The duty is, however, now clear. It is similar to the duty to give notification of decision and reasons under Pt. III of the Housing Act 1985, in respect of applications for accommodation by the homeless. It has been held that the purpose of the requirement to give reasons is to enable the recipient to see whether they might be challengeable in law: see (originally) *Thornton v. Kirklees M.B.C.* [1979] Q.B. 626, C.A. (a judicial summary of counsel's submission, rather than a judicial observation in its own right), see also *R. v. Tynedale D.C., ex p. Shield* (1987) 22 H.L.R. 144, and *R. v. Northampton B.C., ex p. Carpenter* (1992) 25 H.L.R. 349, in which the decision letter was said to be "manifestly defective" because it failed to address the reasons the applicant had left his previous accommodation and accordingly defeated the purpose of the section which was "to enable someone who is entitled to a decision to see what the reasons are for that decision and to challenge those reasons if they are apparently inadequate.".

In *R. v. Croydon L.B.C., ex p. Graham* (1993) 26 H.L.R. 286, C.A., Sir Thomas Bingham M.R. said:

"I readily accept that these difficult decisions are decisions for the housing authority and certainly a pedantic exegesis of letters of this kind would be inappropriate. There is, nonetheless, an obligation under the Act to give reasons and that must impose on the council a duty to give reasons which are intelligible and which convey to the applicant the reasons why the application has been rejected in such a way that if they disclose an error of reasoning the applicant may take such steps as may be indicated."

This quotation was cited with approval in *R. v. Islington L.B.C., ex p. Hinds* (1995) 28 H.L.R. 302, C.A., where the duty to give reasons was found to be complied with as the reasons stated in the decision letter were intelligible and conveyed clearly to the applicant the reason why his application had been rejected.

Save in exceptional circumstances, the courts will not permit the reasons given in the notification to be supplemented by affidavit on a challenge: see *R. v. Croydon L.B.C., ex p. Graham* (1993) 26 H.L.R. 286, C.A., and *R. v. Westminster C.C., ex p. Ermakov* (1995) 8 Admin.L.R. 381; 28 H.L.R. forthcoming, C.A., see also *R. v. Southwark L.B.C., ex p. Dagou* (1995) 28 H.L.R. 72; *cf. R. v. Cardiff C.C., ex p. John* (1982) 9 H.L.R. 56, where the court had held that the fact that the decision letter did not itself disclose the proper reasons for the decision did not prevent the authority from relying on proper reasons and justifying their decision accordingly, and *Hobbs v. Sutton L.B.C.* (1993) 26 H.L.R. 286, C.A., where the Court of Appeal accepted affidavit evidence amplifying and explaining earlier evidence as to reasons).

In *R. v. Westminster C.C., ex p. Augustin* (1993) 25 H.L.R. 281, C.A., however, it was held that a later letter could serve to rectify the shortcomings of an earlier notification (which, however, was not considered defective albeit "sparse"—*per* Auld J. in the court below—or "cryptic" [and brief]—*per* Glidewell L.J. in the Court of Appeal: it was considered to give the applicant the information she needed).

Furthermore, the courts have not always held authorities to the words of their reasons when decisions are challenged: see *De Falco, Silvestri v. Crawley B.C.* [1980] Q.B. 460, C.A.; *R. v. Hillingdon L.B.C., ex p. Islam* [1983] 1 A.C. 688, 1 H.L.R. 107, H.L.; *R. v. Westminster C.C., ex p. Chambers* (1982) 6 H.L.R. 15. It has been held that authorities are entitled to give their reasons quite simply: "their decision and their reasons are not to be analysed in minute detail. They are not to be gone through as it were with a toothcomb. They are not to be criticised by saying: 'They have not mentioned this or that'": *Tickner v. Mole Valley D.C.* [1980] 2 April, C.A. Transcript. In *Kelly v. Monklands D.C.,* July 12, 1985, Ct. of Session (O.H.), a mere recital of the words of the Act was even held sufficient on this point.

The nature and extent of reasons must, however, relate to the substantive issues raised by an applicant or, perhaps, by an applicant's adviser: see, *Re Poyser & Mills Arbitration* [1964] 2 Q.B. 467, approved by the House of Lords in *Westminster C.C. v. Great Portland Estates* [1985] A.C. 661, and again in *Save Britain's Heritage v. Secretary of State for the Environment* [1991] 1 W.L.R. 153: "the reasons that are set out must be reasons which will not only be intelligible, but which deal with the substantial points that have been raised," *per* Megaw J. in *Poyser,* and "The three criteria suggested in the *dictum* of Megaw J. are that the reasons should be proper, intelligible and adequate," *per* Lord Bridge in *Save Britain's Heritage.* See also *Givaudan v. Minister of Housing and Local Government* [1967] 1 W.L.R. 250, *Mountview Court Properties v. Devlin* (1970) 21 P. & C.R. 689. In *Edwin H. Bradley & Sons v. Secretary of State for the*

*Environment* (1982) 266 E.G. 264, 926, Glidewell J. added to the *dictum* of Megaw J. that reasons can be briefly stated (also approved in *Great Portland Street*).

In *R. v. Hillingdon L.B.C., ex p. H* (1988) 20 H.L.R. 559, it was held that while the authority were entitled to express themselves quite simply, and could not be criticised for not having gone into great detail, it was none the less incumbent on them to say what was the deliberate act or omission in consequence of which it had been concluded that the applicant had ceased to occupy accommodation available for his occupation and which it would have been reasonable for him to continue to occupy (definition of intentional homeless, s.60, 1985 Act). In the context of the case, this had required more than a statement that he could have continued to occupy his council tenancy in Northern Ireland.

See also *R. v. Tower Hamlets L.B.C., ex p. Monaf* (1988) 20 H.L.R. 529, C.A.; *R. v. Southwark L.B.C., ex p. Davies* (1993) 26 H.L.R. 677, and *R. v. Slough B.C., ex p. Khan* (1995) 27 H.L.R. 492, in the latter of which a decision letter which addressed only one of a number of grounds on which a local connection was claimed was held to be defective. In *R. v. Brent L.B.C., ex p. Baruwa* (1995) 28 H.L.R. 361, it was impossible to work out from the decision letter any reasoning process, or the primary underlying reasoning, which had led the authority to conclude that the applicant was deliberately declining to pay rent which she could afford.

See also the cases on reasons for the decisions of Housing Benefit Review Boards: *R. v. Housing Benefit Review Board, ex p. Thomas* (1991) 25 H.L.R. 1, Q.B.D.; *R. v. Housing Benefit Review Board for East Devon D.C., ex p. Gibson* (1993) 25 H.L.R. 487 C.A.; *R. v. Sefton M.B.C., ex p. Cunningham* (1991) 23 H.L.R. 534; *R. v. Solihull M.B.C. Housing Benefit Review Board, ex p. Simpson* (1994) 27 H.L.R. 41, C.A.; *R. v. Sutton L.B.C., ex p. Partridge* (1994) 28 H.L.R. 315, Q.B.D.

See notes to s.13, above, for a general statement on what is—and is not—a proper approach to decision generally by local authorities, on which (additional to or independently of challenge based on misinterpretation of the provisions of this Act) a challenge may be made, potentially based on what has been disclosed by the notification.

*Subs. (5)*

This subsection enables re-determination of grant in the event of additional or unforeseeable expenditure, works or costs.

*Subs. (6)*

Grant *conditions* are only those for which provision is made in the following sections, or that are attached with the consent of the Secretary of State. For example, without such consent, the authority could not agree a landlord's conversion application on the basis of a nomination right to some or all of the flats produced.

## Payment of grants

### Payment of grants: general

**35.**—(1) Where the local housing authority have approved an application for a grant, they shall pay the grant, subject to the following provisions of this Chapter.

(2) The grant may be paid—

(a) in whole after the completion of the eligible works, or

(b) in part by instalments as the works progress and the balance after completion of the works.

(3) Where a grant is paid by instalments, the aggregate of the instalments paid before the completion of the eligible works shall not at any time exceed nine-tenths of the amount of the grant.

DEFINITIONS

"eligible works": s.34.

"local housing authority": s.101.

GENERAL NOTE

Grants may be paid after the completion of the eligible works (as to the meaning of which, see s.34, above) or in stage payments ("as the works progress", which seems to imply no *earlier* than commencement and execution of *some* works), but to a maximum of 90 per cent of the total grant due. See notes to s.13, above, on Discretion and Policy. See also s.39, below, as to grant made payable to contractor. See also ss.40–44 for circumstances where payment may not be forthcoming.

See also next section where a mandatory disabled facilities grant is payable.

### Delayed payment of mandatory grant

**36.**—(1) Where the local housing authority are obliged to approve an application for a grant under section 24(1)(a) (mandatory disabled facilities grant), they may do so on terms that payment of the grant, or part of it, will not be made before a date specified in the notification of their decision on the application.

(2) That date shall not be more than twelve months, or such other period as may be specified by order of the Secretary of State, after the date of the application.

DEFINITIONS
  "disabled facilities grant": s.1.
  "local housing authority": s.101.

GENERAL NOTE
  This section is designed to allow an authority to budget where mandatory grants are in issue; it follows a number of incidents over the years in which authorities have complained of inability to pay mandatory grants, partly because of government spending constraints, but on occasion because of difficulty managing the budgetary process. " ... Authorities have little scope to manage their financial resources by prioritising cases where mandatory grant is an issue ... We believe that our proposals will help authorities in their financial management by giving them the discretion to withhold payment of mandatory disabled facilities grants for up to 12 months after the date of the application ... We envisage that authorities should only need to use the measure sparingly and in exceptional cases ... " (*Hansard* (H.L.), Committee, April 18, 1996, col. 1667 (Government Whip) (Lord Lucas)).

  Use of the section is discretionary: on the one hand, it permits an authority to *defer* commencement of payment of a mandatory disabled facilities grant (see s.24, above), insofar as approval must be no later than six months after application (see s.34, above), and stage payments *could* commence almost as soon as works have begun (see notes to last section); on the other hand—if used—it limits the start of payments to a date that is no later than 12 months after the date of the application (unless another date is specified by the Secretary of State), by which time it is unlikely that all works would be completed (see notes to s.37, below), so that—in this sense—its use may positively benefit the applicant. Put another way, the latter effect is the price for the element of discretion.

  The payment may be all or part only of the grant: the section does not appear to be in conflict with the previous section, save as to discretion, and it is accordingly submitted that the 90 per cent limit in s.35, above, is applicable.

### Payment of grants: conditions as to carrying out of the works

**37.**—(1) It is a condition of payment of every grant that the eligible works are carried out within twelve months from—
  (a)  the date of approval of the application concerned, or
  (b)  where section 36 applies (delayed payment of mandatory grant), the date specified in the notification of the authority's decision,
or, in either case, such further period as the local housing authority may allow.

(2) The authority may, in particular, allow further time where they are satisfied that the eligible works cannot be, or could not have been, carried out without carrying out other works which could not have been reasonably foreseen at the time the application was made.

(3) In approving an application for a grant a local housing authority may require as a condition of payment of the grant that the eligible works are carried out in accordance with such specifications as they determine.

(4) The payment of a grant, or part of a grant, is conditional upon—
  (a)  the eligible works or the corresponding part of the works being executed to the satisfaction of the authority, and

(b) the authority being provided with an acceptable invoice, demand or receipt for payment for the works and any preliminary or ancillary services or charges in respect of which the grant or part of the grant is to be paid.

For this purpose an invoice, demand or receipt is acceptable if it satisfies the authority and is not given by the applicant or a member of his family.

<small>DEFINITIONS</small>
"eligible works": s.34.
"local housing authority": s.101.
"member of family": s.98.

<small>GENERAL NOTE</small>
This section contains some important if discrete, elements of the grant process:
(i) *Completion.* All works must be completed within 12 months of approval of application (save if a mandatory disabled facilities grant is deferred, in which case 12 months from the date to which first payment has been deferred: see s.36, above), unless a further period is allowed by the authority, in particular where the works have been prolonged because of added, unforeseeable works—subss. (1), (2).
(ii) *Specifications.* The authority *may* impose a grant condition that the eligible works are carried out in accordance with a specification determined by them, *e.g.* no substitution of different methods or materials—subs. (3).
(iii) *Satisfactory Works.* The authority must be satisfied that the works—or, if a stage payment, the relevant part of the works—have been executed to their satisfaction—subs. (4)(a). (This duty is imposed for the protection of the public purse, and does not create any duty of care on the part of the authority towards the recipient, such as would found an action in tort if the works have not been carried out satisfactorily: see *Curran v. Northern Ireland Co-Ownership Housing Association* [1987] 1 A.C. 718; 19 H.L.R. 318, H.L.)
(iv) *Proof of expenditure.* The authority must be satisfied with the invoices, demands or receipts for payments in respect of which the grant—or part—is payable, which cannot include ones issued by the applicant himself or a member of his family (as to which see notes to s.98, below). See also s.39, below, for grant made payable to contractor.

## Payment of grants: conditions as to contractors employed

**38.**—(1) It is a condition of payment of every grant, unless the local housing authority direct otherwise in any particular case, that the eligible works are carried out by the contractor whose estimate accompanied the application or, where two or more estimates were submitted, by one of those contractors.

(2) The Secretary of State may by regulations make provision as to the establishing and maintaining by local housing authorities of lists of contractors approved by them for the purpose of carrying out grant-aided works.

(3) The regulations may provide that it shall be a condition of payment of every grant by a local housing authority by whom such a list is maintained that, except in such cases as may be prescribed and unless the local housing authority direct otherwise in any particular case, the eligible works are carried out by a contractor who is on the authority's list of approved contractors.

<small>DEFINITIONS</small>
"local housing authority": s.101.

<small>GENERAL NOTE</small>
Grant applications have to be accompanied by estimates from two different contractors: s.2(2)(b). Unless the authority *direct* otherwise, it is a condition of payment that one of those who has provided the original estimate (not necessarily the lowest estimate, or that on which the authority have based the grant) carries out the works. The "direction" power would be available where the authority have (or, since application, have acquired) cause to be dissatisfied with the workmanship or efficiency of a contractor, *e.g.* in relation to completion of works, or other such circumstances.

Where the Secretary of State has used his power to permit authorities to draw up and maintain "approved lists" of grant contractors (subs. (2)), and provided that—absent a direction from the authority to the contrary in a particular case—the works can only be carried out by a contractor on the approved list, it does not seem to be so much a case of the authority "directing" the applicant not to use an estimating (but non-approved) contractor, for unless the applicant does not do so, he will not get his grant by reason of subs. (3); on the other hand, unless the authority do so direct, he will not get his grant for reason of subs. (1). Presumably the confusion will be resolved by the authority directing the applicant to get an additional estimate, from an approved contractor, under s.2(2)(b).

## Payment of grant to contractor

**39.**—(1) The local housing authority may pay a grant or part of a grant—
(a) by payment direct to the contractor, or
(b) by delivering to the applicant an instrument of payment in a form made payable to the contractor.
They shall not do so unless the applicant was informed before the grant application was approved that this would or might be the method of payment.
(2) Where an amount of grant is payable, but the works in question have not been executed to the satisfaction of the applicant, the local housing authority may at the applicant's request and if they consider it appropriate to do so withhold payment from the contractor.
If they do so, they may make the payment to the applicant instead.

DEFINITIONS
"local housing authority": s.101.

GENERAL NOTE
If the applicant was so informed of the possibility before approval, the authority can pay grant directly to the contractor, or else by issuing a cheque or other money instrument payable to the contractor: subs. (1). If the applicant asks the authority not to pay direct, because he is dissatisfied with the works, he may ask the authority to withhold payment and the authority *may* do so and *may* instead make the payment direct to the applicant.
If the authority *decline* to comply with the request, at least so far as it concerns withholding payment from the contractor, they may find themselves joined to any subsequent litigation, and the foundation or parameters of the decision in *Curran v. Northern Ireland Co-Ownership Housing Association* [1987] 1 A.C. 718; 19 H.L.R. 318, H.L. (see note to s.37, above) may be in some doubt.

## Applicant ceasing to be entitled before payment of grant

**40.**—(1) This section applies where an application for a grant is approved but before the certified date the applicant ceases to be a person entitled to a grant of that description.
In the case of a joint application this section does not apply unless all the applicants cease to be so entitled.
(2) Where this section applies—
(a) in the case of a renovation grant, disabled facilities grant or HMO grant, no grant shall be paid or, as the case may be, no further instalments shall be paid, and
(b) in the case of a common parts grant approved on a landlord's application, the local housing authority may refuse to pay the grant or any further instalment,
and the authority may demand that any instalment of the grant which has been paid be repaid forthwith, together with interest from the date on which it was paid until repayment, at such reasonable rate as the authority may determine.
(3) For the purposes of this section an applicant ceases to be a person entitled to a renovation grant—
(a) in the case of an owner's application—
(i) if he ceases to have a qualifying owner's interest, or
(ii) if he ceases to have the intention specified in the owner-occupation certificate or certificate of intended letting which accompanied the application;

(b) in the case of a tenant's application—
    (i) if he ceases to be a qualifying tenant of the dwelling, or
    (ii) if the application was accompanied by a certificate of intended letting and the landlord ceases to have the intention specified in the certificate; or
(c) if the application was approved under section 13(5) (approval of grant in respect of works to unfit premises) and the authority cease to be satisfied of the matters mentioned in that provision.

(4) For the purposes of this section an applicant ceases to be a person entitled to a disabled facilities grant—
(a) in the case of an owner's application—
    (i) if he ceases to have a qualifying owner's interest, or
    (ii) if he ceases to have the intention specified in the owner's certificate which accompanied the application;
(b) in the case of a tenant's application—
    (i) if he ceases to be a qualifying tenant of the dwelling, or
    (ii) if the application was accompanied by an owner's certificate and the landlord ceases to have the intention specified in the certificate.
But if the case falls within section 41 (change of circumstances affecting disabled occupant), the authority shall act under that section.

(5) For the purposes of this section an applicant ceases to be a person entitled to an HMO grant—
(a) if he ceases to have a qualifying owner's interest in the house;
(b) if he ceases to have the intention specified in the certificate of future occupation which accompanied the application; or
(c) if the application was approved under section 28(5) (approval of grant in respect of works to unfit premises) and the authority cease to be satisfied of the matters mentioned in that provision.

(6) For the purposes of this section an applicant whose application is a landlord's application for a common parts grant ceases to be a person entitled to a grant—
(a) if he ceases to have an owner's interest in the building;
(b) if he ceases to have a duty or power to carry out the relevant works; or
(c) if the application was approved under section 18(4) (approval of grant in respect of works to unfit premises) and the authority cease to be satisfied of the matters mentioned in that provision.

(7) This section has effect subject to section 56 (provisions relating to death of applicant).

DEFINITIONS
"certified date": s.44.
"common parts grant": s.1.
"disabled facilities grant": s.1.
"disabled occupant": ss.20, 100.
"HMO grant": s.1.
"local housing authority": s.101.
"owner's application": s.7.
"renovation grant": s.1.

GENERAL NOTE
This section governs changes of circumstances between approval and final payment of grant: it matches the pre-conditions for various grants under ss.7–11, 14–16, 19–22 and 25–26, above, and the circumstances in which grant paid may be repayable (see ss.45–50, below). It is part of the general process of tightening up against abuse: see Introduction to Pt. I, above. See also—
(i) s.41, below, which governs disabled facilities grants when there is a change affecting the disabled occupant (which section, if applicable, takes priority over the provisions of this: see subs. (4)),
(ii) s.42, where grants may be recalculated, withheld or repayable as a result of factors relating to the works as distinct from the factors relating to the applicant,

(iii) s.43, where the applicant—unknown to the authority—was not entitled to the grant at all, and

(iv) s.56, which governs the position on the death of the applicant (in priority to this section: see subs. (7)).

*Subs. (1)*

The section applies where an applicant ceases to be a person entitled to the relevant grant, between approval and the "certified date", which means the date certified by the authority as that on which execution of the works was completed to their satisfaction under s.44(3), below. Where there is a joint application, all of the applicants must so cease before the section can come into play.

*Subs. (2)*

Where the section applies, no grant is payable, or no further instalments are payable, and the authority may demand repayment of grant, together with interest at such reasonable rate as they may determine: subs. (2). The restriction in subs. (2)(b) means that only cessation of qualification by a landlord will lead to these consequences in relation to a common parts grant (reflecting the unfairness to the landlord if payment stopped, or a demand for repayment was made, as a result of a change in the numbers of relevant occupiers under ss.15(1)(b) and 16(1)(b), as well as the difficulties that would arise were grant to be withheld, or demand to be made for repayment, from—for example—one of a number of occupier-applicants, *i.e.* recalculation of grants for the *other* or *remaining* occupier-applicants, possibly to the point that some might claim that they would not have taken on the responsibility if the consequential figures had been known at the outset).

*Subs. (3)*

See s.8(2) and (3) as to the original conditions which would not have been met had these changes occurred before approval; the reference to s.13(5) involves satisfaction as to fitness on completion, satisfactory financial and other arrangements for carrying out the works, and that execution of the works is the most satisfactory course of action.

*Subs. (4)*

This subsection concerns disabled facilities grant. If the change of circumstance is one that falls within the next section, then it is to be applied in place of the provisions of this section.

See s.21 and s.22 as to the original conditions which would not have been met had these changes occurred before approval.

*Subs. (5)*

See s.25 and s.26 as to the original conditions which would not have been met had these changes occurred before approval; the reference to s.28(5) involves satisfaction as to conditions on completion, satisfactory financial and other arrangements for carrying out the works, and that execution of the works is the most satisfactory course of action.

*Subs. (6)*

See s.15(1)(a) and s.16(1)(a) as to the original conditions which would not have been met had these changes occurred before approval; the reference to s.14(4) involves satisfaction as to conditions on completion, satisfactory financial and other arrangements for carrying out the works, and that execution of the works is the most satisfactory course of action.

## Change of circumstances affecting disabled occupant

**41.**—(1) This section applies where an application for a disabled facilities grant has been approved and before the certified date—

    (a) the works cease to be necessary or appropriate to meet the needs of the disabled occupant, or

    (b) the disabled occupant ceases to occupy the dwelling or flat concerned or it ceases to be the intention that he should occupy it, or

    (c) the disabled occupant dies.

Where the application related to more than one disabled occupant, this section applies if any of paragraphs (a) to (c) applies in relation to any of them.

(2) This section applies whether or not the disabled occupant (or any of them) is the applicant (or one of them).

(3) Where this section applies the local housing authority may take such action as appears to them appropriate and may decide—

(a) that no grant shall be paid or, as the case may be, no further instalments shall be paid,

(b) that the relevant works or some of them should be completed and the grant or an appropriate proportion of it paid, or

(c) that the application should be redetermined in the light of the new circumstances.

(4) In making their decision the authority shall have regard to all the circumstances of the case.

(5) If the authority decide that no grant shall be paid or that no further instalments shall be paid, they may demand that any instalment of the grant which has been paid be repaid forthwith, together with interest from the date on which it was paid until repayment, at such reasonable rate as the authority may determine.

DEFINITIONS
"certified date": s.44.
"disabled facilities grant". s.1.
"disabled occupant": ss.20, 100.
"dwelling": s.101.
"flat": s.58.
"local housing authority": s.101.

GENERAL NOTE
Where there is a change of circumstances between grant approval and the "certified date", which means the date certified by the authority as that on which the execution of the works had been completed to their satisfaction under s.44(3), below, which if it had taken place before approval would have meant that no grant would have been available, s.40, above, will normally determine what steps the authority may take to prevent further, or recover, payments of grant. Where the change is one of those identified in subs. (1) (and, if more than one disabled occupant, if the change applies to any one of them—subs. (2)), however, they have a much broader discretion as to what to do in the circumstances, which *may* involve cessation of payments or even demand for repayment (*e.g.* if it is thought that the change may or should have been anticipated by applicant), but equally may involve continuation with grant process in its entirety: see subs. (3). As to Discretion and Policy, see notes to s.13, above.

*Subs. (5)*
The entitlement to interest continues until payment and does not end with (by merger in) the judgment: see *Ealing L.B.C. v. El Isaac* [1980] 1 W.L.R. 932, C.A.

## Cases in which grants may be re-calculated, withheld or repaid

**42.**—(1) This section applies where an application for a grant has been approved by the local housing authority and—

(a) the authority ascertain that the amount was determined under section 30 or 31 on the basis of inaccurate or incomplete information and exceeds that to which the applicant was entitled;

(b) the authority ascertain that without their knowledge the eligible works were started before the application was approved;

(c) the eligible works are not completed to the satisfaction of the authority within the period specified under section 37(1), or such extended period as they may allow under that provision;

(d) the authority ascertain that the aggregate of the cost of completing the eligible works and the costs incurred with respect to preliminary or ancillary services and charges, is or is likely to be lower than the estimated expense; or

(e) the authority ascertain that without their knowledge the eligible works were carried out otherwise than as required by section 38 (conditions as to contractors employed).

(2) Where this section applies, the authority may—

(a) refuse to pay the grant or any further instalment of grant which remains to be paid, or

(b)  make a reduction in the grant which, in a case falling within subsection (1)(d), is to be a reduction proportionate to the reduction in the estimated expense;

and they may demand repayment by the applicant forthwith, in whole or part, of the grant or any instalment of the grant paid, together with interest at such reasonable rate as the authority may determine from the date of payment until repayment.

<small>DEFINITIONS</small>
"eligible works": s.34.
"local housing authority": s.101.
"preliminary or ancillary services and charges": s.2.

<small>GENERAL NOTE</small>
This section identifies a number of circumstances, in the main relating to the property and to the works rather than to the applicant, but including a case where it is ascertained that more grant was awarded than the applicant was entitled to "on the basis of inaccurate or incomplete information", which (a) would clearly cover erroneous assessment by way of means-testing under s.30, landlord's grant under s.31 or allocation of common parts grant under s.32, and (b) is equally clearly not confined to (but will comprise) fraudulent or wilful deception or omission. See also next section where it appears to an authority *post*-approval that the applicant was not entitled to grant at all. The section is another part of the general process of tightening up against abuse: see Introduction to Pt. I, above.

There is also a range of reactions on the part of the authority, in particular to refuse further payment, reduce grant or demand repayment, with interest at such reasonable rate as they may determine: subs. (2). Where the change is that the costs are to be lower than estimated, there is an express obligation to confine any reduction in the grant to an amount that is proportionate to the reduced expenditure: subs. (2)(b). This should not be read as automatically meaning that lower costs will mean no more than reduced grant: lower costs *could* reflect "inaccurate or incomplete information", in which case either there may be somewhat more than reduction, or else the reduction may be under subs. (1)(a). (There is no corresponding limitation on a reduction arising under subs. (1)(a), which supports proposition (b) in the last paragraph.)

*Subs. (2)*
See notes to s.41(5), above.

## Repayment where applicant not entitled to grant

**43.**—(1) This section applies where an application for a grant is approved but it subsequently appears to the local housing authority that the applicant (or, in the case of a joint application, any of the applicants) was not, at the time the application was approved, entitled to a grant of that description.

(2) Where this section applies—

(a)  in the case of a renovation grant, disabled facilities grant or HMO grant, no grant shall be paid or, as the case may be, no further instalments shall be paid, and

(b)  in the case of a common parts grant approved on a landlord's application, the local housing authority may refuse to pay the grant or any further instalment,

and the authority may demand that any grant which has been paid be repaid forthwith, together with interest from the date on which it was paid until repayment, at such reasonable rate as the authority may determine.

(3) For the purposes of this section an applicant is not entitled to a renovation grant—

(a)  in the case of an owner's application if—

(i)  he does not have a qualifying owner's interest, or

(ii)  he does not have the intention specified in the owner-occupation certificate or certificate of intended letting which accompanied the application; or

(b)  in the case of a tenant's application if—

(i)  he is not a qualifying tenant of the dwelling, or

(ii) if the application was accompanied by a certificate of intended letting and the landlord does not have the intention specified in the certificate.

(4) For the purposes of this section an applicant is not entitled to a disabled facilities grant—

(a) in the case of an owner's application—

(i) if he does not have a qualifying owner's interest, or

(ii) if he does not have the intention specified in the owner's certificate which accompanied the application; or

(b) in the case of a tenant's application—

(i) if he is not a qualifying tenant of the dwelling, or

(ii) if the application was accompanied by an owner's certificate and the landlord does not have the intention specified in the certificate.

(5) For the purposes of this section an applicant is not entitled to an HMO grant—

(a) if he does not have a qualifying owner's interest in the house; or

(b) if he does not have the intention specified in the certificate of future occupation which accompanied the application.

(6) For the purposes of this section an applicant whose application is a landlord's application for a common parts grant is not entitled to a grant—

(a) if he does not have an owner's interest in the building; or

(b) if he does not have a duty or power to carry out the relevant works.

DEFINITIONS

"common parts grant": s.1.

"disabled facilities grant": s.1.

"H.M.O. grant": s.1.

"local housing authority": s.101.

"renovation grant": s.1.

GENERAL NOTE

This section is a further part of the general process of tightening up against abuse: see Introduction to Pt. I, above. In the past, there was a mismatch between the intentions declared in the course of applying for a grant, and the circumstances in which grant could be recovered. Where the latter did not apply, but there was a suspicion that an applicant was not entitled to grant in the first place, *i.e.* has lied about his intentions, the remedies open to the authority were few and only occasionally available:

(i) in a particularly blatant case, to invite investigation and possible prosecution by the police, (see, for example, *R. v. Parker* (1993) 26 H.L.R. 508, C.A.) and/or

(ii) to take civil action for recovery for the tort of deceit. Action for deceit can be founded on a statement of intentions. "The state of a man's mind is as much a fact as the state of his digestion. It is true that it is very difficult to prove what the state of a man's mind at a particular time is, but if it can be ascertained it is as much a fact as anything else": *Edgington v. Fitzmorris* (1885) 29 Ch.D. 459.

It is now not necessary to prove dishonesty—or perhaps recklessness—because if it comes to appear to the authority that there was no entitlement to the grant that has been awarded (meaning the grant itself, as distinct from an amount of it, which would fall within s.42, above), then the grant is to cease and so far as any of it has been paid, the authority may demand repayment, together with interest at such reasonable rate as they may determine: subs. (2). The entitlement to interest continues until payment and does not end with (by merger in) the judgment: see *Ealing L.B.C. v. El Isaac* [1980] 1 W.L.R. 932, C.A.

While the provision is couched in the subjective form ("The section is framed in a 'subjective' form ... This form of section is quite well-known and at first sight might seem to exclude judicial review ... " *per* Lord Wilberforce, *Secretary of State for Education and Science v. Tameside M.B.C.* [1977] A.C. 1014, H.L. at p.1047), the decision must none the less be based on the facts:

"If a judgment requires, before it can be made, the existence of some facts, then although the evaluation of those facts is for the Secretary of State alone, the courts must enquire whether those facts exist, and have been taken into account, whether the judgment has been made on a proper self-direction as to those facts, whether the judgment has not been made on other facts which ought not to have been taken into account ..." (*per* Lord Wilberforce, *ibid.*).

See generally notes to s.13, above.

*Subs. (2)*
   See note to s.40(2), above, with particular reference to the distinct position of a common parts grant.

*Subs. (3)*
   See s.8(2) and (3) as to the original conditions which would not have been met had these changes occurred before approval.

*Subs. (4)*
   See s.21 and s.22 as to the original conditions which would not have been met had these changes occurred before approval.

*Subs. (5)*
   See s.25 and s.26 as to the original conditions which would not have been met had these changes occurred before approval.

*Subs. (6)*
   See s.15(1)(a) and s.16(1)(a) as to the original conditions which would not have been met had these changes occurred before approval.

## Grant conditions and repayment

### Grant conditions: introductory

**44.**—(1) The following sections have effect with respect to the conditions to be observed where an application for a grant has been approved by a local housing authority.
   In this Chapter a "grant condition" means a condition having effect in accordance with any of those sections.
   (2) Except as otherwise provided—
   (a) the grant conditions as to repayment on disposal (sections 45 to 47) have effect from the date on which the application is approved until the end of the grant condition period;
   (b) the grant conditions as to occupation (sections 48 to 50) have effect from the certified date until the end of the grant condition period; and
   (c) a grant condition imposed under section 52 (power to impose other conditions with consent of Secretary of State) has effect for such period as may be specified in, or in accordance with, the Secretary of State's consent.
   (3) In this Chapter—
   (a) the "grant condition period" means the period of five years, or such other period as the Secretary of State may by order specify or as may be imposed by the local housing authority with the consent of the Secretary of State, beginning with the certified date; and
   (b) the "certified date" means the date certified by the local housing authority as the date on which the execution of the eligible works is completed to their satisfaction.
   (4) A local housing authority may not impose any condition requiring a grant to be repaid except in accordance with the following sections.
   This applies whether the condition purports to operate as a condition of the grant, as a personal covenant or otherwise.

DEFINITIONS
   "local housing authority": s.101.

GENERAL NOTE
   This section introduces the grant conditions—and the only conditions—which an authority are entitled to enforce by means of repayment: subs. (4) (*cf.* s.34(5) on conditions generally, which are limited to those already considered in the preceding sections, and those in the follow-

ing sections, and can be extended with the consent of the Secretary of State. The apparent exclusion—even with such consent—of a condition requiring repayment, is mitigated by the qualification that the authority may do so as permitted or provided for by the following sections, which includes s.52, below, empowering just such added conditions, albeit with consent).

*Grant conditions involving repayment on disposal* last from the *date of approval* of grant until the end of the grant period, which is five years *from the certified date* (*or* such other period as the Secretary of State may prescribe, *or* such other period as the authority may impose but only with the consent of the Secretary of State): the certified date is the date certified by the authority as that on which the works are completed to their satisfaction (but *n.b. Curran v. Northern Ireland Co-Ownership Housing Association* [1987] 1 A.C. 718; 19 H.L.R. 318, H.L. in notes to s.37, above). The date to be certified is the date on which the works were physically completed to that standard, not the date when the local authority have inspected the finished works and approved them: see *R. v. Westminster C.C., ex p. Hazan* (1988) 20 H.L.R. 205, C.A.

Accordingly, the full period may be as much as six and a half years, or even more (six months from application to approval, s. 44; 12 months from approval to completion, s. 37; five years from certification, this section, but in the case of completion there could be an extension granted by the authority, and of course certification will itself take some period of time, *e.g.* a few days or even weeks).

*Grant conditions involving repayment on change of occupation* last *from the certified date* (as above) until the end of the grant condition period, *i.e.* five years or such other period as may be prescribed or permitted by the Secretary of State.

*Grant conditions on repayment.* Owners and others can "redeem" the condition by repayment of the grant to the authority under s.55, below; conditions also cease when repayment is activated under ss.45–50, below, or if the authority determine not to demand repayment for breach of grant condition under those parts of those sections which allow them a discretion.

## Condition for repayment on disposal: renovation grants

**45.**—(1) It is a condition of a renovation grant that if an owner of the premises to which the application relates makes a relevant disposal (other than an exempt disposal)—

(a) of the whole or part of the premises to which the application relates,

(b) after any instalment of grant has been paid, and

(c) before the certified date,

he shall repay to the local housing authority on demand the amount of grant that has been paid.

(2) It is a condition of a renovation grant that if an owner of the dwelling to which the application relates or, in the case of a conversion application, any dwelling provided by the relevant works, makes a relevant disposal (other than an exempt disposal)—

(a) of the whole or part of the dwelling,

(b) on or after the certified date, and

(c) before the end of the grant condition period,

he shall repay to the local housing authority on demand the amount of grant that has been paid.

In the case of a conversion application the grant shall be treated for this purpose as apportioned equally between the dwellings provided.

(3) A condition under this section is a local land charge and is binding on any person who is for the time being an owner of the premises concerned.

(4) Where the authority have the right to demand repayment of an amount as mentioned in subsection (1) or (2), they may—

(a) if the case falls within subsection (5), or

(b) in any other case, with the consent of the Secretary of State,

determine not to demand payment or to demand a lesser amount.

(5) The cases referred to in subsection (4)(a) are where the authority are satisfied that the owner of the dwelling—

(a) is elderly or infirm and is making the disposal with the intention—

(i) of going to live in a hospital, hospice, sheltered housing, residential care home or similar institution as his only or main residence, or

(ii) of moving to somewhere where care will be provided by any person; or

(b) is making the disposal with the intention of going to live with and care for an elderly or infirm member of his family or his partner's family.

(6) Any condition under this section shall cease to be in force with respect to any premises if there is a relevant disposal of the premises that is an exempt disposal, other than—

(a) a disposal within section 54(1)(a) (disposal to associates of person making disposal), or

(b) a disposal within section 54(1)(b) (vesting under will or on intestacy).

DEFINITIONS
"certified date": s.44.
"conversion application": s.58.
"dwelling": s.101.
"exempt disposal": s.54.
"grant condition period": s.44.
"member of family": s.98.
"owner": s.99.
"partner": s.101.
"relevant disposal": s.53.
"renovation grant": s.1.

GENERAL NOTE

The cornerstone of this section—and those following—is the concept of "the relevant disposal" which is not an "exempt disposal", a concept introduced by the Housing Act 1980 (c. 51) (subsequently, the Housing Act 1985) to govern claw-back of discount on right to buy (and now in use, *inter alia*, in the Housing Act 1996 to govern a new right to buy scheme for the tenants of registered social landlords), albeit not in identical terms. See ss.53, 54, below. Under this Act, as under the 1989 Act, repayment is triggered by a relevant disposal which is not an exempt disposal. In view of the wording of subss. (4), (5), and of ss.46(4), 47(4), 48(4), 49(4), 50(5), 51(5) and 52(4), there is no doubt that the authority have no other discretion not to reclaim the payments of grant in full. There is no discount for "complete years", as in right to buy.

The circumstances governed by this section concern renovation grants: if any owner of premises makes a non-exempt relevant disposal of the whole or part of the premises, after payment of any instalment of grant but before the certified date (see notes to s.44, above), the grant is repayable; likewise, if the owner of a dwelling make such a disposal, on or after the certified date but before the end of the grant condition period (see notes to s.44, above), the grant is repayable, with grant apportioned equally according to the number of dwellings provided by conversion. The distinction between premises and dwellings covers conversion grants, which may start with buildings which are not dwellings.

*Owner.* For this purpose (*cf.* above, s.25, below, s.47, on H.M.O. grants), owner is defined in s.99 and means the person entitled to receive from a lessee a rent of not less than two-thirds of the net annual value of the dwelling, or who would be so entitled if the dwelling were so let, but excluding someone who is only the lessee of the dwelling or of property including the dwelling, and who is bound to pay such a rent to a superior landlord, in which case it is the superior landlord who will be the owner (see also *White v. Barnet L.B.C.* (1989) 21 H.L.R. 346). Thus an owner-occupier will be an owner, even though the premises are not actually let. In a block of flats, it will normally be leaseholders who are on rents lower than the two-thirds criterion, or such leaseholders plus the landlord in respect of flats let on rents at or above the two-thirds criterion, who will qualify as the owner of the block: *Pollway v. Croydon L.B.C.* [1987] A.C. 79, 18 H.L.R. 443, H.L.

The reference to net annual value reflects the replacement of former (and long-standing) references to rents as a proportion of rateable value. Net annual value means the rent at which the dwelling might reasonably be expected to be let if the tenant undertook to pay the usual tenant's rates and taxes and to bear the cost of repair and insurance and other expenses to maintain the dwelling in a state to command such a rent: s.99(2). This definition is modelled on that used for rateable values: see the Local Government Finance Act 1988, Sched. 6, para. 2(1) and see further *Ryde on Rating and Council Tax*, Chaps. E3 and E4. The fact that statute may constrain the recoverable rent will not affect the issue: that which is a statutory will limit what can reasonably be expected—*Rawlance v. Croydon Corporation* [1952] 2 Q.B. 803, C.A. A dispute as to net annual value is referable to the District Valuer: s.97(3).

See also notes to s.82, below.

*Subs. (3)*

*Local land charge.* So long as the grant condition is in force, it binds any owner for the time being. Such a condition creates an incumbrance or burden on the property, binding successive owners, and it is for this reason that it requires to be registered as a local land charge: see *Rignall Developments Ltd. v. Halil* (1988) 20 H.L.R. 7, Ch.D. It should be noted that failure to register the condition as a local land charge does not affect its enforceability against subsequent purchasers (Local Land Charges Act 1975 (c. 76), s.10(1)) but where there has been a failure to register the charge, the local authority operating the register in which the land is situated will be liable to pay compensation for any loss caused: *ibid.*

*Subss. (4), (5)*

These subsections contain the only and limited discretion to *not* recover the grant or all of the grant, which is exercisable *either* with the consent of the Secretary of State, *or* on the authority's own motion because the owner is elderly or infirm and is making the disposal in order to go to live in a hospital, hospice, sheltered housing or residential care home or similar institution (see notes to s.11, above), as his only or main residence (see notes to s.8, above), or of moving somewhere where care will be provided, or else is disposing in order to go and live with and care for an elderly or infirm member of his family, or his partner's family. "Partner" means spouse, or a person with whom the owner lives as husband and wife (see s.101, below).

*Subs. (6)*

Even though it will not cause repayment, the condition ceases to be in force when there is an exempt disposal, other than of the two classes identified, *i.e.* such disposals keep the condition alive (but, because they are exempt, do not activate repayment).

## Condition for repayment on disposal: common parts grants

**46.**—(1) It is a condition of a common parts grant approved on a landlord's application that if the applicant makes a relevant disposal (other than an exempt disposal)—

(a) of the whole or part of the building,

(b) after any instalment of grant has been paid, and

(c) before the certified date,

he shall repay to the local housing authority on demand the amount of grant that has been paid.

(2) It is a condition of a common parts grant approved on a landlord's application that if the applicant makes a relevant disposal (other than an exempt disposal)—

(a) of the whole or part of the building,

(b) on or after the certified date, and

(c) before the end of the grant condition period,

he shall repay to the local housing authority on demand the amount of grant that has been paid.

(3) A condition under this section is a local land charge and is binding on any person who is for the time being a successor in title to the interest in the building by virtue of which the applicant made his application.

(4) Where the authority have the right to demand repayment of an amount as mentioned in subsection (1) or (2), they may, with the consent of the Secretary of State, determine not to demand payment or to demand a lesser amount.

(5) Any condition under this section shall cease to be in force with respect to any premises if there is a relevant disposal of the premises that is an exempt disposal.

DEFINITIONS

"certified date": s.44.

"common parts grant": s.1.

"exempt disposal": s.54.

"grant conditions period": s.44.

"landlord's application": s.15.

"local housing authority": s.101.

"relevant disposal": s.53.

GENERAL NOTE

This section makes provision analogous to the last, governing a landlord's application for common parts grant (see also notes to s.40, above, on the difficulties with recovery of common parts grant where individual leaseholders sell or let their own flats), in two stages, as between approval and certified date, and between certified date and end of grant condition period (see notes to s.44, above).

*Subs. (4)*

*Cf.* above, s.45(4), (5), and General Note on the limited discretion *not* to recover, which here is only exercisable with the consent of the Secretary of State.

*Subs. (5)*

*Cf.* above, s.45(6): the condition does not survive an exempt disposal.

## Condition for repayment on disposal: HMO grants

**47.**—(1) It is a condition of an HMO grant that if an owner of the house makes a relevant disposal (other than an exempt disposal)—

(a)  of the whole or part of the house,

(b)  after any instalment of grant has been paid, and

(c)  before the certified date,

he shall repay to the local housing authority on demand the amount of grant that has been paid.

(2) It is a condition of an HMO grant that if an owner of the house makes a relevant disposal (other than an exempt disposal)—

(a)  of the whole or part of the house,

(b)  on or after the certified date, and

(c)  before the end of the grant condition period,

he shall repay to the local housing authority on demand the amount of grant that has been paid.

(3) A condition under this section is a local land charge and is binding on any person (other than a local housing authority or registered social landlord) who is for the time being an owner of the house.

(4) Where the authority have the right to demand repayment of an amount as mentioned in subsection (1) or (2), they may, with the consent of the Secretary of State, determine not to demand payment or to demand a lesser amount.

(5) Any condition under this section shall cease to be in force with respect to any premises if there is a relevant disposal of the premises that is an exempt disposal.

DEFINITIONS

"exempt disposal": s.54.

"HMO grant": s.1.

"local housing authority": s.101.

"owner": ss.99, 101.

"registered social landlord": s.101.

"relevant disposal": s.53.

GENERAL NOTE

This section makes provision analogous to the last two, governing an HMO grant, in two stages, as between approval and certified date, and between certified date and end of grant condition period (see notes to s.44, above).

*Owner.* For HMO purposes, see notes to s.15, above. There can, accordingly, be more than one "owner" for this purpose (*cf.* above, s.45, note on Owner for renovation grant purposes), who may breach the condition.

*Subs. (3)*

The local land charge is *not* binding on either the local housing authority themselves, or another housing authority, or a "registered social landlord", which is the concept introduced by Pt. I of the Housing Act 1996, to replace registered housing associations, but (a) which still requires registration with the Housing Corporation, and (b) which will include all currently registered housing associations.

*Subs. (4)*
    *Cf.* above, s.45(4), (5), and General Note on the limited discretion *not* to recover, which here is only exercisable with the consent of the Secretary of State.

*Subs. (5)*
    *Cf.* above, s.45(6): the condition does not survive an exempt disposal.

## Condition as to owner-occupation: renovation grants

**48.**—(1) Where an application for a renovation grant was accompanied by an owner-occupation certificate in respect of any dwelling (see section 8(2)), it is a condition of the grant that throughout the grant condition period the dwelling is occupied in accordance with the intention stated in the certificate.
    (2) It is also a condition of the grant that if at any time when that condition is in force the authority serve notice on the owner of the dwelling requiring him to do so, he will within the period of 21 days beginning with the date on which the notice was served furnish to the authority a statement showing how that condition is being fulfilled.
    (3) A condition under this section is a local land charge and is binding on any person who is for the time being an owner of the dwelling.
    (4) In the event of a breach of a condition under this section, the owner for the time being of the dwelling shall on demand repay to the local housing authority the amount of the grant, together with compound interest on that amount as from the certified date, calculated at such reasonable rate as the authority may determine and with yearly rests.
    (5) The local housing authority may determine not to make such a demand or to demand a lesser amount.
    (6) Any condition under this section shall cease to be in force with respect to the dwelling if there is a relevant disposal of the dwelling that is an exempt disposal, other than—
    (a) a disposal within section 54(1)(a) (disposal to associates of person making disposal), or
    (b) a disposal within section 54(1)(b) (vesting under will or on intestacy).

DEFINITIONS
    "dwelling": s.101.
    "exempt disposal": s.53.
    "grant condition period": s.44.
    "local housing authority": s.101.
    "owner": s.99.
    "owner-occupation certificate": s.8.
    "relevant disposal": s.53.
    "renovation grant": s.1.

GENERAL NOTE
    This is the first of the "occupation conditions" (*cf.* above, s.44) and is applicable to renovation grants. It contains two elements. The first is that the intention stated in the owner-occupation certificate (see notes to s.8, above), as applied (in the case of a conversion grant) to any dwelling provided (see s.8(1)), is fulfilled throughout the grant condition period, *i.e.* that he or a member of his family will occupy the dwelling as an only or main residence: subs. (1). The second element is that on demand by the authority, the owner of the dwelling (as to which, see s.99, and also General Note to s.45, above) will within 21 days furnish the authority with a statement showing how the condition is being fulfilled: subs. (2).

*Subss. (4), (5)*
    The "penalty" for breach of *either* condition is repayment of grant, together with *compound interest* (at yearly rests) at such reasonable rate as the authority may determine; however, the

authority *do* enjoy a discretion not to recover the full or any amount (*cf.* above, ss.45(4), 46(4), 47(4)). The entitlement to interest continues until payment and does not end with (by merger in) the judgment: see *Ealing L.B.C. v. El Isaac* [1980] 1 W.L.R. 932, C.A.

*Subs. (6)*
　Even though it will not cause repayment, the conditions cease to be in force when there is an exempt disposal, other than of the two classes identified, *i.e.* such disposals keep the condition alive (but, because they are exempt, do not activate repayment).

### Condition as to availability for letting: renovation grants

**49.**—(1) Where an application for a renovation grant was accompanied by a certificate of intended letting in respect of any dwelling (see section 8(3)), it is a condition of the grant that throughout the grant condition period the dwelling is let or available for letting in accordance with the intention stated in the certificate.

　(2) It is also a condition of the grant that if at any time within the grant condition period the local housing authority by whom the grant was paid serve notice on the owner of the dwelling requiring him to do so, he will within the period of 21 days beginning on the date on which the notice was served furnish to the authority a statement showing how the condition in subsection (1) is being fulfilled.

　(3) A condition under this section is a local land charge and is binding on any person (other than a local housing authority or registered social landlord) who is for the time being the owner of the dwelling.

　(4) In the event of a breach of a condition under this section, the owner for the time being of the dwelling shall on demand repay to the local housing authority the amount of the grant, together with compound interest on that amount as from the certified date, calculated at such reasonable rate as the authority may determine and with yearly rests.

　(5) The local housing authority may determine not to make such a demand or to demand a lesser amount.

　(6) The terms of any tenancy of the dwelling (or any part of it, or any property including the dwelling or part of it) shall be deemed to include a duty on the part of the tenant, if required to do so by the owner of the dwelling, to furnish him with such information as he may reasonably require to enable him to comply with a notice under subsection (2).

DEFINITIONS
　"certificate of intended letting": s.8.
　"dwelling": s.101.
　"grant condition period": s.44.
　"local housing authority": s.101.
　"owner": s.99.
　"renovation grant": s.1.
　"tenant": s.101.

GENERAL NOTE
　This section makes analogous provision to the last, including the two elements—
　(i) compliance with the intention stated in the certificate of intended letting (see notes to s.8, above), as applied (in the case of a conversion grant) to any dwelling provided (see s.8(1)), throughout the grant condition period, *i.e.* let or available for letting (and not for a holiday) to a tenant who is not connected with the landlord (subs. (1)), and
　(ii) on demand by the authority to furnish the authority with a statement showing how the condition is being fulfilled (subs. (2)(a)).
　Corresponding to the second condition, it is to be an implied term of any tenancy of (or of part of) the dwelling that the tenant will provide the owner (as to which, see s.99, and also General Note to s.45, above) with such information as he reasonably requires to comply with the authority's notice: subs. (6).

*Subs. (3)*
  Cf. note to s.47(3), above.

*Subss. (4), (5)*
  See note to s.48(4), (5), above.

### Conditions as to occupation: HMO grants

**50.**—(1) It is a condition of an HMO grant that throughout the grant condition period—
  (a) the house is occupied or available for residential occupation in accordance with the intention stated in the certificate of future occupation that accompanied the application (see section 26(2)); and
  (b) that the house is not so occupied as to cause
      (i) a breach of the duty under section 353A of the Housing Act 1985 (duty to keep premises fit for number of occupants), or
      (ii) a breach of any direction given by the local housing authority under section 354 of that Act (power to limit number of occupants of house).

(2) It is also a condition of the grant that if at any time within the grant condition period the local housing authority by whom the grant was paid serve notice on the owner of the house requiring him to do so, he will within the period of 21 days beginning with the date on which the notice was served furnish to the authority a statement showing how the condition in subsection (1)(a) is being fulfilled.

(3) A condition under this section is a local land charge and is binding on any person (other than a local housing authority or registered social landlord) who is for the time being an owner of the house.

(4) In the event of a breach of a condition under this section, the owner for the time being of the dwelling shall on demand pay to the local housing authority the amount of the grant, together with compound interest on that amount as from the certified date, calculated at such reasonable rate as the authority may determine and with yearly rests.

(5) The local housing authority may determine not to make such a demand or to demand a lesser amount.

(6) The terms of any tenancy of any part of the house shall be deemed to include a duty on the part of the tenant, if required to do so by the owner of the house, to furnish him with such information as he may reasonably require to enable him to comply with a notice under subsection (2).

DEFINITIONS
  "certificate of future occupation": s.26.
  "HMO grant": s.1.
  "local housing authority": s.101.
  "owner": ss.99, 101.

GENERAL NOTE
  This section makes analogous provision to the last two, including the two elements—
  (i) compliance with the intention stated in the certificate of future occupation (see notes to s.26, above), throughout the grant condition period, *i.e.* residential occupation under tenancy or licence by persons who are not connected with the landlord (subs. (1)(a)), and
  (ii) on demand by the authority to furnish the authority with a statement showing how the condition is being fulfilled (subs. (2)(a)).
  Corresponding to the second condition, it is to be an implied term of any tenancy of (or of part of) the dwelling that the tenant will provide the owner (as to which, see s.101, see General Note to s.47, above) with such information as he reasonably requires to comply with the authority's notice: subs. (6).
  The *first* condition is also subject to extension in relation to an HMO grant: that the house is not occupied so as to cause a breach of duty under s.353A, Housing Act 1985, to keep the premises fit for the number of occupants, or so as to cause a breach of direction by the local housing authority under *ibid.* s.354 to limit the number of occupants.

*Housing Act 1985, s.353A* (added by the Housing Act 1996, s.73):

"(1) It is the duty of the person having control of a house in multiple occupation, and of the person managing it, to take such steps as are reasonably practicable to prevent the occurrence of a state of affairs calling for the service of a notice or further notice under section 352 (notice requiring execution of works to render a house fit for number of occupants).

(2) A breach of duty is actionable in damages at the suit of any tenant or other occupant of the premises, or any other person who suffers loss, damage or personal injury in consequence of the breach.

(3) A person who fails to comply with the duty imposed on him by subsection (1) commits a summary offence and is liable on conviction to a fine not exceeding level 5 on the standard scale".

For the relevant provisions of s.352, see notes to s.17 above.

*Housing Act 1985, s.354* (as amended—see words in square brackets—by the Local Government and Housing Act 1988, Sched. 9, para. 52):

"(1) The local housing authority may, for the purpose of preventing the occurrence of, or remedying, a state of affairs calling for the service of a notice or further notice under section 352 ... —

(a) fix as a limit for the house what is in their opinion the highest number of individuals or households, or both, who should, having regard to the [requirements set out in subsection (1A)] of that section, occupy the house in its existing conditions, and

(b) give a direction applying that limit to the house,

(2) The authority may also exercise the powers conferred by subsection (1) in relation to a part of a house; and the authority shall have regard to the desirability of applying separate limits where different parts of a house are, or are likely to be, occupied by different persons".

For the relevant provisions of s.352, see notes to s.17, above.

*Subs. (3)*
*Cf.* note to s.47(3), above.

*Subss. (4), (5)*
See note to s.48(4), (5), above.

## Conditions as to repayment in case of other compensation, &c

**51.**—(1) Where a local housing authority approve an application for a grant they may, with the consent of the Secretary of State, impose a condition requiring the applicant to take reasonable steps to pursue any relevant claim to which this section applies and to repay the grant, so far as appropriate, out of the proceeds of such a claim.

(2) The claims to which this section applies are—

(a) an insurance claim, or a legal claim against another person, in respect of damage to the premises to which the grant relates, or

(b) a legal claim for damages in which the cost of the works to premises to which the grant relates is part of the claim;

and a claim is a relevant claim to the extent that works to make good the damage mentioned in paragraph (a), or the cost of which is claimed as mentioned in paragraph (b), are works to which the grant relates.

(3) In the event of a breach of a condition under this section, the applicant shall on demand pay to the local housing authority the amount of the grant so far as relating to any such works, together with compound interest as from such date as may be prescribed by or determined in accordance with the regulations, calculated at such reasonable rate as the authority may determine and with yearly rests.

(4) The local housing authority may determine not to make such a demand or to demand a lesser amount.

DEFINITIONS
"local housing authority": s.101.

GENERAL NOTE
A new concept, this section permits the local authority—with the consent of the Secretary of State—to impose a condition on a grant approval which requires the applicant to take steps to

pursue claims out of which the grant, or part of it, may be repaid, *i.e.* insurance or legal claim, where the works to which the grant relates are or include works to make good the damage the subject of the claim (see subs. (2)).

"... The new clause will enable the local authority to give grant for essential works in the knowledge that the grant, or the relevant part of it, can be recovered from the applicant if the claim is successfully resolved. That is not possible under current legislation. While the condition will require the consent of the Secretary of State, we envisage there being a general consent, under [s.94, below], covering house insurance and claims for damages to property and to the individual." *Hansard* (H.C.), June 6, 1996, Standing Committee F, Fifth Sitting, col. 199, Parliamentary Under-Secretary of State for the Environment (Mr Clappison).

*Subs. (3)*
The compound interest provision is the same—deliberately penal—provision which governs breach of occupation conditions (as distinct from repayment without interest on a decision to dispose).

*Subs. (5)*
The authority have discretion to waive a claim, or to claim less than the whole of the amount recouped that relates to grant-aided works.

## Power to impose other conditions with consent of Secretary of State

**52.**—(1) Where a local housing authority approve an application for a grant they may, with the consent of the Secretary of State, impose such conditions as they think fit—

(a) relating to things done or omitted before the certified date and requiring the repayment to the local housing authority on demand of any instalments of grant paid, or

(b) relating to things done or omitted on or after that date and requiring the payment to the local housing authority on demand of a sum equal to the amount of the grant paid;

and, in either case, that amount may be required to be paid together with compound interest on that amount as from the date of payment, calculated at such reasonable rate as the authority may determine and with yearly rests.

(2) A condition under this section is a local land charge and is binding on—

(a) any person who is for the time being an owner of the dwelling, house or building, and

(b) such other persons (if any) as the authority may, with the consent of the Secretary of State, specify.

(3) The reference in subsection (2)(a) to the owner of the building shall be construed—

(a) in the case of a grant condition imposed on a landlord's application for a common parts grant, as a reference to the applicant or any successor in title to the interest in the building by virtue of which the applicant made his application;

(b) in the case of a grant condition imposed on an application for an HMO grant, as excluding a local housing authority or registered social landlord.

(4) Where the authority have the right to demand repayment of an amount as mentioned in subsection (1), they may determine not to demand payment or to demand a lesser amount.

(5) Any conditions imposed under this section are in addition to the conditions provided for by sections 45 to 51.

DEFINITIONS
"certified date": s.44.
"common parts grant": s.1.
"HMO grant": s.1.
"landlord's application": s.15.
"local housing authority": s.101.
"owner": ss.99, 101.

GENERAL NOTE
Further conditions (*cf.* subs. (5)) may be imposed on approval, with the consent of the Secretary of State, relating to things done or omitted either before or after the certified date (subs. (1)), which can require repayment of instalment, or of grant, with compound interest at yearly rests, but subject to a discretion on the part of the authority to recoup no, or a lesser, amount (subs. (4)). Examples given were nomination rights, recovery of specialised equipment, insurance and maintenance: *Hansard* (H.C.), June 6, 1996, Standing Committee F, Fifth Sitting, col. 202, Parliamentary Under-Secretary of State for the Environment (Mr Clappison).

## Meaning of relevant disposal

**53.**—(1) A disposal is a relevant disposal for the purposes of the provisions of this Chapter relating to grant conditions if it is—

(a) a conveyance of the freehold or an assignment of the lease, or

(b) the grant of a lease (other than a mortgage term) for a term of more than 21 years otherwise than at a rack rent.

(2) For the purposes of subsection (1)(b) it shall be assumed—

(a) that any option to renew or extend a lease or sub-lease, whether or not forming part of a series of options, is exercised, and

(b) that any option to terminate a lease or sub-lease is not exercised.

(3) The grant of an option enabling a person to call for a relevant disposal shall be treated as such a disposal made to him.

GENERAL NOTE

This section is modelled on the Housing Act 1985, s.159.

A conveyance is "an instrument that transfers property from one person to another" (*Eastbourne Corporation v. A.G.* [1904] A.C. 155, H.L.). An instrument which does not pass a legal estate will not qualify as a conveyance, even if it is sufficient to amount to an enforceable contract for the conveyance and so pass an equitable interest in the property under the rule in *Walsh v. Lonsdale* (1882) 21 Ch.D. 9: see *Rodger v. Harrison* (1893) 1 Q.B. 161; *I.R.C. v. Angus* (1889) 23 Q.B.D. 579.

A sub-letting for the whole of the remainder of a term will take effect as an assignment: *Milmo v. Carreras* [1946] K.B. 306. The fact that there is a right of re-entry or forfeiture will not prevent a lease being for more than 21 years: *Quinlan v. Avis* (1933) 149 L.T. 214.

The term "rack-rent" means a rent of, or near to, the full annual value of a property (*Re Sawyer and Withall* [1919] 2 Ch. 333) determined as at the date of the grant (*London Corporation v. Cusack-Smith* [1955] A.C. 337, H.L.; *cf.*, above, notes to s.45, on net annual value) or the maximum rent which is permitted by law: *Compton Group v. Estates Gazette* (1978) 36 P. & C.R. 148, C.A. "The former meaning is its primary meaning in legal language, although the meaning of the expression may vary according to the context in which it is used": *Woodfall, Landlord and Tenant Law*, para. 7.013, citing *Compton*.

## Meaning of exempt disposal

**54.**—(1) A disposal is an exempt disposal for the purposes of the provisions of this Chapter relating to grant conditions if it is a disposal of the whole or part of the premises to which the application relates of any of the following descriptions—

(a) a conveyance of the freehold or an assignment of the lease where the person, or each of the persons, to whom it is made is a qualifying person (as defined in subsection (2));

(b) a vesting in a person taking under a will or on an intestacy;

(c) a disposal in pursuance of any such order as is mentioned in subsection (3);

(d) a compulsory disposal (see subsection (4));

(e) a disposal of property consisting of land included in the dwelling by virtue of section 184 of the Housing Act 1985 (land let with or used for the purposes of the dwelling-house);

(f) a disposal under which the interest of a person entitled to assistance by way of repurchase under Part XVI of that Act (assistance for owners of defective housing) is acquired in accordance with Schedule 20 to that Act;

(g) a disposal by way of enfranchisement or lease extension under Part I of the Leasehold Reform Act 1967;

(h) a disposal in pursuance of an obligation arising under Chapter I or II of Part I of the Leasehold Reform, Housing and Urban Development Act 1993;

(i) a disposal on the exercise of a right of first refusal under Part I of the Landlord and Tenant Act 1987 or in accordance with an acquisition order under Part III of that Act;

(j) a disposal on the exercise of—
    (i) the right to buy under Part V of the Housing Act 1985, or
    (ii) the right conferred by section 16 of the Housing Act 1996
(right of tenant of registered social landlord to acquire dwelling);

(k) a conveyance of the freehold or an assignment of the lease where
    (i) the person making the disposal is aged at least 70,
    (ii) the disposal is to provide an annuity income, and
    (iii) the person concerned is entitled to continue to occupy the premises as his only or main residence;

(l) a disposal of any other description specified by order of the Secretary of State for the purposes of this section.

(2) A person is a qualifying person for the purposes of subsection (1)(a) if—

(a) in the case of an individual, he is—
    (i) the person, or one of the persons, by whom the disposal is made;
    (ii) the spouse, or former spouse, of that person or one of those persons; or
    (iii) a member of the family of that person or one of those persons; or

(b) in the case of a company, it is an associated company of the company by whom the disposal is made.

Section 416 of the Income and Corporation Taxes Act 1988 (meaning of associated company) applies in determining whether a company is an associated company of another for the purposes of paragraph (b).

(3) The orders referred to in subsection (1)(c) are orders under—

(a) section 24 or 24A of the Matrimonial Causes Act 1973 (property adjustment orders or orders for the sale of property in connection with matrimonial proceedings);

(b) section 2 of the Inheritance (Provision for Family and Dependants) Act 1975 (orders as to financial provision to be made from estate);

(c) section 17 of the Matrimonial and Family Proceedings Act 1984 (property adjustment orders or orders for the sale of property after overseas divorce, etc.); or

(d) paragraph 1 of Schedule 1 to the Children Act 1989 (orders for financial relief against parents).

(4) For the purposes of subsection (1)(d) a compulsory disposal is a disposal of property which is acquired compulsorily, or is acquired by a person who has made or would have made, or for whom another person has made or would have made, a compulsory purchase order authorising its compulsory purchase for the purposes for which it is acquired.

(5) The grant of an option enabling a person to call for an exempt disposal shall be treated as such a disposal made to him.

Definitions
"member of the family": s.98.

General Note
This section defines the exempt disposals, which in some cases (see ss.45(6), 46(5), 47(5), 48(6)) have the incidental effect of bringing a grant condition to a premature end *without* requiring repayment. These disposals are:

(i) *Voluntary re-arrangements.* Disposals by or to oneself together with others, or to one's own spouse, former spouse, or family member, or that of one of the co-disponors, and in the case of a company to an associated company. Note, however, that these disposals, while exempt and so not activating repayment, do not terminate the repayment condition under ss.45 or 48.

(ii) *Death.* Likewise, the vesting in a person under a will or intestacy, while exempt and so not activating repayment, does not terminate the repayment condition under ss.45 or 48.

(iii) *Court ordered transfer.* Orders under the provisions identified in subs. (3) do not activate repayment and do terminate the repayment condition. A property sale under s.24A, Matrimonial Causes Act 1973 (c. 18), is now within the exemption, whereas it would not have been within the analogous provisions of the previous legislation (although see s.141, below), *cf. R. v. Rushmore B.C., ex p. Barrett* (1988) 20 H.L.R. 366, C.A. (under the right to buy provisions of the Housing Act 1985).

(iv) *Compulsory purchase.* This includes a sale by agreement to a person who has made, or could have made, a compulsory purchase order, or for whom another (such as a local authority or the Housing Corporation) could make such an order authorising compulsory purchase: see subs. (4).

(v) *Added land.* Land let together with a dwelling house is treated as part of the dwelling house for the purposes of right to buy, under the Housing Act 1985, s.184(1), unless it is agricultural land exceeding two acres; also, land not within s.184(1) may be added at the request of the purchasing tenant, if it is reasonable to do so and it is land which is or has been used for the purposes of the dwelling—see s.184(2). Such added lands may be disposed of, without activating repayment.

(vi) *Defective dwellings.* Repurchase under Pt. XVI of the Housing Act 1985, see notes to s.6, above.

(vii) *Leaseholders.* Under the Leasehold Reform Act 1967 (c. 88), long leaseholders of houses may be able to require the extension of their leases by 50 years, or their enfranchisement (purchase of freehold); likewise, there are powers for leaseholders of flats to acquire the freeholds of their blocks, under both the Landlord and Tenant Act 1987 (c. 31), and the Leasehold Reform, Housing and Urban Development Act 1993 (c. 28). Any of these disposals—compulsory against the freeholder or person with a superior interest—could mean that a freeholder or person with a superior interest, who has received a grant, finds himself making a disposal he has not initiated and which is against his will, for which reason the disposal is exempt, and the condition comes to an end.

(viii) *Right to buy.* The right to buy under the Housing Act 1985 can in some circumstances be exercisable as against bodies other than local authorities, and the analogous right under the Housing Act 1996, if passed, will be a right against registered social landlords who are not excluded from grant by s.2, above, for which reason these landlords are in the same position as the last, *i.e.* Leaseholders.

(ix) *Annuity disposals.* Some elderly people sell their homes, with the right to continue to reside in them until death, in exchange for an annuity: such disposals are likewise exempt, and the repayment condition ceases to apply.

(x) *Reserve powers.* The Secretary of State has reserve powers to specify additional exempt disposals.

## Cessation of conditions on repayment of grant, &c

**55.**—(1) If at any time while a grant condition remains in force with respect to a dwelling, house or building—

   (a) the owner of the dwelling, house or building to which the condition relates pays the amount of the grant to the local housing authority by whom the grant was made,

   (b) a mortgagee of the interest of the owner in that dwelling, house or building being a mortgagee entitled to exercise a power of sale, makes such a payment,

   (c) the local housing authority determine not to demand repayment on the breach of a grant condition, or

   (d) the authority demand repayment in whole or in part on the breach of a grant condition and that demand is satisfied,

that grant condition and any other grant conditions shall cease to be in force with respect to that dwelling, house or building.

(2) In the case of a grant condition imposed on a landlord's application for a common parts grant the references in subsection (1)(a) and (b) to the owner of the building are to the applicant or any such successor in title as is referred to in section 46(3).

(3) An amount paid by a mortgagee under subsection (1)(b) above shall be treated as part of the sums secured by the mortgage and may be discharged accordingly.

(4) The purposes authorised for the application of capital money by—

(a) section 73 of the Settled Land Act 1925,

(b) that section as applied by section 28 of the Law of Property Act 1925 in relation to trusts for sale, and

(c) section 26 of the Universities and College Estates Act 1925,

include the making of payments under this section.

DEFINITIONS

"common parts grant": s.1.
"dwelling": s.101.
"landlord's application": s 15
"local housing authority": s.101.
"owner": ss.99, 101.

GENERAL NOTE

This section permits an owner voluntarily to repay a grant in order to free himself from all of the conditions attached to it: note that, as with repayment on disposal under ss.45–47, no interest is payable on reimbursement.

An applicant may find that he has effectively or in practice traded away his right to use this right. In *R. v. Hackney L.B.C., ex p. Gransils Investments* (1988) 20 H.L.R. 313, Q.B.D., the landlord had agreed that—in return for the local authority not enforcing a compulsory purchase order—he would convert the property into three flats with assistance by way of grant-aid (under Pt. XV of the Housing Act 1985), subject to certificates of availability for letting (see now the certificate of intended letting under s.8(3)). On completion of the works the landlord sought to repay the grant and sell the flats. The authority responded by seeking to implement the compulsory purchase order, which the court held that they were entitled to do.

The right is available not only to an owner, but also to a mortgagee who is entitled to exercise the power of sale, in which case the amount so repaid is treated as part of the sum secured by the mortgage, *i.e.* may be repaid out of the proceeds of sale: subss. (3), (4).

The section also provides that if the authority determine not to enforce a repayment entitlement, at all or in full, the grant conditions will come to an end, just as if they do so demand and the demand is met. Where an authority make an incorrect determination of the amount owing that is smaller than the amount due, it is arguable that the authority would be estopped from seeking the larger sum, where the applicant has acted in reliance, and to his detriment, on the demand: see *Lombard North Central v. Stobart* [1990] C.C.L.R. 53, C.A.

*Supplementary provisions*

**Provisions relating to death of applicant**

**56.**—(1) References in this Chapter to the applicant, in relation to a grant or an application for a grant, shall be construed in relation to any time after his death as a reference to his personal representatives.

(2) Where the applicant dies after liability has been incurred for any preliminary or ancillary services or charges, the local housing authority may, if they think fit, pay grant in respect of some or all of those matters.

(3) Where the applicant dies after the relevant works have been begun and before the certified date, the local housing authority may, if they think fit, pay grant in respect of some or all of the works already carried out and other relevant works covered by the application.

(4) Nothing in this section shall be construed as preventing the provisions as to grant conditions applying in relation to any payment of grant under subsection (2) or (3).

DEFINITIONS

"local housing authority": s.101.
"preliminary or ancillary services or charges": s.2.
"relevant works": s.2.

GENERAL NOTE

If an applicant dies, the provisions of this Chapter apply to his personal representatives, so that if the grant condition period (see notes to s.44) is still running, they will be bound by it, but so also that if, before approval, they would not in their own right qualify for the grant (whether by reason of means-testing or otherwise, *e.g.* non-compliance with residence intentions), no grant will be available (subs. (1)). However, the authority *may* none the less pay grant in respect of costs incurred before the death, whether in making the application, or preparing for the works, or indeed on relevant works (subss. (2), (3)), in which case the grant conditions will apply to such sums in the same way as if the full grant had been paid (subs. (4)).

## Power of local housing authority to carry out works which would attract grant

**57.**—(1) A local housing authority may by agreement with a person having the requisite interest execute at his expense—

(a) any works towards the cost of which a grant under this Chapter is payable or might be paid on an application duly made and approved, and

(b) any further works which it is in their opinion necessary or desirable to execute together with the works mentioned in paragraph (a).

(2) Except in the case of a common parts grant, the "requisite interest" means a qualifying owner's interest for the purposes of a renovation grant, or an owner's interest for the purposes of a disabled facilities grant or HMO grant, as the case may be.

(3) In the case of a common parts grant, the reference in subsection (1) to a person having the requisite interest is a reference to the person who has—

(a) an owner's interest in the building, or

(b) such an interest in a flat in the building as is mentioned in section 14(2)(a) to (d) (occupying tenants),

and has a power or duty to carry out the relevant works.

DEFINITIONS

"common parts grant": s.1.
"H.M.O. grant": s.1.
"local housing authority": s.101.
"qualifying owner's interest": ss.7, 19, 25.
"renovation grant": s.1.

GENERAL NOTE

This section permits "agency agreements", under which the authority may carry out grant-aided works, or works which could have been grant-aided if an application had been duly paid and approved, and any additional works they consider desirable to carry out together with such works: subs. (1). The person for whom the authority carry out the works must have a "requisite interest" as defined in subss. (2) and (3). A tenant's application under s.9 may still lead to agency works provided the person with whom the arrangement is made has a requisite interest, for the works will still be grant-aided or grant-aidable.

"Execution" is wide enough to cover not only the authority doing the works themselves, *e.g.* by a Direct Labour Organisation, but also commissioning and supervising works: "Many owners have been deterred from improving their homes because they do not know how to set about it, or because they do not relish making detailed arrangements ... The local authority would be in a position to supervise the improvement works: and to make sure that the work was well done at reasonable cost ... " (DoE Circular 63/69, para. 9, of the analogous power in the Local Government and Housing Act 1989, s.135).

## Minor definitions: Chapter I

**58.** In this Chapter—

"common parts", in relation to a building, includes the structure and exterior of the building and common facilities provided, whether in the building or elsewhere, for persons who include the occupiers of one or more flats in the building;

"common parts application", in relation to an application for a disabled facilities grant, means an application in respect of works to the common parts of a building containing one or more flats;

"conversion application"—

    (a) in relation to an application for a renovation grant, means an application in respect of works required for the provision of one or more dwellings by the conversion of a house or other building, and

    (b) in relation to an application for an HMO grant, means an application for a grant in respect of works for the provision of a house in multiple occupation by the conversion of a house or other building;

"flat" means a dwelling which is a separate set of premises, whether or not on the same floor, divided horizontally from some other part of the building.

GENERAL NOTE

    See notes to s.1, above.

## Index of defined expressions: Chapter I

**59.** In this Chapter the expressions listed below are defined by or otherwise fall to be construed in accordance with the provisions indicated—

| | |
|---|---|
| certificate of future occupation (in relation to an application for an HMO grant) | section 26(2) |
| certificate of intended letting (in relation to an application for a renovation grant) | section 8(3) |
| certified date | section 44(3)(b) |
| common parts | section 58 |
| common parts application (in relation to a disabled facilities grant) | section 58 |
| common parts grant | section 1(3) |
| connected (with the owner of a dwelling) | section 98(2) |
| conversion application | section 58 |
| disabled facilities grant | section 1(4) |
| disabled occupant | section 20 |
| disabled person | section 100(1) to (3) |
| dwelling | section 101 |
| elderly | section 101 |
| eligible works | section 34(2)(a) |
| estimated expense | section 34(2) |
| exempt disposal | section 54 |
| fit for human habitation | section 97(1) |
| flat | section 58 |
| grant (without more) | section 1(6) |
| grant condition | section 44(1) |
| grant condition period | section 44(3)(a) |
| HMO grant | section 1(5) |
| house in multiple occupation | section 101 |
| housing action trust | section 101 |
| improvement | section 101 |
| introductory tenant | section 101 |
| landlord's application | |
|   —in relation to a renovation grant | section 10(6) |
|   —in relation to a common parts grant | section 15(1) and (2) |
| local authority | section 101 |
| local housing authority | section 101 |
| long tenancy | section 101 |
| member of family | section 98(1) |
| new town corporation | section 101 |

CHAPTER II

GROUP REPAIR SCHEMES

*Introductory*

### Group repair schemes

**60.**—(1) A local housing authority may prepare a scheme (a "group repair scheme") for the carrying out of works—
    (a) to put in reasonable repair the exterior of the buildings to which the scheme relates, or
    (b) to render the buildings to which the scheme relates structurally stable,
or for both those purposes.
    (2) For the purposes of this Chapter "building" includes the whole or part of a terrace of houses or other units.
    (3) The scheme must satisfy the requirements of sections 61 and 62 as to the buildings to which it relates and the works specified in it.

DEFINITIONS
    "exterior": s.62.
    "local housing authority": s.101.
    "reasonable repair": s.96.
    "structural stability": s.62.

GENERAL NOTE
    "Enveloping is the renovation of the external fabric and curtilage of dwellings which have deteriorated beyond the scope of routine maintenance. ... It includes such items as repair or renewal of roof and chimneys, rainwater goods, work to external walls, repair or replacement of doors and windows and improvements to the curtilages. Whole terraces or blocks are dealt with simultaneously ...": DoE Circular 29/82.
    The practice of enveloping used only to be possible where the authority declared a housing action area or general improvement area, and consequently had the power to carry out works to the housing within the area. The cost of the works was not generally sought from the owners of the properties concerned. Enveloping works can still be carried out in a renewal area, under Pt. VII of the Local Government and Housing Act 1989 (particularly, s.93). In addition, they can be carried out—not only in renewal areas (but *cf.* below, s.67(4)(a), for lower contributions in a renewal area)—by way of grant-aided group repair scheme, a concept first introduced by that Act, Pt. VIII, and repeated here, subject to some amendment.
    Group repair schemes require the approval of the Secretary of State if they are to lead to any activity: see s.63, below.

*Subs. (1)*
    Works extend both to putting the building into reasonable repair (which would have included works necessary thereto which amounted to works of structural stability), and those merely intended to achieve structural stability (*Hansard* (H.C.), Report, July 8, 1996, col. 64, Parliamentary Under-Secretary for State for the Environment (Mr Clappison)). See also s.62, below.

*Subs. (2)*
    The group repair scheme is concerned with "buildings", defined to include "the whole or part of a terrace of houses or other units": this definition is intended to extend the natural meaning of building, to include terrace, rather than to confine the operation of the grant to what is or originally was built as what might be considered a house. While one of the buildings must still be a primary building, within s.61(3), below, that definition is now left to regulations, and no longer includes the former requirement (1989 Act, s.128(2)), that, as constructed, it contained no less than four separate houses.
    The definition is clearly used to render unnecessary recourse to the extensive case-law on the meaning of the word "house", although insofar as regulations on the meaning of primary and qualifying buildings may yet rely on the word house, and insofar as the historical genesis of a concept is never irrelevant to statutory interpretation (either to show what it means or, some-

times, to show what it does *not* mean), it is still useful to summarise it here. (See also, on purpose-built HMOs treated as "houses", notes to s.1, above).

The word "house" has in any event never had any very precise meaning (*Quilotex Co. v. Minister of Housing and Local Government* [1966] 1 Q.B. 704, C.A.), being a mixed question of law (involving construction of the Act in question) and fact (*In Re Butler, Camberwell (Wingfield Mews) No. 2 Clearance Order 1936* [1939] 1 K.B. 570, C.A.) to be left in the first instance to the decision-maker, with whose decision the courts can only interfere on conventional (administrative law) grounds (*cf.* notes to s.13, above): *Re South Shields (D'Arcy Street) Compulsory Purchase Order 1937* [1939] 1 All E.R. 419, C.A.; *Ashbridge Investments v. Minister of Housing and Local Government* [1965] 1 W.L.R. 1320, C.A.

A house is a "building for human habitation": *Reed v. Hastings Corporation* (1964) 62 L.G.R. 588, C.A., or a "building constructed or adapted for use as or for the purposes of a dwelling" (*Ashbridge Investments*, above). A garage or workshop with a dwelling above was held to be a house in *In Re Butler* (above)—see also *Re Hammersmith (Bergham Mews) Clearance Order 1936* [1937] 3 All E.R. 539. Where a building is used partly for residential purposes, and partly for others, it has to be looked at as a whole to ascertain whether, as a question of degree, it can properly be described as a house: *Annicola Investments v. Minister of Housing and Local Government* [1968] 1 Q.B. 631, C.A. It need not be shown that all the rooms in a building are in residential use: *Premier Garage Co. v. Ilkeston Corporation* (1933) 97 J.P. 786.

Although original construction is important (*In Re Butler*, above), use at the time the question falls to be determined is also relevant (*ibid.*, see also *Grosvenor v. Hampstead Junction Railway* [1957] L.J. Ch. 731; an unfinished house may qualify as a house—*Alexander v. Crystal Palace Railway* (1862) 30 Beav. 556; a building constructed as a house but used for other purposes has been considered to remain a house—*Howard v. Ministry of Housing and Local Government* (1967) 65 L.G.R. 257.

A building subdivided into flats can remain a house, whether or not so constructed: *Annicola* (above), *Quilotex* (above), *Benabo v. Wood Green B.C.* [1946] 1 K.B. 38, *Critchell v. Lambeth L.B.C.* [1957] 2 Q.B. 535, C.A., *Okereke v. Brent L.B.C.* [1967] 1 Q.B. 42, C.A. A flat itself however, is not a house, nor for like reasons a building (*R. v. Lambeth L.B.C., ex p. Clayhope* (1987) 19 H.L.R. 426, C.A.), even although for most housing purposes it is not so treated, and it clearly is a dwelling, or can be premises. In *Lake v. Bennett* [1970] 1 Q.B. 663, C.A., under the Leasehold Reform Act 1967, Lord Denning M.R. doubted whether a tower block could *ever* reasonably be called a house, but Salmon L.J. emphasised that the decision did not necessarily affect the Housing Acts, and the wording of the 1967 Act does refer to a house "reasonably so-called".

It has commonly been noted that care must be taken when applying case-law that is derived from other legislation, and even from other parts of the Housing Acts: see *Quilotex* (above), *Annicola* (above), *R. v. Cardiff C.C., ex p. Cross* (1981) 1 H.L.R. 54, Q.B.D. (upheld on appeal at (1982) 6 H.L.R. 1, C.A.); in view of the definition of building, there will be no such difficulties in relation to group repair schemes.

## Qualifying buildings

**61.**—(1) The buildings to which a group repair scheme relates must be qualifying buildings.

(2) A building is a qualifying building if at the time the scheme is prepared it satisfies the conditions prescribed for qualifying buildings in relation to a group repair scheme.

(3) A group repair scheme must relate to at least one qualifying building which at the time the scheme is prepared satisfies the conditions prescribed for a primary building in relation to a group repair scheme.

(4) Each of the other qualifying buildings to which a group repair scheme relates must satisfy the conditions prescribed for an additional building in relation to a group repair scheme.

DEFINITIONS
"building": s.60.

GENERAL NOTE
A group repair scheme concerns (a) a primary building, and (b) other qualifying buildings (additional buildings). The conditions for each of these concepts is to be defined in regulations. By virtue of the definition of building in s.60(2), above, the primary building itself may be the whole or part of a terrace of houses (or other units, *e.g.*, former offices or warehousing converted into housing, or shops with flats above which might or more not, in their own rights, have fallen to be considered houses—see notes to s.60(2), above).

**Scheme works**

**62.**—(1) The works specified in a group repair scheme ("scheme works") must be works of the following descriptions.

(2) In the case of works to put in reasonable repair the exterior of the buildings to which the scheme relates, the works must be—

(a) works to the exterior of the buildings to which the scheme relates, or

(b) so far only as may be necessary to give satisfactory effect to such works, additional works to other parts of the buildings,

and must be such that on completion of the works the exterior of the buildings will be in reasonable repair.

(3) In the case of works to render the buildings to which the scheme relates structurally stable, the works must be—

(a) works to the structure or to the foundations of the buildings to which the scheme relates, or

(b) other works necessary to give satisfactory effect to such works,

and must be such that on completion of the works the buildings will be structurally stable.

(4) For the purposes of this Chapter the exterior of a building means—

(a) any part of the building which is exposed to the elements of wind and rain or otherwise faces into the open air (including, in particular, roofs, chimneys, walls, doors, windows, rainwater goods and external pipework), and

(b) the curtilage of the building, including any wall within the curtilage which is constructed as a retaining wall or otherwise to protect the structure of the building.

(5) In relation to works to the curtilage of a building the reference in subsection (2)(b) to additional works to other parts of the building includes additional works on land outside the curtilage.

(6) For the purposes of this Chapter the exterior of a building shall not be regarded as in reasonable repair unless it is substantially free from rising or penetrating damp.

Definitions

"building": s.60.
"group repair scheme": s.60.

General Note

The works in a group repair scheme must either be—

(a) to put the "exterior of the buildings" in reasonable repair (save so far as additional works are necessary to give satisfactory effect to external works), and they must be such that on completion, the exterior of the buildings will be in reasonable repair (see notes to s.96, below), which has an expanded definition for the purposes of such schemes, that a building will not be regarded as in reasonable repair unless on completion of the works it is "substantially free from rising or penetrating damp" (subs. (6)); or

(b) to render the building itself structurally stable, meaning works to the foundations (save so far as additional works are necessary to give satisfactory effect to works to the foundation).

*Subs. (4)*

*Curtilage.* The meaning of "curtilage" was considered in *Dyer v. Dorset C.C.* [1989] Q.B. 346, 20 H.L.R. 490, C.A., in relation to the exemption from the right to buy in what is now Sched. 5, para. 5, to the Housing Act 1985, where it was held to involve some small and necessary extension to the property to which the word is attached. An area of land could not properly be described as a curtilage unless it formed part and parcel of the house or building which it contains or to which it is attached. See also *Barwick v. Kent C.C.* (1992) 24 H.L.R. 341, C.A.

*Exterior.* See also cases on "structure and exterior" in notes to s.1, above, although this statutory definition is relatively comprehensive and comprises all that would be so defined.

### Approval of scheme by Secretary of State

**63.**—(1) If a group repair scheme prepared by a local housing authority is approved by the Secretary of State, the authority may, with the consent of the persons participating in the scheme, enter into agreements to secure the carrying out of the works specified in the scheme.

(2) The approval of the Secretary of State may be given either to a specific scheme or generally to schemes which fulfil such criteria as he may from time to time specify.

(3) Different criteria may be specified for different types of scheme and for different areas.

(4) The approval of a scheme may be made conditional upon compliance with requirements specified by the Secretary of State.

DEFINITIONS
"group repair scheme": s.60.
"local housing authority": s.101.
"persons participating in the scheme": s.64.

GENERAL NOTE
This section requires the approval of the Secretary of State to a group repair scheme, without which there can be no agreements to effect the works.

*Participation in group repair scheme*

### Persons eligible to participate in group repair scheme

**64.**—(1) A person is eligible to participate in a group repair scheme if at the date of the approval of the scheme—
  (a) he has an owner's interest in a dwelling or other premises comprised in a building to which the scheme relates, and
  (b) as respects the dwelling or other premises in which he has an owner's interest he either—
      (i) is able to give possession of any part of the building to which scheme works are proposed to be carried out, or
      (ii) has the consent of the occupier of that part to the carrying out of those works.
In the case of a scheme not submitted for specific approval, the date of approval shall be taken to be the date on which the authority decide that the scheme fulfils the criteria for general approval.

(2) A person eligible to participate in a group repair scheme may participate as an assisted participant—
  (a) if the owner's interest which he has is an interest in a dwelling and he gives an owner-occupation certificate or a certificate of intended letting, or
  (b) if the owner's interest which he has is an interest in a house in multiple occupation and he gives a certificate of future occupation.
This is subject to the exceptions specified in subsection (7) or by order under that subsection.

(3) An "owner-occupation certificate" certifies that the person concerned—
  (a) has an owner's interest in the dwelling, and
  (b) intends that throughout the protected period he, or a member of his family, will live in the dwelling, as his (or that member's) only or main residence.

(4) A "certificate of intended letting" certifies that the person concerned—
  (a) has an owner's interest in the dwelling, and
  (b) intends that throughout the protected period the dwelling will be let or available for letting as a residence and not for a holiday to someone other than a member of his family.

In paragraph (b) "letting" does not include a letting on a long tenancy.

(5) In subsection (4) references to letting include the grant of a licence to occupy premises.

References in this Chapter to tenants, and other expressions relating to tenancies, in the context of a certificate of intended letting, shall be construed accordingly.

(6) A "certificate of future occupation" certifies that the person concerned—

(a) has an owner's interest in the house, and

(b) intends that throughout the protected period the house or a part of it (specified in the certificate) will be residentially occupied, or available for residential occupation, under tenancies or licences by persons who are not connected with the owner for the time being of the house.

In paragraph (b) "residential occupation" does not include occupation for a holiday, and "tenancies" does not include a long tenancy.

(7) The following may not participate in a group repair scheme as an assisted participant—

(a) a local authority;

(b) a new town corporation;

(c) the Development Board for Rural Wales;

(d) a health authority, special health authority or NHS trust;

(e) a police authority established under section 3 of the Police Act 1964;

(f) a housing action trust;

(g) a registered social landlord;

(h) any other authority, body or other person excluded by order of the Secretary of State.

(8) An order under subsection (7)(h) may proceed wholly or in part by reference to the provisions relating to entitlement to housing benefit, or any other form of assistance, as they have effect from time to time.

(9) A person eligible to participate in a group repair scheme who is unable to participate as an assisted participant may participate as an unassisted participant.

DEFINITIONS
"building": s.60.
"dwelling": s.101.
"group repair scheme": s.60.
"house in multiple occupation": s.101.
"housing action trust": s.101.
"local authority": s.101.
"long tenancy": s.101.
"new town corporation": s.101.
"member of family": s.98.
"owner's interest": s.101.
"registered social landlord": s.101.

GENERAL NOTE
This section defines the participants eligible to participate in an approved group repair scheme. Participation is by the consent (s.65(1)) of eligible participants, whether or not assisted participants, but the contribution of an assisted participant is at a lower level than that (100 per cent) of an unassisted participant: s.67. See s.68, below, for variation of schemes, including as to participation. See also ss.69 *et seq.*, for conditions attached to reduced contributions.

*Participants.* The applicant must have an owner's interest in *a* dwelling (therefore, including the owner of a flat or something less than the whole of a building—see notes to s.1, above) or other premises to which the scheme relates (subs. (1)(a)): see notes to s.7, above. He must be able to give up sufficient possession of the premises to enable the works to be carried out, or else have the consent of the occupier: subs. (1)(b). These qualifications have to be established as at the date of approval or—if the scheme is not subject to specific approval, but instead to a general approval under s.63, above—on the date when the authority decide that the scheme so qualifies.

(Or, in the case of a scheme that is varied to allow new participants, at the date of the variation specific approval, or qualification under a general approval: see s.68(3), below). Even if the participant does not qualify as an assisted participant, he can still participate as an *un*assisted participant: subs. (7).

*Assisted Participants*. A participant can only be an *assisted* participant (*i.e.* enjoy the benefit of grant assistance under ss.67 *et seq*., below), if (subs. (2)):
(i) he is not one of the public or quasi-public landlords identified in or prescribed under subs. (6), and
(ii) (a) *either* he has an owner's interest in a dwelling, *i.e.* not merely in a property which has dwellings within it or other property to be dealt with under the scheme, (b) *or* he has an owner's interest in an HMO (as to the meaning of which, see notes to s.1, above), and
(iii) he gives one of the two classes of certificate—for an owner of a dwelling, an owner-occupation certificate or a certificate of intended letting; for an owner of an HMO, a certificate of future occupation.

*Owner-Occupation certificate*. See notes to s.8, above—but a certificate of *proposed* acquisition will not here qualify.

*Certificate of intended letting*. See notes to s.8, above—again, a certificate of *proposed* acquisition will not here qualify.

*Certificate of future occupation*. See notes to s.26, above—with the same exception for certificate of *proposed* acquisition.

## Scheme consent and restriction on works

**65.**—(1) The persons who are eligible to participate in a group repair scheme do so by signifying consent ("scheme consent"), in accordance with the terms of the scheme, to the proposals to carry out the works specified in the scheme.
(2) No scheme works shall be carried out to a part of a building which consists of premises in respect of which no person eligible to participate has signified scheme consent, except as mentioned below.
(3) The restriction in subsection (2) does not apply to works carried out to premises in respect of which there is no person (or no ascertainable person) eligible to participate in the scheme.
(4) The restriction in subsection (2) does not apply to works—
(a) which are carried out to premises in respect of which the person eligible to participate consents to their being carried out but has not signified scheme consent (and, accordingly, is not liable to contribute), and
(b) which it is necessary to carry out in order satisfactorily to carry out any works specified in the scheme to another part of the same building in respect of which a person eligible to participate has signified scheme consent.

DEFINITIONS
"eligible to participate": s.64.
"group repair scheme": s.60.
"scheme works": s.62.

GENERAL NOTE
The burden of participation is contribution: s.67. Contribution is confined to those who are eligible participants (s.64) who consent to the scheme works: subs. (1). Scheme works cannot normally be carried out to parts of a building which consist of premises in respect of which there is no eligible participant who has signified his consent: subs. (2). This restriction is lifted where there is *no one* (or no ascertainable person) who is eligible to participate (*i.e.* eligible, but declines consent, so that he will not become a contributor): subs. (3).
The restriction also does not apply where there is an eligible participant (in respect of part of a building) who declines consent (and, therefore, cannot be a contributor), where it is *necessary* to carry out works satisfactorily to another part of that building which is within the scheme

(because someone who is eligible in respect of that part has consented and is therefore participating): subs. (4).

## Certificate of completion date

**66.**—(1) When the works specified in a group repair scheme are completed, the local housing authority shall send to each assisted participant a certificate specifying the date on which the works were completed to the authority's satisfaction.

(2) In this Chapter that date is referred to as "the completion date".

DEFINITIONS
  "assisted participant": s.64.
  "group repair scheme" ; s.60,
  "local housing authority": s.101.

GENERAL NOTE
  Once the works have been completed to their satisfaction (*cf.* notes to s.44, above), the authority are to notify each assisted participant (see notes to s.64, above) specifying the date on which the works were so completed (*i.e.* the date on which the works were physically completed to that standard, not the date when the local authority have inspected the finished works and approved them: *R. v. Westminster C.C., ex p. Hazan* (1988) 20 H.L.R. 205, C.A.). This date is the completion date: subs. (2).

## Contributions by participants

**67.**—(1) The participants in a group repair scheme are liable to contribute to the cost, as notified to them under the scheme, of scheme works relating to the premises in which they have an interest, at a rate determined in accordance with this section.

(2) The cost of the works shall be apportioned between the several buildings and premises in such way as may be agreed between the participants with owner's interests in them or, in default of agreement, equally.

(3) In the case of an unassisted participant, the rate of contribution is 100 per cent.

(4) In the case of an assisted participant whose owner's interest is in premises other than a dwelling or house in multiple occupation, the rate of contribution is—

(a) 25 per cent. where the building is in a renewal area, and

(b) 50 per cent. in any other case.

The Secretary of State may by order amend paragraph (a) or (b) so as to specify a different percentage.

(5) In the case of any other assisted participant, the rate of contribution is a percentage determined by the local housing authority not exceeding that which would apply under subsection (4).

(6) In making their determination the authority shall have regard to the way in which—

(a) section 30 (means-testing in case of application by owner-occupier or tenant), or

(b) section 31 (determination of amount of grant in case of landlord's application),

would apply if he were an applicant for a renovation grant or, as the case may require, an HMO grant.

(7) They shall also have regard to any guidance given by the Secretary of State for the purposes of this section.

Different guidance may be given for different cases, different descriptions of cases and different areas and, in particular, with respect to different local housing authorities or descriptions of authority (including a description framed by reference to authorities in a particular area).

Definitions

Definitions
   "assisted participant": s.64.
   "group repair scheme": s.60.
   "house in multiple occupation": s.101.
   "participants": s.64.
   "owner's interest": s.101.
   "renewal area": s.101.
   "scheme works": s.62.
   "unassisted participant": s.64.

General Note
   Consent to the scheme (s.65) means paying a contribution to the costs, the level of which depends on the considerations set out in this section: subs. (1). See also ss.69 *et seq.*, for conditions attached to reduced contributions.
   The cost is apportioned by agreement between all those having owner's interests (see s.64), or otherwise equally between all the buildings and premises.
   Premises would normally seem to be capable of including flats: yet the requirement for equal division between buildings and premises (in default of agreement) cannot here mean, *e.g.* an equal amount for a building and a flat, and if it did so it would encourage refusal to agree an apportionment—the omission of the word "dwelling" suggests therefore that it is buildings as a whole which are in mind at this stage, although this leaves aside division between owners of flats in buildings: subs. (2). (The provisions of subss. (4), (5), assist in determining level of contribution to apportionment, and not only does not resolve this problem but supports the risk that it will occur.)
   An unassisted participant must pay a contribution of 100 per cent (subs. (3)). Assisted participants pay different contributions as follows:
      (i) Owner's contribution *not* in a dwelling or an HMO, 25 per cent in a renewal area and 50 per cent otherwise (subs. (4)—but *n.b.* power of Secretary of State to prescribe different percentage (*ibid.*);
      (ii) Owner's contribution in a dwelling or an HMO, of *no more than* 25 per cent or 50 per cent or other prescribed percentage (as above), but otherwise calculated having regard to the calculation of renovation grant under s.30 or landlord's grant under s.31 (subss. (5), (6)).
   The authority are not *bound* to pay in accordance with ss.30, 31 (see notes to s.31, above, on the obligation "to have regard", but if less is offered, it would seem to require explanation—see *ibid.*; see also notes to s.13, above, on Discretion and Policy). The authority are also bound to have regard to guidance issued for the purposes of the section by the Secretary of State (subs. (7)).

*Variation of group repair scheme*

## Variation of group repair scheme

   **68.**—(1) A group repair scheme may be varied at any time before the completion date.
   The variation may relate to the participants in the scheme, the buildings to which the scheme relates, the scheme works or any other matter.
   (2) A variation is not effective unless approved by the Secretary of State.
   The provisions of section 63(2) to (4) (supplementary provisions as to approval of scheme) apply to approval of a variation.
   (3) Where a scheme is varied to enable other persons to participate section 64 (persons eligible to participate) applies in relation to new participants with the substitution for the reference to the date of approval of the scheme of a reference to the date of approval of the variation.
   In the case of a variation not submitted for specific approval, the date of approval shall be taken to be the date on which the authority decide that the variation fulfils the criteria for general approval.
   (4) Before varying a group repair scheme the local housing authority shall consult the existing participants and consider any representations made by them.
   (5) Fresh scheme consent is required in the case of an existing participant as to whom the authority are satisfied that his interests are adversely affected by the variation.

In any other case the existing scheme consent shall be treated as extended to the scheme as varied.

"completion date": s.66(2).
"group repair scheme": s.60.
"participants": s.64.

GENERAL NOTE

This section is intended to "allow late participants to join an approved scheme once it has been approved thus creating greater facility. The amendments contain safeguards for existing participants, and enable schemes to be varied": *Hansard* (H.C.), June 11, 1996, Standing Committee F, Sixth Sitting, col. 213, Parliamentary Under-Secretary of State for the Environment (Mr Clappison).

The basic power is to vary a scheme at any time until the completion date (under s.66, above): subs. (1). The variation may be to participants, property or works: *ibid*. The variation requires the consent of the Secretary of State: subs. (2). (Consent may be specific or general, and may be subject to different criteria for different schemes or areas, and may be conditional: see s.63(2)-(4), above, applied to this section by subs. (3)). Participation qualification is on the same terms as under s.64, but with the substitution of the date of approval of variation, or date when the authority consider that the variation qualifies within a variation general approval: subs. (3).

*Subs. (4)*
*Consultation.*

"... [T]he essence of consultation is the communication of a genuine invitation to give advice and a genuine consideration of that advice ... To achieve consultation sufficient information must be supplied by the consulting to the consulted party to enable it to tender helpful advice. Sufficient time must be given by the consulting to the consulted party. Sufficient, in that context, does not mean ample, but at least enough to enable the relevant purpose to be fulfilled. By helpful advice, in this context, I mean sufficiently informed and considered information or advice about aspects of the form or substance of the proposals, or their implications for the consulted party, being aspects material to the implementation of the proposal as to which the party consulted might have relevant information nor advice to offer." (*per* Webster J., *R. v. Secretary of State for Social Services, ex p. Association of Metropolitan Authorities* [1986] 1 W.L.R. 1 at p.4).

See also *R. v. Brent L.B.C., ex p. Gunning* (1985) 84 L.G.R. 168, *R. v. Warwickshire D.C., ex p. Bailey* [1991] C.O.D. 284.

### *Conditions of participation*

## Conditions of participation: general

**69.**—(1) The following sections have effect with respect to the conditions of participation in a group repair scheme as an assisted participant.

(2) Except as otherwise provided those conditions have effect for the period of five years, or such other period as may be prescribed, beginning with the completion date.

That period is referred to in this Chapter as "the protected period".

(3) For the purposes of those conditions the "balance of the cost" is the difference between—

    (a) the cost as notified to the participant under the scheme of such of the works specified in the scheme as relate to the premises in which his owner's interest subsisted, and

    (b) the amount of the contribution in respect of that cost paid by him by virtue of section 67.

"assisted participant": s.64.
"completion date": s.66.
"group repair scheme": s.60.

GENERAL NOTE
A reduced contribution is analogous to a grant: see s.67(5), (6), above. Accordingly, conditions analogous to grant conditions are applied to assisted participants for the "protected period" of five years or such other period as may be prescribed, commencing with the completion date defined by s.66 (subs. (2)). The amount to which they are applied is the "balance of the cost", meaning the difference between the amount of the cost of the scheme as whole, notified under s.67(1), as apportioned under s.67(2), and the amount of the contribution that the applicant will have paid under s.67(5), (6). The grant conditions operate as conditions of participation in the scheme (ss.70(1), 71(1)).

## Condition as to payment of balance of cost on disposal

**70.**—(1) It is a condition of participation in a group repair scheme as an assisted participant that if, at any time after signifying scheme consent and before the end of the protected period, he makes a relevant disposal (other than an exempt disposal) of the premises in which he had an owner's interest at the date of the approval of the scheme, he shall pay to the local housing authority on demand the balance of the cost.

(2) The condition under this section is a local land charge and is binding on any person who is for the time being an owner of the premises concerned.

(3) Where the authority have the right to demand payment of an amount as mentioned in subsection (1), they may determine not to demand payment or to demand a lesser amount.

(4) The condition under this section shall cease to be in force with respect to any premises if there is a relevant disposal of the premises that is an exempt disposal, other than—

(a) a disposal within section 54(1)(a) (disposal to associates of person making disposal), or

(b) a disposal within section 54(1)(b) (vesting under will or on intestacy).

DEFINITIONS
"assisted participant": s.64.
"exempt disposal": s.72.
"group repair scheme": s.60.
"owner's interest": s.101.
"protected period": s.69.
"relevant disposal": s.72.
"scheme consent": s.65.

GENERAL NOTE
This section identifies the first condition of participation (see also s.71, below), which corresponds to the grant conditions under ss.44 *et seq.*, above. As with those conditions, it operates in relation to a "relevant disposal" which is not an "exempt disposal" (defined in s.72, below by cross reference): see notes to ss.53, 54, above. The condition comprises (subs. (1)) an obligation to pay (on demand by the authority) the balance of the cost (as defined in s.69(3), above), if such a disposal of the premises in which he had an owner's interest (above, s.64) takes place between (a) the date when he signified consent to the scheme under s.65(1), above, and (b) the end of the protected period, *i.e.* five years (or other prescribed period) from completion date (under s.66): see s.69(2)).

Repayment is at the discretion of the authority: subs. (3). "... We recognise the concern among local authorities that the requirement to pay the balance of the cost might deter some people from joining a group repair scheme if they were uncertain as to whether they could meet the conditions. We want to encourage authorities to take a strategic approach to renewal. [The amendments] will help to increase the flexibility of group repair by giving local authorities full discretion in determining the amount, if any, to be recovered from participants if the property is disposed of during the five-year protected period ... Although we would still expect authorities to demand payment where the owner can clearly afford it, they will be able to waive or abate payments where payment in full would cause hardship ..." (*Hansard* (H.L.), Report, April 18, 1996, col. 881, Government Whip, (Lord Lucas)).

See the discussion of Discretion and Policy in notes to s.13, above.

*Subs. (2)*
See notes to s.45(3), above.

*Subs. (4)*
The condition remains in force only until the relevant disposal which is not an exempt disposal, *save* that in two classes the condition remains in force even if there is such a disposal, in which case it will continue to bind under subs. (2). See notes to s.45(6), above. See also notes to s.54, above.

### Conditions as to occupation

**71.**—(1) It is a condition of participation in a group repair scheme as an assisted participant—
> (a) where the participant gave an owner-occupation certificate, that throughout the protected period the dwelling is occupied in accordance with the intention stated in the certificate;
> (b) where the participant gave a certificate of intended letting, that throughout the protected period the dwelling is let or available for letting in accordance with the intention stated in the certificate; and
> (c) where the participant gave a certificate of future occupation, that throughout the protected period the house is residentially occupied, or available for residential occupation, in accordance with the intention stated in the certificate.

(2) It is also a condition of participation as an assisted participant that if at any time when any of the above conditions is in force the authority serve notice on the owner of the dwelling or house requiring him to do so, he will within the period of 21 days beginning with the date on which the notice was served furnish to the authority a statement showing how that condition is being fulfilled.

(3) A condition under this section is a local land charge and is binding on any person who is for the time being an owner of the dwelling or house.

(4) In the event of a breach of a condition under this section, the owner for the time being of the dwelling or house shall pay to the local housing authority on demand the balance of the cost.

(5) The local housing authority may determine not to make such a demand or may demand a lesser amount.

(6) Any condition under this section shall cease to be in force with respect to any premises if there is a relevant disposal of the premises which is an exempt disposal other than a disposal within section 54(1)(a) (disposal to associates of person making disposal).

DEFINITIONS
> "assisted participant": s.64.
> "balance of cost": s.69.
> "certificate of intended letting": s.64.
> "dwelling": s.101.
> "group repair scheme": s.60.
> "local housing authority": s.101.
> "owner": ss.99, 101.
> "owner occupation certificate": s.64.
> "protected period": s.69.

GENERAL NOTE
This is the second condition on participation: see notes to s.70, above. The condition is to pay the authority on demand the balance of the cost (see s.69, above), if the intentions in the relevant occupation certificate (see notes to s.64, above) are breached as specified in subs. (1) (as to which, see notes to ss.48(1), 49(1), 50(1), above, to which the conditions in this section correspond). There is also a condition requiring the owner to provide the authority with a statement showing how the occupation requirement is being fulfilled, within 21 days of a demand to do so

by the authority: subs. (2): this corresponds to ss.48(2), 49(2)(a) and 50(2)(a), above, but there is no provision requiring a tenant or occupier to comply with a request from the owner for information, corresponding to ss.49(2)(b) and 50(2)(b).

The demand is at the authority's discretion: subs. (5). See the discussion of Discretion and Policy in notes to s.13, above.

## Meaning of relevant disposal and exempt disposal

**72.** Sections 53 and 54 (meaning of "relevant disposal" and "exempt disposal") apply for the purposes of this Chapter.

## Payment of balance of cost, &c: cessation of conditions

**73.**—(1) If at any time while a condition of participation under section 70 or 71 remains in force—

(a) the assisted participant pays the balance of the cost to the local housing authority,

(b) a mortgagee of the interest of the assisted participant in the premises being a mortgagee entitled to exercise a power of sale, makes such a payment,

(c) the authority determine not to demand payment on the breach of a condition of participation, or

(d) the authority demand payment in whole or in part on the breach of a condition of participation and that demand is satisfied,

that condition and any other conditions of participation shall cease to be in force with respect to the premises of that assisted participant.

(2) An amount paid by a mortgagee under subsection (1)(b) above shall be treated as part of the sums secured by the mortgage and may be discharged accordingly.

(3) The purposes authorised for the application of capital money by—

(a) section 73 of the Settled Land Act 1925,

(b) that section as applied by section 28 of the Law of Property Act 1925 in relation to trusts for sale, and

(c) section 26 of the Universities and College Estates Act 1925,

include the making of payments under this section.

DEFINITIONS
"assisted participant": s.64.
"local housing authority": s.101.

GENERAL NOTE
This makes provision corresponding to s.55, above.

*Supplementary provisions*

## Power of Secretary of State to modify operation of Chapter

**74.**—(1) If the Secretary of State so directs in the case of any scheme or any description of scheme, such of the preceding provisions of this Chapter as are specified in the direction shall not apply in relation to that scheme or, as the case may be, in relation to a scheme of that description.

(2) The power under this section to give directions may be so exercised as to make different provision with respect to different local housing authorities or descriptions of authority (including a description framed by reference to authorities in a particular area).

DEFINITION
"local housing authority": s.101.

GENERAL NOTE
The Secretary of State has power to disapply any of the provisions of this Chapter to any particular scheme or description of scheme, including as to categories of authority or parts of the country.

## Index of defined expressions: Chapter II

**75.** In this Chapter the expressions listed below are defined by or otherwise fall to be construed in accordance with the provisions indicated—

### Chapter III

#### Home repair assistance

## Home repair assistance

**76.**—(1) A local housing authority may, on application being made to them, give assistance under this Chapter ("home repair assistance") in the form of a grant or the provision of materials for the carrying out of works of repair, improvement or adaptation to a dwelling.

(2) The Secretary of State may by order make provision as to the total amount or value of home repair assistance that may be given—

(a) on any one application, or

(b) in respect of the same dwelling in any period of three years.

(3) Home repair assistance shall not be given in respect of works—

(a) for which a grant under Chapter I has been approved or in respect of which an application for a grant is pending, or

(b) which are specified in a group repair scheme approved under Chapter II or prepared and awaiting the approval of the Secretary of State.

DEFINITIONS
"dwelling": s.101.
"local housing authority": s.101.

GENERAL NOTE
The home repair grant replaces the minor works grant under the Local Government and Housing Act 1989. It is a discretionary grant, an alternative (not supplement) to grant aid under Chap. I or group repair under Chap. II (see subs. (3)), and is expected to be (see subs. (2)) at a level of £2,000 in any one year, and £4,000 in any three year period: *The Future of Private Housing Renewal Programmes, Explanatory Paper* linked to the White Paper "*Our Future Homes*", June 1995, s.5.

### Entitlement to home repair assistance

**77.**—(1) Subject to the following provisions of this section, a local housing authority shall not entertain an application for home repair assistance unless they are satisfied—

(a) that the applicant is aged 18 or over on the date of the application,

(b) that he lives in the dwelling as his only or main residence,

(c) that he has an owner's interest in the dwelling, or is a tenant of the dwelling, alone or jointly with others,

(d) that he has a duty or power to carry out the works in question, and

(e) that he or his partner is in receipt of income support, family credit, housing benefit, council tax benefit or disability working allowance.

(2) In the case of an application in respect of works to adapt a dwelling to enable an elderly, disabled or infirm person to be cared for, the condition in subsection (1)(b) shall be treated as met if the elderly, disabled or infirm person (whether or not the applicant) lives or proposes to live in the dwelling as his only or main residence.

(3) For the purposes of the condition in subsection (1)(c) "tenant" includes—

(a) a secure tenant or statutory tenant,

(b) a protected occupier under the Rent (Agriculture) Act 1976 or a person in occupation under an assured agricultural occupancy within the meaning of Part I of the Housing Act 1988, and

(c) an employee (whether full-time or part-time) who occupies the dwelling or flat concerned for the better performance of his duties;

but does not include a tenant of an authority or body mentioned in section 3(2) (authorities and bodies not eligible to apply for grants under Chapter I).

(4) An application may be made by a person who does not satisfy the condition in subsection (1)(c) but who occupies the dwelling under a right of exclusive occupation granted for his life or for a period of more than five years.

But except in the case of—

(a) works to adapt a dwelling to enable an elderly, disabled or infirm person, who lives or proposes to live in the dwelling as his only or main residence, to be cared for,

(b) works relating to means of escape from fire or other fire precautions, or

(c) any works to a dwelling in a renewal area,

the local housing authority shall not entertain an application made by virtue of this subsection unless they are satisfied that the applicant has occupied the dwelling as his only or main residence for a period of at least three years immediately preceding the date of the application.

(5) The condition in subsection (1)(e) does not apply—

(a) to an applicant who is elderly, disabled or infirm, or

(b) to an application in respect of works to adapt a dwelling to enable an elderly, disabled or infirm person, who lives or proposes to live in the dwelling, to be cared for.

DEFINITIONS
"disabled person": s.100.
"dwelling": s.101.
"elderly person": s.101.

"owner's interest": s.101.
"partner": s.101.
"secure tenant": s.101.
"statutory tenant": s.101.

GENERAL NOTE
This section contains the limitations on availability of home repair assistance. There are five principal conditions which must be fulfilled by an applicant.
(i) The applicant must be aged 18 or more on the date of the application—see notes to s.3, above.
(ii) The applicant must live in the dwelling as his only or main residence—see notes to s.8, above; in the case of an application to adapt a dwelling for an elderly, disabled or infirm person, this condition may be fulfilled by intended occupation (subs. (2)).
(iii) The applicant must either have an owner's interest in the dwelling (see notes to s.7, above) or be a tenant (in either case, alone or jointly with another); tenants include secure and statutory tenants, protected and assured agricultural occupiers, and service occupiers (see notes to s.19, above), including someone with a right to occupy for life (see notes to s.19, above) or for more than three years (subss. (3), (4)), but *not* if the tenancy is held from one of the public bodies disqualified from the principal, Chap. I grants by s.3 above (see notes thereto) (subs. (3)); the applicant must normally have occupied the dwelling (as an only or main residence) for a period of at least three years before the application (see s.10, above), *save*
   (a) in the case of works to adapt a dwelling for an elderly, disabled or infirm person, or
   (b) in the case of works relating to means of escape from fire or other fire precautions (see s.12, above), or
   (c) in the case of works to a dwelling in a renewal area (see notes to s.10, above) (subs. (4)).
(Note the extension to occupiers of houseboats and mobile homes, below, s.78.)
(iv) The applicant has a duty or power to carry out the works (*cf.* notes to s.15, above).
(v) *Either* the applicant or his partner is in receipt of one of the identified social security benefits, *or* the applicant is elderly, disabled or infirm, *or* the application is for works to adapt a dwelling for an elderly, disabled or infirm person who lives or proposes to live in the dwelling (subs. (5)).

## Assistance in respect of house-boats and mobile homes

**78.**—(1) Subject to the following provisions of this section, sections 76 and 77 (home repair assistance) apply in relation to a house-boat or mobile home as in relation to a dwelling.

(2) For the purposes of those sections as they apply in relation to a house-boat or mobile home, any person lawfully in occupation of the house-boat or mobile home shall be treated as a person with an owner's interest in or a tenant of a dwelling.

But except in the case of—
   (a) works to adapt a house-boat or mobile home to enable an elderly, disabled or infirm person, who lives or proposes to live there as his only or main residence, to be cared for, or
   (b) works relating to means of escape from fire or other fire precautions,
the local housing authority shall not entertain an application for home repair assistance unless the residence requirement is met.

(3) The residence requirement in the case of a house-boat is that the local housing authority are satisfied that—
   (a) the applicant has occupied the boat as his only or main residence for a period of at least three years immediately preceding the date of the application;
   (b) the boat has for that period had its only or main mooring in the same locality on an inland waterway or in marine waters within the boundary of the authority; and
   (c) the applicant had a right to moor his boat there.

(4) The residence requirement in the case of a mobile home is that the local housing authority are satisfied that—
   (a) the applicant has occupied the mobile home as his only or main residence for a period of at least three years immediately preceding the date of the application;

(b) the mobile home has for that period been on land forming part of the same protected site within the meaning of the Mobile Homes Act 1983; and

(c) the applicant occupied it under an agreement to which that Act applies or under a gratuitous licence.

(5) In this section—

"house-boat" means a boat or similar structure designed or adapted for use as a place of permanent habitation, and

"mobile home" means a caravan within the meaning of Part I of the Caravan Sites and Control of Development Act 1960 (disregarding the amendment made by section 13(2) of the Caravan Sites Act 1968),

which is a dwelling for the purposes of Part I of the Local Government Finance Act 1992 (council tax).

Definitions
"disabled person": s.100.
"elderly person": s.101.
"local housing authority": s.101.

General Note
This section extends home repair assistance to the occupiers of house-boats and mobile homes (as defined), in which cases "any person lawfully in occupation" is treated as fulfilling the condition in s.77(1)(c), above, that he has an owner's interest in or is a tenant of the house-boat or mobile home.

The applicant must have occupied the house-boat or mobile home as his only or main residence (see notes to s.8, above) for at least three years preceding the application, unless the works are either to adapt the property for an elderly, disabled or infirm person who lives in the house-boat or mobile home or who intends to do so, or for works relating to means of escape from fire or other fire precautions (see s.77(4), above): subss. (2)–(4).

In addition, however, and if this residence requirement requires to be fulfilled (*i.e.* not if the works are for an elderly, etc., person or fire-related),

(i) in the case of a houseboat, the applicant must have had the right to a mooring, which has been its only or main mooring for the same period, but whether or not the same mooring throughout, within the authority's boundaries, and

(ii) in the case of a mobile home, the applicant must have had an agreement in relation to a protected site within the meaning of the Mobile Homes Act 1983 (c. 34), or a free licence to occupy such a site (subss. (3), (4)).

*Houseboat.* The houseboat—a boat or similar structure designed or adapted for use as a place of permanent habitation (subs. (5))—must qualify as a dwelling for the council tax purposes of Pt. I of the Local Government Finance Act 1992 (c. 14), *i.e.* "any property" which *would have been* a hereditament for rating purposes under the General Rate Act 1967 (c. 9) if that Act had remained in force, and is *not* on a non-domestic rating list, and is *not* exempt from local non-domestic rating, *nor* is a yard, garden, outhouse or other appurtenance, or a private garage, or private storage premises, forming part of a larger property which is a dwelling—1992, s.3.

*Mobile home.* This means a caravan which is a dwelling within Pt. I of the Local Government Finance Act 1992 (see last note), and which is within the meaning of Pt. I of the Caravan Sites and Control of Development Act 1960 (c. 62), *i.e.* a structure designed or adapted for human habitation and capable of being moved from one place to another, and any motor vehicle so designed, but not including railway rolling-stock or a tent—1960, s.29. Thus, a large van used, but neither designed nor adapted, for human habitation was not a caravan in *Backer v. Secretary of State for the Environment* [1983] J.P.L. 602.

*Protected site.* This means (Mobile Homes Act 1983, s.5) a site requiring a licence for use as a caravan site under s.1, Caravan Sites Act 1968 (c. 52) (see *Balthazar v. Mullane* (1985) 17 H.L.R. 561, C.A.; *Adams v. Watkins* (1990) 22 H.L.R. 107, C.A.).

## Power to make further provision by regulations

**79.**—(1) The Secretary of State may by regulations make provision as to—

(a) the manner of making an application for home repair assistance and the contents of such an application;

(b) the procedure for dealing with applications for home repair assistance and for ensuring that works are carried out to any standard specified in the regulations;

(c) the way in which the amount of home repair assistance to be given on any application is to be determined; and

(d) the taking into account (in such manner and to such extent as may be prescribed) of the financial circumstances of the applicant.

(2) The Secretary of State may by regulations make provision extending or restricting the availability of home repair assistance, by reference to such description of persons, circumstances or other factors as the Secretary of State thinks fit.

(3) Regulations under subsection (2) may proceed wholly or in part by reference to the provisions relating to entitlement to housing benefit, or any other form of assistance, as they have effect from time to time.

GENERAL NOTE

The bulk of the provisions—including how to apply for home repair assistance, approval and determination procedure and means-testing—will be governed by regulations made by the Secretary of State, which regulations may also extend or limit those who may apply for such assistance, or otherwise extend or limit the assistance, *e.g.* to particular categories of work.

## Index of defined expressions: Chapter III

**80.** In this Chapter the expressions listed below are defined by or otherwise fall to be construed in accordance with the provisions indicated—

| | |
|---|---|
| disabled person | section 100(1) to (3) |
| dwelling | section 101 |
| elderly | section 101 |
| home repair assistance | section 76(1) |
| improvement | section 101 |
| local housing authority | section 101 |
| owner's interest | section 101 |
| partner | section 101 |
| prescribed | section 101 |
| renewal area | section 101 |
| secure tenant | section 101 |
| statutory tenant | section 101 |
| tenancy and tenant (generally) | section 101 |

CHAPTER IV

DEFERRED ACTION NOTICES, &C.

*Deferred action notices*

## Deferred action notices

**81.**—(1) If the local housing authority are satisfied that a dwelling-house or house in multiple occupation is unfit for human habitation, but are satisfied that serving a deferred action notice is the most satisfactory course of action, they shall serve such a notice.

(2) A deferred action notice is a notice—

(a) stating that the premises are unfit for human habitation,

(b) specifying the works which, in the opinion of the authority, are required to make the premises fit for human habitation, and

(c) stating the other courses of action which are available to the authority if the premises remain unfit for human habitation.

(3) The notice becomes operative, if no appeal is brought, on the expiry of 21 days from the date of the service of the notice and is final and conclusive as to matters which could have been raised on an appeal.

(4) A deferred action notice which has become operative is a local land charge so long as it remains operative.

(5) The fact that a deferred action notice has been served does not prevent the local housing authority from taking any other course of action in relation to the premises at any time.

DEFINITIONS
  "dwelling-house": s.90.
  "house in multiple occupation": s.90.
  "local housing authority": s.101.
  "unfit for human habitation": s.97.

GENERAL NOTE
*Introduction.* This Chapter is in a different category to those which have gone before: it creates no grant entitlement; it is in substance amendment of other legislation; it is related to the earlier Chapters, but only in practice, not in theory. What the first group of sections (ss.81–85, see also ss.86–98 which have a wider application) in this Chapter does—on the demise of the mandatory grant to remedy or prevent unfitness and serious disrepair—is to empower the local authority to serve a "deferred action notice" where currently they would be *obliged* to serve notice under s.189 of the Housing Act 1985, whether the property is a house, a dwelling-house (therefore, including a flat), or a house in multiple occupation, which is unfit (*unless* not satisfied that to do so would be the most satisfactory course of action, in which case they would be obliged to take the alternative action of closing the property to human habitation or even demolishing it under *ibid.*, Pt. IX).

*The notice.* The deferred action notice is, in substance, an early warning notice that the authority consider the premises unfit, identifying the works which the authority consider are required to make the premises fit, and identifying the courses of action other than deferred action (therefore, repair notice, or closing or demolition order) which are available to the authority if the premises remain unfit: subs. (2). The deferred action notice is without prejudice to recourse to their other powers, at any time: subs. (5).

It may be that the courts would consider that service of a deferred action notice has created a legitimate expectation that there will be no recourse to other powers, at least without fore-warning and/or other than in changed circumstances, although highly unlikely—in the light of subs. (5)—to go further than this in limiting by case-law what Parliament has expressly left unlimited. Further, s.86 provides the Secretary of State with express power to impose procedural requirements, including by way of forewarning, on the service of notices under the relevant provisions of the Housing Act 1985 (and indeed on the service of a deferred action notice: see s.86(1)(a)). While the existence of or failure to use these powers cannot be fatal to a claim based on legitimate expectation, they must also serve to make it less likely.

*Most satisfactory course of action.* The notice may only be served if the authority are satisfied that to do so is the most satisfactory course of action (subs. (1)): in reaching this decision, the authority are to have regard to such guidance as may from time to time be given by the Secretary of State (prepared in accordance with the requirements of the Housing Act 1985, s.604A(2)–(4), which, *inter alia*, require that the guidance be laid in draft before Parliament)—see s.85, below. As to the duty imported by the expression "have regard to", see notes to ss.12, 31, above.

*Appeal and challenge.* Unless there is an appeal against the notice (under s.83, below), the notice becomes operative 21 days from date of service of notice, and is final and conclusive as to matters which could have been raised on appeal (subs. (3)). Matters which go to the *vires* of the authority in serving the notice *can* be raised on an appeal: see *Wandsworth L.B.C. v. Winder* [1985] A.C. 461, 17 H.L.R. 196, H.L.; *Elliott v. Brighton B.C.* (1980) 258 E.G. 441, C.A., and *Nolan v. Leeds C.C.* (1990) 23 H.L.R. 135, C.A.; see also *R. v. Hackney L.B.C., ex p. Teepee Estates (1956)*, (1967) 19 P. & C.R. 87, D.C.; *Minford Properties v. Hammersmith L.B.C.* (1978) 247 E.G. 561, D.C.

It may be arguable, therefore, that as they *can* so be raised, they cannot be raised by way of judicial review, although the opposite is also arguable: compare *Smith v. East Elloe R.D.C.* [1956] A.C. 736, H.L., applied in *R. v. Secretary of State for the Environment, ex p. Ostler* [1977] Q.B. 122, C.A., distinguishing *Anisminic v. Foreign Compensation Commission* [1969] 2 A.C. 147, H.L., on the side of "final and conclusive", and *Pearlman v. Keepers & Governors of Harrow School* [1979] Q.B. 56, C.A., and *Meade v. Haringey L.B.C.* [1979] 1 W.L.R. 637, C.A., on the side of recourse to judicial review notwithstanding the "final and conclusive" clause.

*Dwelling-house.* See s.90, below. It includes any yard, garden, outhouses and appurtenances belonging to the dwelling-house: the Housing Act 1985, s.207(2)—see notes to s.1, above. A flat can be a dwelling-house: see 1985 Act, ss.189(2), 207(2). Where a building is divided horizontally, the horizontal divisions are flats: 1985 Act, ss.207(2), s.183. Where a building is not structurally detached, and any material part of it overlaps or underlaps another part of the structure, it is also a flat: *ibid.*

*House in multiple occupation.* See s.90, below. It means a house which is occupied by persons who do not form a single household: the Housing Act 1985, s.345—see notes to s.1, above. For this purpose, it includes a part of a building which would not in its own right be considered a house, and which was constructed or has been adapted for occupation by a single household: s.345(2). A flat in multiple occupation is a reference to any part of a building—whether as a result of this extended definition or not—which is itself occupied by persons who do not form a single household: *ibid.*

*Unfit for human habitation.* See notes to s.97, below.

*Subs. (4)*
   See notes to s.45(3), above.
   The notice remains operative until *either* there is a successful appeal (under s.83—in itself or as applied by s.84(4), below), *or* on a s.84 review the authority cease to be satisfied that it is the most satisfactory course of action, *or* the authority take action within s.84(6), below.

## Service of deferred action notices

   **82.**—(1) The local housing authority shall serve a deferred action notice—
   (a) in the case of a notice relating to a dwelling-house, on the person having control of the dwelling-house as defined in section 207 of the Housing Act 1985;
   (b) in the case of a notice relating to a house in multiple occupation, on the person having control of the house as defined in section 398 of that Act.
   (2) Where the authority are satisfied that a dwelling-house which is a flat, or a flat in multiple occupation, is unfit for human habitation by virtue of section 604(2) of the Housing Act 1985, they shall also serve the notice on the person having control (as defined in section 207 of that Act) of the building or part of the building in question.
   (3) In the case of a house in multiple occupation, the authority may serve the notice on the person managing the house instead of the person having control of the house.
   (4) Where the authority serve a notice under subsection (1), (2) or (3)—
   (a) they shall also serve a copy of the notice on any other person having an interest in the premises concerned, whether as freeholder, mortgagee or lessee (within the meaning of Part VI of the Housing Act 1985), and
   (b) they may serve a copy of the notice on any person having a licence to occupy the premises.
   (5) Section 617 of the Housing Act 1985 (service of notices) applies for the purpose of this section as it applies for the purpose of that Act.

DEFINITIONS
   "deferred action notice": s.81.
   "dwelling-house": s.90.
   "flat": s.90.
   "flat in multiple occupation": s.90.
   "house in multiple occupation": s.90.
   "local housing authority": s.101.
   "owner": s.90.
   "unfit for human habitation": s.97.

GENERAL NOTE
   The deferred action notice is served on the person having control of the house, meaning as defined in s.207 of the Housing Act 1985 in the case of a dwelling-house, and *ibid.*, s.398, in the case of an HMO. The authority *must* also serve the notice on the person having control of a building or part of a building, where satisfied that a flat or a flat in multiple occupation is unfit (subs. (2)). The authority *may* also serve the notice of the manager of an HMO instead of the person having control (subs. (3)): see notes to s.90, below. The authority *must* also serve a copy of the notice on any other person having an interest in either dwelling-house or HMO, as

freeholder, mortgage or lessee, and *may* serve a copy on a licensee (see notes to s.7, above): subs. (4). A notice served on entirely the wrong person may simply be ignored, and does not become final and conclusive under s.80, above: *Pollway Nominees v. Croydon L.B.C.* [1987] A.C. 79, 18 H.L.R. 443, H.L.

*Person having control*. This is the person who receives the rack-rent of the premises, meaning a rent that is not less than two-thirds of the net annual value, whether on his own account or as agent or trustee for another, or who would so receive it if it were so let: 1985 Act, ss.207, 398. The freeholder of a block of flats is not the person having control of it as, although the common parts may be said to remain in his possession in the sense that he could let them out, he could not let out the block: only the individual leaseholders, who were occupying on leases at less than a rack-rent, could let out their individual flats, so that the person in control would seem to be all of the long leaseholders, plus the freeholder in respect of (a) common parts, and (b) any flats let out at a rack-rent: *Pollway*.

The fact that there may be rent controls is unlikely to affect what comprises the net annual value: *Rawlance v. Croydon Corporation* [1952] 2 Q.B. 803, C.A. The question is to be determined at the date of the letting, so that a subsequent variation in value will not affect the matter: *London Corporation v. Cusack-Smith* [1955] A.C. 337, H.L. If there is a letting at a rack-rent, there is no need to look further and see whether someone else might in some circumstances be able (also) to let at a rack-rent: *Kensington B.C. v. Allen* [1926] 1 K.B. 576. Where there is a chain of lettings at less than a rack-rent, only the person in possession will be in a position to let *at* a rack-rent: *Truman, Hanbury, Buxton & Co. v. Kerslake* [1894] 2 Q.B. 774; *Pollway*.

*Subs. (5)*

Under the Housing Act 1985, s.617, the authority must take reasonable steps to identify anyone who may be a person having control, or managing, or having an estate or interest in premises: s.617(1). Persons merely having an estate or interest can serve notice of their interest on the authority, who are bound to record it: s.617(2). If not reasonably practicable to ascertain the name or address of a person to be served, it may be served by addressing it to the person having control of (the address in question), and delivering it to some person on the premises or, if no such, by fixing it to some conspicuous part of the premises: s.617(3). Where there is more than one person who qualifies to be served, more than one of them may be served: s.617(4).

## Appeals against deferred action notices

**83.**—(1) A person aggrieved by a deferred action notice may within 21 days after the service of the notice appeal to the county court.

(2) Without prejudice to the generality of subsection (1), it is a ground of appeal that serving a notice under section 189 of the Housing Act 1985, or making a closing order under section 264 of that Act or a demolition order under section 265 of that Act, is a more satisfactory course of action.

(3) Where the grounds on which an appeal is brought are or include that specified in subsection (2), the court, on the hearing of the appeal, shall have regard to any guidance given to the local housing authority under section 604A of the Housing Act 1985 or section 85 of this Act.

(4) On an appeal the court may make such order either confirming, quashing or varying the notice as it thinks fit.

(5) Where the appeal is allowed and the reason or one of the reasons for allowing the appeal is that serving a notice under section 189 of that Act or making a closing order under section 264 of that Act or a demolition order under section 265 of that Act is a more satisfactory course of action, the judge shall, if requested to do so by the appellant or the local housing authority, include in his judgment a finding to that effect.

(6) If an appeal is brought, the deferred action notice does not become operative until—

   (a) a decision on the appeal confirming the notice (with or without variation) is given and the period within which an appeal to the Court of Appeal may be brought expires without any such appeal having been brought, or

   (b) if a further appeal to the Court of Appeal is brought, a decision on that appeal is given confirming the notice (with or without variation);

and for this purpose the withdrawal of an appeal has the same effect as a decision confirming the notice or decision appealed against.

DEFINITIONS
"deferred action notice": s.81.
"local housing authority": s.21.

GENERAL NOTE
*Appeal.* Within 21 days of service (not including the day of service itself: *Goldsmith's Co. v. West Metropolitan Ry. Co.* [1904] 1 K.B. 1, C.A.), a person aggrieved (*i.e.* some deprived of a legal entitlement, or subject to a legal burden, but not necessarily a pecuniary grievance—*Ex p. Sidebotham* (1880) 14 Ch.D. 458; *R. v. London Quarter Sessions, ex p. Westminster Corporation* [1951] 2 K.B. 508) may appeal to the county court (subs. (1)), in which case the deferred action notice does not become operative until a final decision of the court below or at the Court of Appeal confirming the notice (with or without variation), or withdrawal of an appeal: subs. (6).

*Leave for further appeal.* It does not seem that leave is needed to appeal to the Court of Appeal, because the court would not seem here to be sitting in an appellate capacity within County Courts Appeals Order 1991, art. 2(1)(b), which applies where the court is sitting at second instance, *i.e.* on appeal from the District Judge: see the commentary in the Supreme Court Practice, at para. 59/1/34; see also *Sherred & Tarling v. Dover D.C.*, September 26, 1995, Mr Registrar Adams, Transcript.

*Grounds.* The grounds for appeal are not specified, nor are they confined by subs. (2) (see also *Elliott v. Brighton B.C.* (1980) 258 E.G. 441, C.A., and *Nolan v. Leeds C.C.* (1990) 23 H.L.R. 135, C.A.; see generally note on Appeal and Challenge, notes to s.81, above).

*Powers of court.* When determining what is the most satisfactory course of action, both under s.81 (see notes thereto), and under the relevant provisions of the Housing Act 1985, the authority are bound to have regard to (see notes to s.85, below) guidance issued by the Secretary of State: s.81(1), above and s.85, below; 1985 Act, ss.189(1), (2), 264(1), 265(2) and 604A(1). So also must the court: subs. (3). The court may make an order confirming, quashing or varying the notice: subs. (4).

*Subs. (5)*
If the authority omit to ask the judge to make a finding, it will not be possible to return at a later date for this purpose: *Victoria Square Property Co. v. Southwark L.B.C.* [1978] 1 W.L.R. 463, C.A.

## Review of deferred action notices

**84.**—(1) The local housing authority may at any time review any deferred action notice served by them, and they shall do so not later than two years after the notice becomes operative and at intervals of not more than two years thereafter.

The Secretary of State may by order amend this subsection so as to specify such other period or periods as he considers appropriate.

(2) The authority shall for the purposes of any such review inspect the premises concerned.

For this purpose sections 197 (powers of entry) and 198 (penalty for obstruction) of the Housing Act 1985 apply as they apply for the purposes of Part VI of that Act.

(3) If the authority are satisfied that the deferred action notice remains the most satisfactory course of action, they shall renew the notice and serve notice of their decision.

(4) The provisions of section 82 (service of deferred action notice) and section 83(1) to (5) (appeals against deferred action notices) apply in relation to the authority's decision to renew a deferred action notice as in relation to the original notice.

(5) If an appeal is brought against the decision to renew a deferred action notice, the notice remains operative until any decision on the appeal, or any further appeal, quashing or varying the notice.

(6) If the authority take action in relation to the premises under any of the provisions listed in section 604A(1) of the Housing Act 1985, the deferred

action notice shall cease to be operative on the relevant notice, order or declaration becoming operative.

DEFINITIONS
"deferred action notice": s.81.
"local housing authority": s.101.

GENERAL NOTE
*Review and inspection.* The deferred action notice may be reviewed at any time, but no later than two years (or such other period as the Secretary of State may specify by amendment by order) after it became operative, *i.e.* 21 days after service if no appeal (s.81(3), above), or on the final determination or withdrawal of appeal under s.83(6), above: subs. (1). A review involves a mandatory inspection: subs. (2). (See s.87, below, for the costs of inspection). If satisfied that deferred action remains the most satisfactory course of action, the authority renew it and serve notice of their decision (subs. (3)), in which case the provisions as to service (s.82) and appeal (s.83) apply to the notice of renewal in like manner as they applied to the initial notice: subs. (4). In this case, however, the deferred action notice *remains* operative pending the final outcome of the appeal: subs. (5).

*Alternative courses of action.* The notice ceases to be operative, independently of review, if the authority take action within subs. (6):
(i) Under s.189(1) or (1A) of the Housing Act 1985 (see notes to s.12, above);
(ii) Under *ibid.*, s.264(1) or (2), ordering a dwelling-house, HMO or the whole or part of a building containing unfit flats to be closed to human habitation;
(iii) Under *ibid.*, s.265(1) or (2), ordering a dwelling-house which is not a flat, or an HMO which is not a flat in multiple occupation (in each case, see notes to s.89, below), or the whole or part of a building containing unfit flats to be demolished; or
(iv) Declaring a clearance area over land which includes the dwelling-house, HMO or building under *ibid.*, s.289.

*Subs. (2)*
For the purpose of inspection, the provisions of 1985 Act, ss.197 and 198 are applied. The former permits a person authorised in writing by the local authority, on seven days' notice to the occupier, and to the owner if known, to enter at any reasonable time; the written authorisation must be produced for inspection on demand by the occupier (or someone acting on his behalf). The latter makes it a summary offence, punishable by a fine not exceeding level 3 on the standard scale, to obstruct an officer of the authority, or person authorised by the authority to enter, in the performance of the function for which he was authorised to enter.

## Guidance by Secretary of State

**85.**—In deciding for the purposes of section 81 (deferred action notices) or section 84 (review of deferred action notices) what is the most satisfactory course of action in relation to any premises, the local housing authority shall have regard to such guidance as may from time to time be given by the Secretary of State.

(2) The provisions of section 604A(2) to (4) of the Housing Act 1985 (supplementary provisions as to guidance) apply in relation to such guidance.

GENERAL NOTE
See notes to ss.12, 31, above.

*Power to improve enforcement procedures*

## Unfitness for human habitation etc.: power to improve enforcement procedures

**86.**—(1) The Secretary of State may by order provide that a local housing authority shall act as specified in the order before taking action of any of the following kinds—
  (a) serving a deferred action notice under section 81 or renewing such a notice under section 84;
  (b) serving a notice under section 189 of the Housing Act 1985 (repair notice in respect of house which unfit for human habitation);

(c) serving a notice under section 190 of that Act (repair notice in respect of house in state of disrepair but not unfit for human habitation);

(d) making a closing order under section 264 of that Act;

(e) making a demolition order under section 265 of that Act.

(2) An order under this section may provide that the authority—

(a) shall as soon as practicable give to the person against whom action is intended a written notice which satisfies the requirements of subsection (3); and

(b) shall not take any action against him until after the end of such period beginning with the giving of the notice as may be determined by or under the order.

(3) A notice satisfies the requirements of this subsection if it—

(a) states the nature of the remedial action which in the authority's opinion should be taken, and explains why and within what period;

(b) explains the grounds on which it appears to the authority that action might be taken as mentioned in subsection (1); and

(c) states the nature of the action which could be taken and states whether there is a right to make representations before, or a right of appeal against, the taking of such action.

(4) An order under this section may also provide that, before the authority takes any action against any person, they—

(a) shall give to that person a written notice stating—

(i) that they are considering taking the action and the reasons why they are considering it; and

(ii) that the person may, within a period specified in the notice, make written representations to them or, if the person so requests, make oral representations to them in the presence of a person determined by or under the order; and

(b) shall consider any representations which are duly made and not withdrawn.

(5) An order under this section may in particular—

(a) make provision as to the consequences of any failure to comply with a provision made by the order;

(b) contain provisions (including provisions modifying enactments relating to the periods within which proceedings must be brought) which are consequential upon, or supplemental or incidental to, the provisions made by the order.

(6) Nothing in any order made under this section shall—

(a) preclude a local housing authority from taking immediate action against any person, or from requiring any person to take immediate remedial action to avoid action being taken against him, in any case where it appears to them to be necessary to take such action or impose such a requirement; or

(b) require such an authority to disclose any information the disclosure of which would be contrary to the public interest.

Definitions
"deferred action notice": s.81.
"local housing authority": s.101.
"unfit for human habitation": s.97.

General Note
*Introduction.* There is in general no requirement to give any warning before action is taken under housing enforcement procedures such as a repairs notice (ss.189, 190 of the Housing Act 1985—see notes to s.12, above), closing order under *ibid.*, s.264 or demolition order under *ibid.*, s.265, although in the last two cases, such action formerly only followed a "time and place" procedure at which the future of the property would be discussed and an undertaking to repair could be accepted—see 1985 Act, s.264, as enacted (before it was replaced under the Local Government and Housing Act 1989, Sched. 9, para. 14). While informal procedures may be

available, many authorities do not in practice use them, for a number of reasons, *e.g.* they rarely lead to works and commonly lead to waste of time, there is no recoupment of the cost of the informal procedures (but see now s.87, below), there is a risk of abuse by officers (and a probably greater risk of accusation of such abuse).

*Pre-notice procedures.* This section empowers the Secretary of State by order to introduce a code of forewarning in relation to the actions specified in subs. (1), including the deferred action notice itself (subs. (2)), which, *inter alia*, will provide the person served with the opportunity to take pre-emptive voluntary action, and may also provide him with the right to make representations (subs. (3)), in which case the authority must serve notice of their reasons for considering action and give the person served a period in which to make representations, and indeed must take those representations into account (subs. (4)). The provisions take effect subject to the subs. (6) "necessity" override.

Reasons: see notes to s.34, above.

*Subs. (6)*
Where the authority consider it *necessary* to take immediate action, or to require immediate action to be taken, the requirements of an order need not cause them to delay. Nor, in the context of the requirement to give reasons in subs. (4)(a)(i) does the duty require the disclosure of information contrary to the public interest.

## Power to charge for enforcement action

### Unfitness for human habitation, etc.: power to charge for enforcement action

**87.**—(1) A local housing authority may make such reasonable charge as they consider appropriate as a means of recovering certain administrative and other expenses incurred by them in taking action of any of the following kinds—

(a) serving a deferred action notice under section 81 or deciding to renew such a notice under section 84;

(b) serving a notice under section 189 of the Housing Act 1985 (repair notice in respect of house which unfit for human habitation);

(c) serving a notice under section 190 of that Act (repair notice in respect of house in state of disrepair but not unfit for human habitation);

(d) making a closing order under section 264 of that Act;

(e) making a demolition order under section 265 of that Act.

(2) The expenses are, in the case of the service of a notice under section 81 of this Act or section 189 or 190 of the Housing Act 1985, the expenses incurred in—

(a) determining whether to serve the notice,

(b) identifying the works to be specified in the notice, and

(c) serving the notice.

(3) The expenses are, in the case of a decision to renew a notice under section 84 of this Act, the expenses incurred in—

(a) deciding whether to renew the notice, and

(b) serving notice of the authority's decision.

(4) The expenses are, in the case of a closing order under section 264 of the Housing Act 1985 or a demolition order under section 265 of that Act, the expenses incurred in—

(a) determining whether to make the order, and

(b) serving notice of the order.

(5) The amount of the charge shall not exceed such amount as is specified by order of the Secretary of State.

(6) Where a court allows an appeal against the underlying notice, decision or order mentioned in subsection (1), it may make such order as it thinks fit reducing, quashing or requiring the repayment of any charge under this section made in respect of the notice, decision or order.

DEFINITIONS
"local housing authority": s.101.
"unfit for human habitation": s.97.

GENERAL NOTE

*Introduction.* Local authorities' powers to charge were considered in *McCarthy & Stone v. Richmond L.B.C.* [1992] 2 A.C. 48, H.L., in relation to charges for "pre-application" planning inquiries (for which *applications* scale fees were set), which were held to be *ultra vires.* Where a statute provides its own comprehensive code of powers, there is no room for the implication of further powers (of the order governed by the code) under s.111 of the Local Government Act 1972: *ibid.*; see also *Hazell v. Hammersmith L.B.C.* [1992] 2 A.C. 1, H.L.; see further *Crédit Suisse v. Allerdale B.C., Same v. Waltham Forest L.B.C., The Times,* May 20, 1996, C.A.

Whatever the position may be in other cases, the express power to execute works in default of compliance with a repairs notice under the Housing Act 1985, ss.189, 190, to be found in *ibid.*, s.193, backed by the right to recover their expenses of so doing (under *ibid.* Sched. 10), and other analogous provisions (see, *e.g.*, ss.271–272, 288), suggested that any attempt to seek to recover any *other* costs associated with these functions would be doomed to failure.

The Local Government and Housing Act 1989 does, however, contain power for the Secretary of State to prescribe circumstances in which authorities may make charges.160.

*Chargeable functions.* The new power is to make reasonable charges in order to recover their administrative and other expenses incurred in taking action to serve or renew a deferred action notice, or to serve a repairs notice under ss.189, 190 of the Housing Act 1985, or to make a closing order under *ibid.*, s.264 or a demolition order under *ibid.*, s.265: subs. (1). In the case of a deferred action or repairs notice, the expenses in question are those incurred in deciding whether or not to serve the notice, identifying the works and actually serving the notice (subs. (2)). In the case of the renewal of a deferred action notice, the expenses are those incurred in deciding whether to renew, and serving notice of renewal (the inspection function already being a statutory part of the decision-making process, by s.84(2), above): subs. (3). In the case of a closing or demolition order, the expenses are likewise those of deciding whether or not to make—and of serving—the order: subs. (4).

Interestingly, there is no express inclusion of charging for compliance with any requirements under s.86, above. However, if these are statutorily required pre-conditions of the decision-making process, there would seem to be no reason why they should not be comprised within the expression "determining whether to" serve or renew the notice, or make the order.

*Expenses incurred.* Expenditure is incurred when the payer comes under a liability to make a payment, rather than when the payment itself is made, but not a loss or expenditure which is no more than impending, threatened or anticipated: see, *e.g.*, *Capital and Counties Freehold Equity Trust v. B.L.* [1987] 2 E.G.L.R. 49, *West Ham Corporation v. Grant* (1888) 40 Ch.D. 331, *Law v. Coburn* [1972] 1 W.L.R. 1238; see also *New Zealand Flax Investments v. Federal Commissioner* (1938) 61 C.L.R. 179 at p.207, *Federal Commissioner for Taxation v. James Flood Pty.* (1953) 88 C.L.R. 492, *King v. Commissioner of Inland Revenue* [1974] 2 N.Z.L.R. 190.

*Amount of charge.* The Secretary of State may set a maximum charge: subs. (5). Subject thereto, the amount must be (a) reasonable, and (b) *as a means of* recovering administrative and other expenses incurred in following the course of action in question: see, generally, discussion of administrative law in notes to s.13, above. The Secretary of State has power to prescribe both a form for a demand for a charge (under s.88(3)), *and* the particulars to be contained in it: s.89, below.

*Appeal.* On an appeal under s.84, the court has jurisdiction to make such order as it thinks fit in respect of any charge made under this section.

*Recovery.* See following section.

### Recovery of charge for enforcement action

**88.**—(1) The following provisions have effect with respect to the recovery of a charge under section 87.

(2) The charge may be recovered by the authority concerned from—

(a) in the case of a notice under section 81 of this Act, or section 189 or 190 of the Housing Act 1985, any person on whom the notice is served;

(b) in the case of a renewal of a notice under section 84 of this Act, any person on whom notice of the decision to renew the notice is served;

(c) in the case of an order under section 264 or 265 of the Housing Act 1985, any person on whom notice of the order is served as an owner of the premises.

(3) A demand for payment of the charge shall be served on the person from whom the authority seeks to recover it.

(4) The demand becomes operative, if no appeal is brought against the underlying notice, decision or order, on the expiry of the period of 21 days from the service of the demand.

(5) The sum recoverable by the authority is, until recovered, a charge on the premises concerned; and—

(a) the charge takes effect when the demand becomes operative,

(b) the authority have for the purpose of enforcing the charge the same powers and remedies under the Law of Property Act 1925 and otherwise as if they were mortgagees by deed having powers of sale and lease, of accepting surrenders of leases and of appointing a receiver, and

(c) the power of appointing a receiver is exercisable at any time after the expiration of one month from the date when the charge takes effect.

GENERAL NOTE

This section governs from whom the administration charge in s.87, above, may be recovered. The demand becomes operative on the expiry of 21 days from service, unless an appeal is brought: subs. (4). If such an appeal is brought, then the powers of the court are those to be found in s.87(6), above.

## *Supplementary provisions*

## Power to prescribe forms

**89.**—The Secretary of State may by regulations prescribe the form of and the particulars to be contained in—

(a) a deferred action notice, or a notice of an authority's decision to renew a deferred action notice, or

(b) a demand for payment of any charge under section 87 (power to charge for enforcement action).

GENERAL NOTE

Deferred action notices—or notices of their renewal—may need to be in prescribed form, if the Secretary of State so provides; the same may be true of a demand for payment of a charge.

## Minor definitions: Chapter IV

**90.** In this Chapter—

(a) "dwelling-house", "flat" and references to the owner of a dwelling-house or flat, have the same meaning as in Part VI of the Housing Act 1985 (repair notices); and

(b) "house in multiple occupation", "flat in multiple occupation" and references to the owner of or person managing such a house or flat, have the same meaning as in Part XI of that Act.

GENERAL NOTE

*Dwelling-house.* This includes any yard, garden, outhouses and appurtenances belonging to the dwelling-house: Housing Act 1985, s.207(2)—see notes to s.1, above. A flat can be a dwelling-house: see 1985 Act, ss.189(2), 207(2). Where a building is divided horizontally, the horizontal divisions are flats: 1985 Act, ss.207(2), 183. Where a building is not structurally detached, and any material part of it overlaps or underlaps another part of the structure, it is also a flat: *ibid.*

The owner of a dwelling-house means a person (other than a mortgagee not in possession) entitled to dispose of the fee simple of the premises, and includes a person holding or entitled to the rents and profits under a lease of which there is at least three years unexpired: 1985 Act, s.207.

*House in multiple occupation.* This means a house which is occupied by persons who do not form a single household: the Housing Act 1985, s.345—see notes to s.1, above. For this purpose, it includes a part of a building which would not in its own right be considered a house, and which was constructed or has been adapted for occupation by a single household: s.345(2). A flat in multiple occupation is a reference to any part of a building—whether as a result of this extended definition or not—which is itself occupied by persons who do not form a single household: *ibid.*

"Owner" of a house in multiple occupation has the same meaning as of a dwelling-house: 1985 Act, s.398(3). "Person managing" a house in multiple occupation means an owner or lessee (including a statutory tenant: 1985 Act, s.398(2)) who, directly or through an agent or trustee, receives rents or other payments from tenants or lodgers of parts of the premises or would so receive those rents or other payments but for having entered into an arrangement (whether pursuant to a court order or otherwise) with another person, who is not an owner or lessee of the premises, by virtue of which that other person receives the rents or other payments: 1985 Act, s.398(6), as to be amended by the Housing Act 1996, s.79(2). If received through an agent or trustee, the agent or trustee is also a person managing the HMO: *ibid.*

## Index of defined expressions: Chapter IV

**91.** In this Chapter the expressions listed below are defined by or otherwise fall to be construed in accordance with the provisions indicated—

| | |
|---|---|
| deferred action notice | section 81 |
| dwelling-house | section 90(a) |
| flat | section 90(a) |
| flat in multiple occupation | section 90(b) |
| house in multiple occupation | section 90(b) |
| local housing authority | section 101 |
| owner | |
|   –in relation to a dwelling-house or flat | section 90(a) |
|   –in relation to a house or flat in multiple occupation | section 90(b) |
| person managing (a house or flat in multiple occupation) | section 90(b) |
| prescribed | section 101 |
| unfit for human habitation | section 97 |

CHAPTER V

SUPPLEMENTARY PROVISIONS

*Contributions by Secretary of State*

## Contributions by the Secretary of State

**92.**—(1) The Secretary of State may pay contributions to local housing authorities towards such expenditure incurred by them under this Part as he may determine.

(2) The rate or rates of the contributions, the calculation of the expenditure to which they relate and the manner of their payment shall be such as may be determined by the Secretary of State with the consent of the Treasury.

(3) A determination under subsection (1) or (2)—

(a) may be made generally or with respect to a particular local housing authority or description of authority, including a description framed by reference to authorities in a particular area, and

(b) may make different provision in relation to different cases or descriptions of case.

(4) Contributions under this section shall be payable subject to such conditions as to records, certificates, audit or otherwise as the Secretary of State may, with the approval of the Treasury, impose.

(5) If, before the declaration of a renewal area, a local housing authority are satisfied that the rate of contributions which, in accordance with a determination under subsection (2), would otherwise be applicable to the authority will not be adequate, bearing in mind the action they propose to take with regard to the area, they may, before making the declaration, apply to the Secretary of State for contributions at a higher rate in respect of that area.

(6) An application under subsection (5) shall be made in such form and shall contain such particulars as the Secretary of State may determine; and, if

such an application is made, the authority shall not declare the area concerned to be a renewal area until the application is approved, refused or withdrawn.

(7) If an application under subsection (5) is approved, the Secretary of State may pay contributions under subsection (1) in respect of the area concerned at such higher rate as he may determine under subsection (2).

DEFINITIONS
"local housing authority": s.101.
"renewal area": s.101.

GENERAL NOTE
This section provides for central government subsidy to be provided by the Secretary of State, with the consent of the Treasury, which may be general, specific or differential between types of scheme, or different categories of authority, including by reference to parts of the country. The express power for authorities to apply for a higher level of subsidy in respect of a renewal area (pending the outcome of which the renewal area is not to be declared: subs. (6)), to be found in subs. (5), corresponds to the provision made by s.99 of the Local Government and Housing Act 1989, governing subsidy for renewal areas generally.

## Recovery of contributions

**93.**—(1) Where the Secretary of State has paid contributions under section 92 to a local housing authority, he may recover from the authority such amount as he determines to be appropriate in respect of repayments of grant under this Part.

(2) For the purposes of this section—

(a) a "grant" includes the cost of scheme works for a group repair scheme (see section 62(1)), and

(b) "repayment of grant" includes the payment to the authority of the balance of the cost (see section 69(3)) by assisted participants in such a scheme.

(3) The amount shall be calculated by reference to the amount appearing to the Secretary of State to represent his contribution to—

(a) grants in respect of which repayments have been made to the authority, or

(b) grants in respect of which repayments could have been recovered if reasonable steps had been taken by the authority,

together with an appropriate percentage of any interest received by the authority, or which would have been received if reasonable steps had been taken by the authority.

(4) The question what steps it would have been reasonable for the authority to take shall be determined by the Secretary of State.

In determining whether the authority took reasonable steps, the Secretary of State may consider whether the authority properly exercised its discretion not to demand repayment of grant or to demand payment of a lesser sum.

DEFINITIONS
"local housing authority": s.101.

GENERAL NOTE
This is a new power, designed to encourage enforcement of grant conditions (defined to include reduced contributions to group repair schemes under Chap. II—see subs. (2)): see the *Explanatory Paper, The Future of Private Housing Renewal Programmes*, June 1995, linked to the White Paper, *Our Future Housing*—see Introduction to Pt. I, above. It empowers the Secretary of State to recover subsidy under s.92 where grants have been or could have been recovered by an authority, for breach of condition (see ss.45–52, and 70 and 71, above): subs. (2). The recoupment may be together with the interest which has been received or could have been charged by the authority: *ibid.*

The question of what steps it would have been reasonable for the authority to take, when deciding recoupment on the ground of repayment and interest which an authority have not, but could have, claimed, is described (subs. (3)) as one for the Secretary of State, which may be considered to pre-empt challenge that it is extremely unlikely would in any event have been successful, but will still have to be determined properly, within the usual principles of administrative law, including the requirements of fairness, *i.e.* to give the authority forewarning of what he is minded to consider reasonable and an opportunity to comment (see notes to ss.5, 13, 34, above).

This power is independent of the right of the Secretary of State to recoup any overpayment of subsidy on other grounds, *e.g.* error of law or mistake of fact: see *R. v. Secretary of State for the Environment, ex p. Camden L.B.C.* (1995) 28 H.L.R. 321, Q.B.D. In such a case, which will be based on the principle of restitution (unjust enrichment), the Secretary of State may deduct the amount from a subsequent payment of subsidy (*Auckland Harbour Board v. R.* [1924] A.C. 318, P.C.), although the defence of "change of position" may be available: *Lipkin Gorman v. Karpnale* [1991] 2 A.C. 548, H.L. If it is raised as a defence to a recoupment by way of deduction, it is a matter for the Secretary of State whether or not he accepts it; *he* is not obliged to refer it to a court to be tested, although the authority could still do so (see *Camden*).

## Consent of the Secretary of State

## Consent of the Secretary of State

**94.** The consent of the Secretary of State for the purposes of—
(a) section 45(4)(b), 46(4) or 47(4) (consent to waiver of liability to repay renovation grant, common parts grant or HMO grant on disposal), or
(b) section 34(6)(b), 44(3)(a), 51 or 52 (conditions imposed with consent of Secretary of State),
may be given either generally or in relation to any one or more specified authorities or descriptions of authority or in relation to particular cases or descriptions of case.

## Parsonages, charities, etc.

## Parsonages, charities, etc.

**95.**—(1) The provisions of Chapter I (main grants) mentioned below do not apply to—
(a) an application for a grant in respect of glebe land or the residence house of an ecclesiastical benefice, or
(b) an application for a grant made by a charity or on behalf of a charity by the charity trustees of the charity.
(2) Those provisions are—
(a) sections 7 to 11 (conditions for application for renovation grant);
(b) sections 19, 21 and 22 (conditions for application for disabled facilities grant);
(c) sections 25 and 26 (conditions for application for HMO grant).
(3) In considering under section 31 the amount (if any) of the grant where the applicant is a charity or the application is in respect of glebe land, the local housing authority shall have regard, in addition to the matters mentioned in that section, to any obligation or practice on the part of the applicant to let dwellings at a rent less than that which could be obtained on the open market.
(4) In Chapter II (group repair schemes), in section 64(2) (persons eligible to participate in group repair scheme as assisted participants), the requirement in paragraph (a) that a person give an owner-occupation certificate or a certificate of intended letting does not apply if—
(a) the person concerned is a charity or the trustee of a charity, or
(b) the dwelling is the residence house of an ecclesiastical benefice;
and the requirement in paragraph (b) that a person give a certificate of future occupation does not apply if the person concerned is a charity or the trustee of a charity.

(5) In Chapter III (home repair assistance), section 77(1)(c) (condition that applicant have owner's interest or tenancy) does not apply to an application by an individual in respect of glebe land or the residence house of an ecclesiastical benefice.

(6) In this section "charity" does not include a registered social landlord but otherwise has the same meaning as in the Charities Act 1993.

GENERAL NOTE

This section disapplies occupation certificates and conditions in the stated cases.

"Charity" does not include a registered social landlord under Pt. I of the Housing Act 1996. It means any institution—corporate or not—established for charitable purposes, and which is subject to the control of the High Court (in the exercise of its jurisdiction over charities); Charities Act 1993 (c. 10), s.96(1). Of the four principal categories of charity (*Income Tax Special Purposes Commissioners v. Pemsel* [1891] A.C. 531, H.L.)—for the relief of poverty, for the advancement of education, for the advancement of religion, and for other purposes beneficial to the community—it is the last, and in some circumstances the first, which will be most likely to be relevant under this Act.

*Interpretation*

## Meaning of "reasonable repair"

**96.** In determining for the purposes of this Part what is "reasonable repair", in relation to a dwelling, house or building, a local housing authority—

(a) shall have regard to the age and character of the dwelling, house or building and the locality in which it is situated, and

(b) shall disregard the state of internal decorative repair.

DEFINITIONS

"dwelling": s.101.
"local housing authority": s.101.

GENERAL NOTE

The definition of reasonable repair by reference to the "age and character of the dwelling, house or building and the locality in which it is situated" is drawn from the case-law on the meaning of "good tenantable repair" in a lease: see *Proudfoot v. Hart* (1890) 25 Q.B.D. 42, see also *Jaquin v. Holland* [1960] 1 W.L.R. 258. There has not been much judicial consideration of what the words actually mean, beyond the oft-cited observation in *Proudfoot* that different standards will apply by reference to "the occupation of a reasonable minded tenant of the class who would be likely to take" a property, so that different standards were to be expected in Grosvenor Square than in Spitalfields.

## Fitness for human habitation

**97.**—(1) Section 604 of the Housing Act 1985 (fitness for human habitation) applies for the purposes of this Part as it applies for the purposes of that Act.

(2) In deciding whether they are satisfied that the carrying out of the relevant works is the most satisfactory course of action in a case where the house or dwelling concerned is unfit for human habitation, the local housing authority shall have regard to any guidance given under section 604A of the Housing Act 1985 and section 85 of this Act.

For that purpose the authority shall treat any guidance given in respect of the serving of a repair notice under section 189(1) of the Housing Act 1985 as guidance given in respect of the completion of the relevant works.

DEFINITIONS

"local housing authority": s.101.
"relevant works": s.2.

GENERAL NOTE

By Housing Act 1985, s.604(1), as substituted by the Local Government and Housing Act 1989, Sched. 9, para. 83, a house is unfit for human habitation if in the opinion of the authority it fails to meet one or more of the following requirements, and by reason of that failure, it is not reasonably suitable for occupation:

"(a) it is structurally stable;

(b) it is free from serious disrepair;

(c) it is free from dampness prejudicial to the health of the occupants (if any);

(d) it has adequate provision for lighting, heating and ventilation;

(e) it has an adequate supply of wholesome water;

(f) there are satisfactory facilities in the dwelling-house for the preparation and cooking of food, including a sink with a satisfactory supply of hot and cold water;

(g) it has a suitably located water-closet for the exclusive use of the occupants (if any);

(h) it has, for the exclusive use of the occupants (if any), a suitably located fixed bath or shower and wash-hand basin each of which is provided with a satisfactory supply of hot and cold water; and

(i) it has an effective system for the draining of foul, waste and surface water".

By *ibid.*, s.604(2), even if a dwelling which is a flat satisfies the foregoing definition, it will still be unfit for human habitation if the building or some part of the building outside of the flat fails to meet one of the following requirements and, by reason of that failure, the flat is not reasonably suitable for occupation:

"(a) the building or part is structurally stable;

(b) it is free from serious disrepair;

(c) it is free from dampness;

(d) it has adequate provision for ventilation; and

(e) it has an effective system for the draining of foul, waste and surface water".

By *ibid.*, s.604(3), s.604(1) applies to a house in multiple occupation by reference to the house itself.

By s.8 of the Landlord and Tenant Act 1985, there is a statutorily implied term that a property will be both put into a state of fitness for human habitation at the commencement of, and kept in such a state during, the tenancy. This, however, applies to lettings at extremely low rents (at their *highest*, £80 p.a. in London and £52 p.a. elsewhere, for lettings from July 6, 1957), and it does not apply at all to a letting for three years or more which is on terms that the tenant put the premises into a condition reasonably fit for human habitation. Unfitness for the purposes of this covenant has the same meaning as it originally had under the Housing Act 1985, s.604, before it was amended by the 1989 Act (Landlord and Tenant Act 1985, s.10):

"In determining for the purposes of this Act whether a house is unfit for human habitation, regard shall be had to its condition in respect of the following matters—

repair,

stability,

freedom from damp,

internal arrangement,

natural lighting,

ventilation,

water supply,

drainage and sanitary conveniences,

facilities for preparation and cooking of food and for the disposal of waste water;

and the house shall be regarded as unfit for human habitation if, and only if, it is so far defective in one or more of those matters that it is not reasonably suitable for occupation in that condition".

*Most satisfactory course of action.* See notes to s.12, above.

## Members of a person's family and connected persons

**98.**—(1) Section 113 of the Housing Act 1985 (meaning of "members of a person's family") applies in determining whether a person is a member of another's family for the purposes of this Part.

(2) For the purposes of this Part a person is connected with the owner for the time being of a dwelling if—

    (a) in a case where personal representatives or trustees are the owner, he is a person who under the will or intestacy or, as the case may be, under the terms of the trust concerned is beneficially entitled to an interest in the dwelling or to the proceeds of sale of the dwelling;

    (b) in any other case, he is a member of the family of the owner.

GENERAL NOTE

Section 113 of the Housing Act 1985, defines "member of the family" in term of spouses, persons living together as husband and wife, parents, grandparents, children, grandchildren, siblings, aunts, uncles, nephews and nieces, treating relationships by marriage as if by blood, half blood and whole blood, step-relationships as real and illegitimacy as legitimacy (although this last is a reference otiose in the light of the Family Law Reform Act 1987 (c. 42)).

*Cohabitation.* It is self-evident that cohabitants can be living together as husband and wife, but that does not mean that every cohabitation so qualifies (nor does homosexual cohabitation so qualify: see *Harrogate B.C. v. Simpson* (1984) 17 H.L.R. 205, C.A.).

Sexual relations are not determinative. In *Adeoso v. Adeoso* [1980] 1 W.L.R. 1535, C.A., it was held that a couple living in a two-room flat (*i.e.* one bedroom and a living room) had to be considered to be living in the same household "as husband and wife", albeit that for months they had not spoken, had communicated only by notes, that each slept in one of the rooms and kept the doors locked, but shared the rent and electricity charge. (This was for the purposes of Domestic Violence and Matrimonial Proceedings Act 1976 (c. 50), s.1(2) and, as such, should be treated with some caution insofar as words must always be read in context).

Whether or not persons are living together as husband and wife is in part a question of intention: in *City of Westminster v. Peart* (1992) 24 H.L.R. 389, C.A., a couple who had reconciled were held not to be living together as husband and wife, on the particular facts of the case including particularly that the defendant had retained another flat.

Under the Rent Acts, it was initially held that a cohabitant could not succeed as a member of the family of a deceased tenant: see *Brock v. Wollams* [1949] 2 K.B. 388, C.A., *Gammans v. Ekins* [1950] 2 K.B. 328, C.A. In *Hawes v. Evenden* [1953] 1 W.L.R. 1169, C.A., however, a woman who had lived with a man for 12 years without taking his name, and who had two children by him, was held to be a member of his family. In *Dyson Holdings v. Fox* [1976] 1 Q.B. 503, C.A., a stable, 20-year period of cohabitation without marriage, but in which the woman had taken the man's name, was held to be a family relationship, having regard to changing popular meaning of the word "family".

This last approach was rejected in *Helby v. Rafferty* [1979] 1 W.L.R. 13, C.A., wherein was held that the word family should have the meaning applicable when first used by Parliament; a man, accordingly, was unable to succeed to the tenancy of a woman with whom he had lived for approximately five years, as her lover, sharing expenses, caring for her while she was dying, but neither having taken the other's name. In *Watson v. Lucas* [1980] 1 W.L.R. 1493, C.A., conversely, and considering themselves bound by *Dyson,* the Court of Appeal held that a man who had lived with a woman for nearly 20 years, even although he had never divorced his lawful wife, was a member of her family.

*Children.* It is unclear whether a *de facto*—but not *de jure*—adopted child can fall within the definition: see *Brock v. Wollams* (above), where this was allowed under the Rent Acts, even though by the time the question arose the child had achieved his majority. As there can be no *de jure* adoption between adults, there can accordingly be no *de facto* such adoption: see *Carega Properties S.A. v. Sharratt* [1979] 1 W.L.R. 928, H.L.

## Meaning of "owner" of dwelling

**99.**—(1) In this Part "owner", in relation to a dwelling, means the person who—

(a) is for the time being entitled to receive from a lessee of the dwelling (or would be so entitled if the dwelling were let) a rent at an annual rate of not less than two-thirds of the net annual value of the dwelling; and

(b) is not himself liable as lessee of the dwelling, or of property which includes the dwelling, to pay such a rent to a superior landlord.

(2) For this purpose the net annual value of a dwelling means the rent at which the dwelling might reasonably be expected to be let from year to year if the tenant undertook to pay all usual tenant's rates and taxes and to bear the cost of repair and insurance and the other expenses, if any, necessary to maintain the dwelling in a state to command that rent.

(3) Any dispute arising as to the net annual value of a dwelling shall be referred in writing for decision by the district valuer.

In this subsection "district valuer" has the same meaning as in the Housing Act 1985.

GENERAL NOTE

See General Note to s.45, above.

## Disabled persons

**100.**—(1) For the purposes of this Part a person is disabled if—
(a)  his sight, hearing or speech is substantially impaired,
(b)  he has a mental disorder or impairment of any kind, or
(c)  he is physically substantially disabled by illness, injury, impairment present since birth, or otherwise.

(2) A person aged eighteen or over shall be taken for the purposes of this Part to be disabled if—
(a)  he is registered in pursuance of any arrangements made under section 29(1) of the National Assistance Act 1948 (disabled persons' welfare), or
(b)  he is a person for whose welfare arrangements have been made under that provision or, in the opinion of the social services authority, might be made under it.

(3) A person under the age of eighteen shall be taken for the purposes of this Part to be disabled if—
(a)  he is registered in a register of disabled children maintained under paragraph 2 of Schedule 2 to the Children Act 1989, or
(b)  he is in the opinion of the social services authority a disabled child as defined for the purposes of Part III of the Children Act 1989 (local authority support for children and their families).

(4) In this Part the "social services authority" means the council which is the local authority for the purposes of the Local Authority Social Services Act 1970 for the area in which the dwelling or building is situated.

(5) Nothing in subsection (1) above shall be construed as affecting the persons who are to be regarded as disabled under section 29(1) of the National Assistance Act 1948 or section 17(11) of the Children Act 1989 (which define disabled persons for the purposes of the statutory provisions mentioned in subsections (2) to (4) above).

GENERAL NOTE
The social services authority are the authority having responsibility under the Local Authority Social Services Act 1970 (c. 42), which means a London borough council or the Common Council of the City of London or the Council of the Isles of Scilly, in England, in the area of a unitary authority that authority, and otherwise, in a metropolitan county the district council, and in a non-metropolitan county the county council and, in Wales the county or county borough council: the Local Government Acts 1972 and 1992; 1970 Act (as amended), s.1—s.98(4).

## Minor definitions: Part I

**101.** In this Part—
"dwelling" means a building or part of a building occupied or intended to be occupied as a separate dwelling, together with any yard, garden, outhouses and appurtenances belonging to it or usually enjoyed with it;
"elderly" means aged 60 years or over;
"house in multiple occupation" has the same meaning as in Part VII of the Local Government and Housing Act 1989;
"housing action trust" means a housing action trust established under Part III of the Housing Act 1988 and includes any body established by order under section 88 of the Housing Act 1988;
"improvement" includes alteration and enlargement;
"introductory tenancy" and "introductory tenant" have the same meaning as in Chapter I of Part V of the Housing Act 1996;

"local authority" and "local housing authority" have the same meaning as in the Housing Act 1985;

"long tenancy" has the meaning assigned by section 115 of that Act;

"new town corporation" has the same meaning as in the Housing Act 1985 and includes any body established by order under paragraph 7 of Schedule 9 to the New Towns Act 1981;

"owner", in relation to a dwelling, has the meaning given by section 99, and, in relation to a house in multiple occupation, has the same meaning as in Part XI of the Housing Act 1985;

"owner's interest", in relation to any premises, means—

  (a) an estate in fee simple absolute in possession, or

  (b) a term of years absolute of which not less than five years remain unexpired at the date of the application,

whether held by the applicant alone or jointly with others;

"partner", in relation to a person, means that person's spouse or a person other than a spouse with whom he or she lives as husband or wife;

"prescribed" means prescribed by regulations made by the Secretary of State;

"registered social landlord" has the same meaning as in Part I of the Housing Act 1996;

"renewal area" has the same meaning as in Part VII of the Local Government and Housing Act 1989;

"secure tenancy" and "secure tenant" have the same meaning as in Part IV of the Housing Act 1985;

"statutory tenancy" and "statutory tenant" mean a statutory tenancy or statutory tenant within the meaning of the Rent Act 1977 or the Rent (Agriculture) Act 1976;

"tenancy" includes a sub-tenancy and an agreement for a tenancy or sub-tenancy;

"tenant" includes a sub-tenant and any person deriving title under the original tenant or sub-tenant;

"urban development corporation" has the same meaning as in the Housing Act 1985 and includes any body established by order under section 165B of the Local Government, Planning and Land Act 1980.

GENERAL NOTE

For the main definitions, see as follows:

Notes to s.1, above—dwelling, house in multiple occupation, improvement, local housing authority;

Notes to s.3, above—housing action trust, local authority, new town corporation, urban development corporation;

Notes to s.7, above—owner's interest, tenancy, tenant;

Notes to s.8, above—long tenancy;

Notes to s.10, above—renewal area;

Notes to s.14, above—statutory tenancy;

Notes to s.25, above—owner of HMO;

Notes to s.45, above—owner;

Notes to s.47, above—registered social landlord;

Notes to s.98, above—living together as husband and wife.

*Transitional and consequential provisions*

**Transitional provisions**

**102.**—(1) The provisions of Chapters I to III of this Part have effect in place of Part VIII of the Local Government and Housing Act 1989 (grants towards cost of improvements and repairs, etc.).

(2) Subject as follows, the provisions of that Part continue to apply to applications for grant of the descriptions mentioned in section 101 of that Act made before the commencement of this Part.

(3) Sections 112 and 113 of that Act (which require a local housing authority to approve certain grant applications) do not apply to an application under that Part made after 2nd February 1996 which has not been approved or refused before the commencement of this Part, unless—

(a) the six month period under section 116(1) of that Act (period within which applicant to be notified of decision) has elapsed before commencement, or

(b) the works were begun on or before 2nd February 1996—

(i) in an emergency, or

(ii) in order to comply with a notice under section 189, 190 or 352 of the Housing Act 1985.

(4) An application to which section 112 or 113 of the Local Government and Housing Act 1989 would have applied but for subsection (3) above shall be dealt with after the commencement of this Part as if those sections were omitted from Part VIII of that Act.

(5) The above provisions do not affect the power conferred by section 150(4) to make transitional provision and savings in relation to the commencement of this Part, including provision supplementary or incidental to the above provisions.

Supplementary and incidental provision may, in particular, be made adapting the provisions of Part VIII of that Act in the case of applications to which section 112 or 113 would have applied but for the above provisions.

GENERAL NOTE

This section contains the transitional provisions which effectively terminate rights to grants under Pt. VIII of the Local Government and Housing Act 1989—including the broader range of mandatory grants available thereunder. The provisions of this Part are expected to be brought into force "about 2 months after Royal Assent" (D.o.E. letter to Chief Executives of local authorities and the Town Clerk of the City of London, February 2, 1996). The former provisions will, however, continue to apply *if either*

(i) the application was made before February 2, 1996 (when the original Bill was introduced), *or*

(ii) the application was made after February 2, 1996 (but before the commencement of this Part), and this Part is brought into force after August 2, 1996, and the application had not been determined, in accordance with the six month requirement under s.116 of the 1989 Act, corresponding to s.34(1), above, *or*

(iii) the application was made after February 2, 1996, (but before the commencement of this Part), but the works were commenced on or before February 2, 1996 (*i.e.* pre-application, *cf.* above, s.29) because of an emergency, or in order to comply with a notice under ss.189, 190 of the Housing Act 1985 (see notes to s.12, above) or under *ibid.*, s.352 (see notes to s.17, above).

Where an application not thus permitted to continue *post*-commencement has not been determined by the time this Part commences, it continues subject to the conditions of Pt. VIII of the 1989 Act *without* the benefit of ss.112 and 113, *i.e.* those provisions which render some applications mandatory. Such applications will be treated as discretionary applications instead (see DOE letter, above). The letter continued:

"Local authorities should inform grant applicants of the detail and timescale of the proposed changes making clear that they are subject to Parliament's approval. It is for authorities to decide how to ensure those who have already received initial enquiry forms and other information on the current regime are notified of the possible changes. For example an authority may take the view that it is sufficient to outline the changes as a Public Notice in two or more local newspapers. Another approach might be for an authority that has been in correspondence with people seeking grant assistance to write to notify them of the possible changes".

This (understandably) begs the questions which may well yet arise, in relation to applicants under the 1989 Act for mandatory grants, as to any entitlement to damages either for non-compliance with this suggestion or for other action which may have been taken in the past which may be construable as designed to deter applicants (in extreme cases, even to mislead them as to entitlement, albeit almost certainly only by omission), so that they at no time came within

Pt. VIII of the 1989 Act, or, of definition, within these transitional provisions. (See also Introduction to Pt. I, above.)

The former omission is unlikely to lead to redress—amounting to no more than a non-statutory suggestion in relation to prospective legislation (at a later rather than earlier stage in the life of a Parliament, so that some may legitimately and reasonably have considered that it was unlikely to complete its passage). Omission at an earlier time, when only the 1989 Act fell to be considered (without the prospect of this legislation), is also unlikely to lead to redress, reflecting no breach of statutory duty (*e.g.* to publicise or promote grants, *cf.* Social Security and Housing Benefits Act 1982, s.31—the only relevant duty was under the Housing Act 1985, s.605, at least annually to *consider* what action to take under Pt. VIII of the 1989 Act, as, now the duty extends to grants under this Part [see Sched. 1, para. 10, below]. The position *may* also be different in a renewal area, under Pt. VII of the 1989 Act, where the authority have a duty to provide an information and advice service to residents and owners of property in the area "who wish to carry out works to housing accommodation": 1989 Act, s.91).

Communications with individual applicants which were somewhat more active in their intentions to deter (if any), however, *may* be in a somewhat different category (*cf. X v. Bedfordshire C.C.* [1995] 2 A.C. 633, H.L. The decision in *Curran v. Northern Ireland Co-Ownership Housing Association* [1987] 1 A.C. 817; 19 H.L.R. 318, H.L.—see notes to ss.37, 44, above—would not seem to have any bearing on this question).

## Consequential amendments: Part I

**103.** The enactments mentioned in Schedule 1 have effect with the amendments specified there which are consequential on the provisions of this Part.

## Part II

### Construction contracts

Introduction

Part II of this Act stemmed from the Final Report produced by Sir Michael Latham in July 1994 entitled "*Constructing the Team*" (H.M.S.O. publication). This was a joint government and industry review of procurement and contractual arrangements in the U.K. construction industry. Sir Michael Latham had commenced work on the Review in September 1993. The terms of reference for the Review involved a consideration of:

(i) Current procurement and contractual arrangements; and
(ii) Current roles, responsibilities and performance of the participants, including the client.

A principle recommendation of the Report was that the industry should only use standard form contracts. Latham specifically recommended the use of the *New Engineering Contract* (NEC) published by Thomas Telford Services Ltd for the Institution of Civil Engineers (now in its second edition and renamed, the *Engineering and Construction Contract*) but recognised the need for the continuance of the standard forms of contract published by the Joint Contracts Tribunal (JCT) and its civil engineering counterpart, the Conditions of Contract Standing Joint Committee (CCSJC), provided that they were amended in accordance with the principles of a modern contract listed in Chap. 5.18 of the Report. These included matters such as adjudication; "secure trust fund routes of payment"; assessment of interim payments by methods other than monthly valuations; and incentives for exceptional performance. If the standard forms were amended in accordance with these principles, it was the Reviewer's opinion that the use of standard forms would increase. However, he went further:

"All parties in the construction process should then be encouraged to use those Standard Forms without amendment. To aid confidence and promote the use of such forms, their central provisions should be underpinned by legislation. This might best be done by a 'Construction Contracts Bill' which extended, *inter alia*, unfair contracts legislation".

Where one of the standard forms (including sub-contracts) is used (i.e. NEC, JCT and CCSJC contracts), the Reviewer recommended that the legislation should declare unfair or invalid certain actions. These included:

(i) Attempts to amend/delete sections relating to times and conditions of payment including a right of interest for late payment;
(ii) Denial or frustration of the right of immediate adjudication where it had been requested by a party;
(iii) Refusal to implement an adjudicator's decision;
(iv) The exercise of rights of set-off without advance notification and without giving specific reasons for the proposed deduction(s) and not being prepared to go to adjudication and accept the result thereof;

(v) Setting-off monies in respect of any contract other than the one in progress.

Recognising that the industry would continue to use bespoke forms, the Reviewer further recommended that the legislation should be extended to all construction contracts. Furthermore, clauses in bespoke forms which have the *"effect of introducing pay-when-paid conditions should be expressly declared unfair and invalid"* (Chap 8.10).

*Insolvency Protection*

The Reviewer also strongly recommended that *"mandatory trust funds for payment"* should apply to all construction work governed by *"formal conditions of contract"*. This would require both public and private sector clients to deposit monies in a trust fund at the beginning of each payment period. In the event of insolvency of the main contractor, payments would be made out of the trust fund directly to sub-contractors. Similarly, if the client failed, payments would be made out of the fund to the contractor. The same arrangement would also cover retention monies.

In this context, the Reviewer advocated the reversal of the House of Lords' decision in *British Eagle International Airlines v. Compagnie Nationale Air France* [1975] 1 W.L.R. 758. Although this case was concerned with the operation of a clearing-house scheme for airline ticket sales, it has been generally assumed that its effect is to rule out direct payments from clients to subcontractors in the event of the insolvency of a main contractor (*Joo Yee Construction Pte (in liquidation) v. Diethelm Industries Pte* (1991) 7 Const. L.J. 53; In *Re Right Time Construction Co. (in liquidation)* (1990) 52 B.L.R. 117; *B. Mullan & Sons (Contractors) v. John Ross and Malcolm London* (1996) C.I.L.L. 1149; but see *Glow Heating v. Eastern Health Board* (1992) 8 Const. L.J. 56).

*Construction Liability*

The Reviewer finally recommended for inclusion in a Construction Contracts Bill a package of measures to reform the law on liability in the construction industry including the introduction of compulsory latent defects insurance. These included;

   (i) Introduction of a system of proportionate liability in place of joint and several liability;

  (ii) A single limitation period of 10 years to commence from the date of practical completion or *"effective occupation"*.

 (iii) The transfer of a client's contractual rights where all or any part of a project is transferred by the client to a purchaser or tenant.

The Reviewer proposed that the liability period should be underwritten by compulsory latent defects insurance for 10 years from completion of the works. This would apply to all new commercial, retail and industrial building work.

*The Government's Position*

The Department of the Environment (DoE) launched a consultation exercise in mid-1995 to gauge reaction to its proposals for incorporating Latham's recommendations in legislation. In its consultation paper, "Fair Construction Contracts", the DoE stated: "The reform of current contractual relations is … central to the competitiveness of the industry in both the short and long term".

In the consultation paper, the DoE concluded that the industry's standard forms of contract (or packages of standard forms) could be given statutory recognition after taking into account, "the presence, fairness and adequacy" of the terms dealing with:

   (i) dispute resolution

  (ii) right of set-off

 (iii) prompt payment

 (iv) protection against insolvency.

The DoE was of the view that little could be done to curb the use of bespoke contracts.

Furthermore, the Government was prepared to legislate only in respect of those matters on which there was a broad industry consensus and for which there was a workable and practical legislative solution.

Part II was drafted following the responses to the DoE's consultation exercise and further consultation with industry representative organisations.

During this process it was generally recognised that statutory approval for certain standard forms could have the opposite effect by encouraging the use of bespoke contracts. Therefore, any statutory requirements would have to apply to all forms of contract. This would necessitate a statutory mechanism for ensuring that such requirements were part of all contracts in the event of non-compliance with the statute. The result was the Secretary of State's Scheme for Construction Contracts (see below).

*What is Omitted from Part II of the Act?*

*Construction Liability*
The recommendations in relation to statutory reform of liability law for construction and compulsory latent defects insurance were not included in Pt. II. Concerns about the implications for ring-fencing construction (as far as the reform of liability law was concerned) proved a formidable obstacle to the inclusion of the Reviewer's recommendations in legislation.

A consultation paper issued by the Department of Trade and Industry in early 1996: "*Feasibility Investigation of Joint and Several Liability*" (carried out by the Law Commission), concluded that the rule on joint and several liability should be retained. The DTI will be issuing a further paper following responses to its consultation paper.

The Law Commission is currently undertaking a comprehensive review of the law relating to limitation periods with a view to its simplification and rationalisation (item 3 in the Law Commission's 6th programme of law reform). A consultation paper is likely to be published in the early part of 1997. Also the Law Commission has recently published its Report, "*Privity of Contract: Contracts for the Benefit of Third Parties*" (Law Commission Paper No.242, Cmd 3329). The Report includes a draft Bill which may go some way towards enabling third parties (such as purchasers or tenants) to acquire rights under construction contracts or professional terms of engagement.

In the absence of any statutory ring-fencing for construction liability, the proposal for compulsory latent defects insurance fell by the wayside, but, in any event, there was considerable reluctance to give statutory legitimacy to existing policies which, in the opinion of some industry bodies, were very limited in scope.

*Trust Funds*
A failure on the part of construction industry representative bodies to agree on a suitable statutory framework for setting up trust funds was a barrier to the Government's preparedness to legislate on trust funds. But there was also reluctance by the Government to embrace trust funds primarily because of its unwillingness to disturb the well-established rules relating to the distribution of an insolvent's assets. It was also for this reason that the Government refused to legislate to overturn the perceived effect of the *British Eagle* decision so far as the construction industry was concerned. This was in spite of the fact that there already exists a statutory precedent in s.159 of the Companies Act 1989 (c. 40) for exempting the rules of distribution of an insolvent's assets. The exemption applies to schemes operated by investment exchanges and finance clearing houses in relation to the settlement of debts arising under market contracts.

"The concept of trust funds is contentious in the construction industry ... There are several problems. The first is that trust funds may fundamentally alter the cash flow of contractors in that sums of money will have to be set aside regularly to maintain and to replenish the fund, and they will therefore be unusable while they are in the fund. That is a prospect which is attractive neither to clients nor to most contractors simply because it is expensive to have considerable sums of money lying idle. The construction industry always has considerable cash flow difficulties and if one locks away a certain slice of cash into a trust fund that may exacerbate the difficulties with which businesses have to deal.

The Government are not convinced that trust funds are consistent with well established practice in respect of insolvency. Parliament has agreed an order of creditors if a company is liquidated under the Insolvency Acts. Trust funds would change that order by ring-fencing payments owed on construction contracts from the main assets of the insolvent company. That may be very convenient for the unsecured creditors who are on construction contracts but it would be very much less acceptable to secured creditors who are claiming on a depleted stock of assets." (*per* Earl Ferrers, Government spokesman, H.L. Committee Stage: *Hansard*, H.C. Vol. 570, col. 1921 1–2).

*Interest on Late Payment*
Although there was industry agreement on the inclusion of a right of interest for late payment, the Government—reflecting the views of the Confederation of British Industry—has always refrained from making this compulsory for any sector of British industry.

*Cross-Contract Set-off*
Cross-contract set-off is not expressly forbidden by Pt. II of the Act—again, this reflects the fact that there was no industry agreement on this point. The Government was, no doubt, also concerned about losing Crown set-off rights by which a Government Department is enabled to

set-off monies against a contractor in respect of outstanding claims against that contractor from other Departments.

*Synopsis of the Act*

*Scope*

The Act applies to construction contracts involving the carrying out of "construction operations". Much of the core of construction activity is included within the definition section— s.105—but some construction activity is excluded and some is not included at all. The main express exclusions are:
  (i) Extraction of oil, natural gas and minerals and any works incidental thereto;
 (ii) Supply and installation of plant for the process industries, e.g. plant for the processing of chemicals, pharmaceuticals, oil, gas, food and drink, etc.;
(iii) On-site fabrication or manufacture of building/engineering components/equipment, etc., and of components for systems of heating, power supply, ventilation, communications etc.;
 (iv) Making, installation and repair of artistic works, e.g. sculptures.

Construction of dwellings which the other contracting party occupies or intends to occupy is specifically excluded. It was never the intention to include such work but the exclusion does not extend to the construction of speculative housing developments.

The Act applies only where the agreement for construction operations is in writing but this requirement is widely defined. Thus, if the parties orally agree on work to be done and the agreement incorporates one of the industry's standard forms of contract, this would be sufficient to satisfy the Act.

*Payment*

There are seven elements to the payment provisions:
  (i) A statutory right to payment by instalments;
 (ii) Contracts to have an *"adequate mechanism"* for determining what and when payments become due;
(iii) Contracts to specify period for discharge of due payments;
 (iv) Contracts to provide for giving of notice specifying the amount of the instalment payment and the basis of the calculation;
  (v) Statutory restrictions on rights to withhold monies;
 (vi) Statutory right of suspension for non-payment;
(vii) Restrictions on use of pay-when-paid provisions.

*Dispute Resolution*

The adjudication provisions in Pt. II of the Act were the subject of intense debate during the Bill's passage through Parliament. Under s.108 a party has a *"right to refer a dispute arising under the contract"* to an adjudicator in accordance with the procedure in s.108(2). Much of that debate arose because the Government and the industry were at cross-purposes as to the meaning of "adjudication". Initially, the Government seemed to regard it as a form of "fast-track" arbitration with the adjudicator having the power to issue a final award. The industry regarded it a "stop-gap" procedure for dealing with disputes quickly and cheaply without a forensic inquiry involving legal representation and the paraphernalia associated with arbitral or court proceedings. Adjudicators' decisions should reflect soundly-rooted commercial commonsense rather than any detailed application of technical legal principle.

It remains to be seen whether the courts will adopt a similar view rather than being over-anxious to overturn an adjudicator's decision on the grounds that he has erred in applying the law. The statutory procedure for adjudication only provides a very basic framework. Contracts should be drafted to steer the courts in the direction desired by the parties.

"Where parties have agreed on machinery ... for the resolution of disputes, it is not for the court to intervene and replace its own process for the contractual machinery agreed by the parties" (*per* Dunn L.J. in *Northern Regional Health Authority v. Derek Crouch Construction Co.* ([1984] Q.B. 644).

Lord Ackner's contribution to the debate at Report Stage in the House of Lords, no doubt, reflected the construction industry's view of adjudication:

"What I have always understood to be required by the adjudication process was a quick, enforceable interim decision which lasted until practical completion when, if not acceptable, it would be the subject matter of arbitration or litigation. That was a highly satisfactory process. It came under the rubric of 'pay now argue later', which was a sensible way of dealing expeditiously and relatively inexpensively with disputes which might hold up the completion of important contracts" (*Hansard*, H.L. Vol. 571, cols. 989, 990).

In fact, precedents already exist in the standard forms of building sub-contract used with the main contract forms published by the Joint Contracts Tribunal. Adjudication in these sub-contracts is confined to set-off disputes but other standard forms of contract in the industry have made provision for adjudication on a wider variety of matters. These include the Supplementary Provisions to the Standard Form of Building Contract with Contractors' Design (1981) published by the Joint Contracts Tribunal, forms published by the Association of Consulting Architects and, also, the *Engineering and Construction Contract*.

Prior to the Committee Stage in the House of Lords, the Government issued draft proposals for the *Scheme for Construction Contracts*. The Scheme is a default mechanism to be incorporated in the contract if there was no contractual procedure to adjudicate disputes. Unfortunately, these proposals generated more heat than light since they tended to confuse adjudication with arbitration. Thus it was stated that, "an adjudicator's award, unless expressly provisional, shall be final and binding". Matters were not helped by the reference in the Bill (now s.108(6) of the Act) to the possibility that the Scheme would apply the provisions of the Arbitration Act 1996 (c. 23) (albeit "with such adaptations and modifications as appear to the Minister making the scheme to be appropriate").

The essential difference between adjudication and arbitration is that the former does not involve a final disposal of the dispute between the parties. In *A Cameron v. John Mowlem and Co.* (1990) 25 Con L.R. 11, the Court of Appeal had to deal with a dispute over the enforceability of an adjudicator's award under the set-off provisions of DOM/1 (the standard domestic sub-contract for use with the Standard Form of Building Contract 1980 published by the Joint Contracts Tribunal). The Court had to consider an application under s.26 of the Arbitration Act 1950 (c. 27) for leave to enforce the decision of an adjudicator in the same manner as a judgment of the court. Section 26 allows enforcement only of an "award on an arbitration agreement". The Court rejected the application and upheld the first instance decision of H.H. Judge Esyr Lewis Q.C. that, "the adjudicator . . . does not perform an arbitral function and does not make any final award definitive of the parties' rights". Since the sub-contract provided that the adjudicator's decision was binding until final determination of the dispute by an arbitrator, the Court held that, "The decision has an ephemeral and subordinate character which, in our view, makes it impossible for the decision to be described as an award on an arbitration agreement. The structure of the sub-contract is against that conclusion" (*per* Mann L.J. at p.25).

However, in Ord. 14 proceedings, the courts have been prepared to enforce the award of an adjudicator even though it is of "an ephemeral and subordinate character" (see, e.g. *Drake & Scull Engineering v. McLaughlin and Harvey* (1992) 60 B.L.R. 102; *Mellowes PPG v. M Fitzpatrick & Sons* (1991) (unreported)).

Following intense industry lobbying, the Bill underwent substantial surgery. The original wording of the Bill referred to "resolution" by an adjudicator. The use of the word "resolution" could have been construed as giving finality to the process but the word was removed from the Bill during its passage in the Commons. The matter is now put beyond doubt by s.108(3) which was inserted as a Government amendment. This makes clear that an adjudicator's decision is of temporary effect until finally resolved by agreement of the parties, by arbitration or by the courts. The parties remain free to accept that the adjudicator's decision is final.

As already mentioned, the contractual adjudication procedure required by Pt. II of the Act is fairly minimal; it envisages the adjudicator reaching a decision within 28 days of referral of a dispute although the period can be extended. The contract must provide a timetable to enable an adjudicator to be appointed and disputes to be referred to him within seven days of notification of a dispute. Other provisions in the Act deal with the immunity of the adjudicator and the need for him to act impartially.

The effect of adjudication (as is, no doubt, intended by s.108) will be to substantially reduce the number of disputes going to arbitration, the standard dispute resolution procedure in the industry. Therefore, the decision of an adjudicator will often amount to a final disposal of the dispute in question. The downside is that parties may resort to the courts to overturn an adjudicator's decision probably on unmeritorious procedural or technical grounds—to avoid the waiting for arbitration.

*Scheme For Construction Contracts*

Both the payment and adjudication provisions (with the exception of ss.111(1) and 112) have a requirement that, in the event that contracts do not conform to the legislation, the Secretary of State's Scheme for Construction Contracts shall apply. As already explained, the proposals for such a Scheme were published for consideration by the House of Lords at Committee Stage but were withdrawn after considerable criticism. A draft Scheme is likely to be published in October 1996 for full industry-wide consultation.

*Conclusion*

In introducing the legislation at Second Reading in the House of Commons, Robert Jones, the Minister for Construction, Planning & Energy Efficiency, said: "Our aim is to encourage the industry to get its contracts right" (*Hansard*, H.C. Vol. 277, col. 53).

Part II may help to establish benchmarks for commercial activity and shape the culture of the industry particularly at site level where prevailing attitudes often lead to unnecessary conflict and disputes. Sir Michael Latham's conclusion was that standards of commercial dealing in the industry would have to improve so that every participant would have a real stake in the process, thereby promoting teamwork. The Act, whilst implementing a key recommendation in "Constructing the Team", also represents part of a finely-balanced package which has as its primary objective the reduction of construction costs by 30 per cent by the turn of the century.

In the meantime, the Government has undertaken to monitor the legislation to ensure that it is working in practice.

"Clearly, as time goes on, we shall be able to monitor the success of this legislation. In an industry where contracts are frequently very long, it might take us quite a while to be sure whether or not we have got matters right. If events show that we have missed the mark in significant ways, we will revisit the issue of fair contracts legislation and make the appropriate changes.

However, legislation should not be seen as an end in itself. The Bill is meant only to be a stepping-stone in the drive to build better relationships within the construction industry and to work towards the wider aims outlined by Sir Michael Latham in Constructing the Team" (*per* Lord Lucas, Government spokesman, during final stage of the Bill in the House of Lords: *Hansard*, H.L. Vol. 574, col. 1350).

*Commencement*

Part II will not be implemented until the Scheme for Construction Contracts has been settled following industry-wide consultation. Therefore, implementation is unlikely to be before May 1, 1997.

Part II will be brought into force on a day appointed by order of the Secretary of State (s.150(3)). The Secretary of State is likely to lay two orders simultaneously before Parliament to vary the definition of "Construction Operations" in s.105 (see s.105(3) and s.106(1)(b)) and to introduce the *Scheme for Construction Contracts* under s.114(1). For technical reasons, it is likely that both orders will have to be approved under the affirmative resolution procedure of each House before Pt. II can come into force. The date of the commencement order for Scotland will not necessarily coincide with that for England and Wales.

## *Introductory provisions*

### Construction contracts

**104.**—(1) In this Part a "construction contract" means an agreement with a person for any of the following—

(a) the carrying out of construction operations;

(b) arranging for the carrying out of construction operations by others, whether under sub-contract to him or otherwise;

(c) providing his own labour, or the labour of others, for the carrying out of construction operations.

(2) References in this Part to a construction contract include an agreement—

(a) to do architectural, design, or surveying work, or

(b) to provide advice on building, engineering, interior or exterior decoration or on the laying-out of landscape,

in relation to construction operations.

(3) References in this Part to a construction contract do not include a contract of employment (within the meaning of the Employment Rights Act 1996).

(4) The Secretary of State may by order add to, amend or repeal any of the provisions of subsection (1), (2) or (3) as to the agreements which are construction contracts for the purposes of this Part or are to be taken or not to be taken as included in references to such contracts.

No such order shall be made unless a draft of it has been laid before and approved by a resolution of each of House of Parliament.

(5) Where an agreement relates to construction operations and other matters, this Part applies to it only so far as it relates to construction operations.
An agreement relates to construction operations so far as it makes provision of any kind within subsection (1) or (2).
(6) This Part applies only to construction contracts which—
(a) are entered into after the commencement of this Part, and
(b) relate to the carrying out of construction operations in England, Wales or Scotland.
(7) This Part applies whether or not the law of England and Wales or Scotland is otherwise the applicable law in relation to the contract.

DEFINITIONS
"construction contract": subss. (1), (2) and (3).

GENERAL NOTE

*Subs. (1)*
A construction contract is a contract for the provision of work and materials but the definition of construction contract has been considerably extended by this Act to include agreements for professional services; for the provision of surveys and reports or the giving of advice as long as they are all related to "construction operations" as defined in s.105.
It is not clear why there is a need for both subss. (1)(b) and 1(c). The essence of both is that it is immaterial that the "construction operations" are procured from others in the contractual chain including, for example, sub-sub-contractors and labour-only contractors. However, subs. (1)(c) is couched in fairly wide terms; it could, for example, apply to employment agencies supplying labour to contractors and sub-contractors.

*Subs. (2)*
This makes clear that services provided by contractors such as design and advice are within the definition of "construction operations"; in the original draft of the Bill there was some doubt as to whether this was the position.

*Subs. (3)*
As already indicated, construction contracts will include labour only sub-contracts (where they involve the carrying out of "construction operations"). However, to the chagrin of the Inland Revenue and Contributions Agency, many labour-only sub-contractors are, in fact, engaged under a contract of service rather than for services. Therefore, subs. (3) ensures that employed people are not within the scope of the legislation.

*Subs. (4)*
The Secretary of State is likely to make an order prior to the commencement date of the Act which will exclude from the definition of "construction contract", contracts entered into under Private Finance Initiative arrangements. It is understood that certain types of private sector agreements will also be excluded. These are likely to include loan agreements for financing "construction operations" and joint venture or partnership agreements for the carrying out of "construction operations" for a third party.

*Subs. (5)*
It would have been much "cleaner" if the whole agreement was made subject to the Act in the event that only part of it was within the scope of the Act. Where there are disputes it could be difficult to disentangle the subject-matter of a dispute where an element of the work is outside the scope of the Act. For example, a steelwork fabricator enters into an agreement to manufacture off-site certain steelwork. In the same agreement he also provides a design service in relation to the fixing of the steelwork (which is to be carried out by a third party). His design service will be within scope but the off-site fabrication will be outwith the Act (see s.105(2)(d)). In the event of any dispute about the steelwork, it could be difficult to separate issues concerning the design input from those relating to the fabrication and fixing processes.

*Subs. (6)*
In relation to subs. (6)(a) it should be noted that the Act is likely to apply to works which have started prior to the commencement of Pt. II although the contract is not executed until after Pt. II has taken effect. Normally express or implied acceptance of a bid or tender would create a contract, even though execution of the documentation is much later. It is a matter of construc-

tion whether the execution of a formal contract is a necessary pre-requisite to contractual liability.

> "It appears to be well settled by the authorities that if the documents or letters relied on as constituting a contract contemplate the execution of a further contract between the parties, it is a question of construction whether the execution of the further contract is a condition of terms of the bargain or whether it is a mere expression of the desire of the parties as to the manner in which the transaction already agreed to will in fact go through. In the former case there is no enforceable contract either because the condition is unfulfilled or because the law does not recognise a contract to enter into a contract. In the latter case there is a binding contract and the reference to the more formal document may be ignored" (*per* Parker J. in *Von Hatzfeldt-Wildenburg v. Alexander* [1912] I Ch 284 at pp.28 8–9; see also *Chillingworth v. Esche* [1924] 1 Ch 978).

Where there is a chain of contracts and sub-contracts, the Act may apply to agreements lower down the chain but not to agreements higher up the chain if they were entered into prior to the date of commencement

The Act will be extended to Northern Ireland by Order in Council (s.149).

## Meaning of "construction operations"

**105.**—(1) In this Part "construction operations" means, subject as follows, operations of any of the following descriptions—

(a) construction, alteration, repair, maintenance, extension, demolition or dismantling of buildings, or structures forming, or to form, part of the land (whether permanent or not);

(b) construction, alteration, repair, maintenance, extension, demolition or dismantling of any works forming, or to form, part of the land, including (without prejudice to the foregoing) walls, roadworks, power-lines, telecommunication apparatus, aircraft runways, docks and harbours, railways, inland waterways, pipe-lines, reservoirs, water-mains, wells, sewers, industrial plant and installations for purposes of land drainage, coast protection or defence;

(c) installation in any building or structure of fittings forming part of the land, including (without prejudice to the foregoing) systems of heating, lighting, air-conditioning, ventilation, power supply, drainage, sanitation, water supply or fire protection, or security or communications systems;

(d) external or internal cleaning of buildings and structures, so far as carried out in the course of their construction, alteration, repair, extension or restoration;

(e) operations which form an integral part of, or are preparatory to, or are for rendering complete, such operations as are previously described in this subsection, including site clearance, earthmoving, excavation, tunnelling and boring, laying of foundations, erection, maintenance or dismantling of scaffolding, site restoration, landscaping and the provision of roadways and other access works;

(f) painting or decorating the internal or external surfaces of any building or structure.

(2) The following operations are not construction operations within the meaning of this Part—

(a) drilling for, or extraction of, oil or natural gas;

(b) extraction (whether by underground or surface working) of minerals; tunnelling or boring, or construction of underground works, for this purpose;

(c) assembly, installation or demolition of plant or machinery, or erection or demolition of steelwork for the purposes of supporting or providing access to plant or machinery, on a site where the primary activity is—

(i) nuclear processing, power generation, or water or effluent treatment, or

(ii) the production, transmission, processing or bulk storage (other than warehousing) of chemicals, pharmaceuticals, oil, gas, steel or food and drink;

(d) manufacture or delivery to site of—

(i) building or engineering components or equipment,

(ii) materials, plant or machinery, or

(iii) components for systems of heating, lighting, air-conditioning, ventilation, power supply, drainage, sanitation, water supply or fire protection, or for security or communications systems,

except under a contract which also provides for their installation;

(e) the making, installation and repair of artistic works, being sculptures, murals and other works which are wholly artistic in nature.

(3) The Secretary of State may by order add to, amend or repeal any of the provisions of subsection (1) or (2) as to the operations and work to be treated as construction operations for the purposes of this Part.

(4) No such order shall be made unless a draft of it has been laid before and approved by a resolution of each House of Parliament.

DEFINITIONS

"construction operations": subss. (1)(a) to (1)(f).

GENERAL NOTE

*Subs. (1)*

The base definition of "construction operations" was taken from s.567 of the Income and Corporation Taxes Act 1988 (c. 1). However, a definition which might be appropriate for one piece of legislation is not necessarily appropriate to advance the objectives of another. Since the Act is designed to encourage sound contractual practice, its ambit should, arguably, extend towards a more liberal definition of construction such as that found in *Reg. 2, Construction (Design and Management) Regulations 1994* (S.I. 1994 No. 3140).

Definitional disputes often result in litigation (see, e.g. the volume of litigation over the definition of "factory" in the Factories Act 1961 (c. 34)) but it is to be hoped that the courts will place greater emphasis on overcoming the mischief addressed by the Act rather than being too astute in finding gaps in the definition.

The major change to the definition of "construction operations" in the draft Bill was the inclusion of maintenance which generated much of the debate at Committee Stage in the Commons on subs. (1). The Government was concerned that the inclusion of maintenance would unnecessarily widen the scope of the Act so that it would apply to general maintenance work. Since repair was already included, the Government felt this was sufficient.

The Opposition view was that the exclusion of maintenance would remove a substantial slice of construction activity from the scope of the legislation and could also encourage unnecessary disputes. As the Opposition spokesman for construction, Nick Raynsford, said in Committee, "When does maintenance cease to be maintenance and become a repair?" (House of Commons, Official Report—Standing Committee F: June 13, 1996, col. 279). However, the Act is now likely to apply to contracts such as facilities management contracts where there is an element of building maintenance.

The reference to "fittings forming part of the land" in subs. (1)(c) includes: "Control systems, fire alarms, close circuit television systems, lifts and other such objects ..." (*per* Robert Jones, Minister for Construction, etc., House of Commons, Official Report—Standing Committee F: June 13, 1996, col. 288). In considering whether "fittings" have become a "part of the land", the courts are likely to draw on the wealth of precedent relating to the distinction between fixtures and chattels.

> "materials worked by one into the property of another become part of that property. This is equally true whether it be fixed or moveable property. Bricks built into a wall become part of the house, thread stitched into a coat which is under repair, or planks and nails and pitch worked into a ship under repair, become part of the coat or the ship" (*per* Blackburn J. in *Appleby v. Myers* [1867] L.R. 2 C.D. 651 at p.659).

Subsection (1)(e) is extremely wide: it could include, for example, anything from geotechnical surveys to fitting-out or finishing work. At Committee Stage in the Commons, the Construction Minister opined that subs. (1)(e) would include dredging, exploration work and the provision and relaying of services by utilities although some of the latter work could be regarded as work forming part of the land in subs. (1)(b).

*Subs. (2)*

Subsection (2) was the most contentious part of s.105 since it excludes matters which, within the industry, are normally considered to be construction activities.

Subsection (2)(c) is an illogical exemption which was achieved through persistent lobbying by an organisation using the unfortunate acronym PILG—Process Industries Latham Group. This body represented the interests of clients in the process industries who maintained that they were not affected by the ills associated with the rest of the construction industry; therefore, the legislation was not relevant to their needs.

During the passage of the Bill the scope of the process plant exemption was significantly reduced.

"I want to make it clear that we do not intend all work on a process engineering site to be excluded from fair contracts provision. We want to exclude only work on the machinery and plant that is highly specific to the process industry, together with work on steelwork that is so intimately associated with that plant and machinery that it could not possibly be reasonably considered apart. To that end, we have made it clear that the steelwork mentioned in the exclusion is only that which relates to support and access . . . I repeat that all normal construction activities on a process engineering site will be subject to the provisions of the Bill. That includes building roads, erecting fences, laying foundations, and building offices or factories—even if they are made of steel" (*per* Robert Jones, M.P., Minister for Construction etc., at Committee Stage in the Commons, House of Commons, Official Report—Standing Committee F: June 13, 1996, cols. 301–2).

However, in some instances such as sewerage and power generation plant, the distinction between that which constitutes plant and construction can become fairly blurred. This distinction has been considered by the courts in connection with the legislation relating to capital allowances (now the Capital Allowances Act 1990 (c. 1)). Thus, for example, it has been held that expenditure on an underground sub-station for transforming electricity was not expenditure on plant (*Bradley (Inspector of Taxes) v. London Electricity, The Times*, August 1, 1996). The test appears to be whether the structure in question is performing a "plant-like function" (*per* Blackburne J.; see also, e.g., *Schofield v. R & H Hall* (1974) 49 TC 538 where a grain silo was held to be plant).

Rather more surprising is the exclusion of components and materials manufactured off-site in subs. (2)(d) (unless the contract for their supply also provides for their fixing). A substantial amount of construction work is now carried out off-site as a way of reducing construction costs. In fact, much off-site fabrication (not involving a fixing element) is carried out under forms of construction contract/sub-contract generally in use within the industry. The Government's position was that it would be extremely difficult to include bespoke off-site work since there was a risk that this could let in supply contracts for items such as bricks, nails, etc. which were for general use. Nevertheless, the Act will apply to a supply-only contract to the extent that the supplier is also engaged in a "construction operation". For example, if a supplier of a boiler also agrees as part of his contract to test and commission it on installation, this would be for "rendering complete [a construction operation]".

*Subss. (3) & (4)*

It is likely that the Secretary of State will closely monitor the operation of subss. (1) and (2) to ensure that any significant anomalies or omissions are dealt with fairly speedily (see commentary on s.104(4)).

## Provisions not applicable to contract with residential occupier

**106.**—(1) This Part does not apply—

(a) to a construction contract with a residential occupier (see below), or

(b) to any other description of construction contract excluded from the operation of this Part by order of the Secretary of State.

(2) A construction contract with a residential occupier means a construction contract which principally relates to operations on a dwelling which one of the parties to the contract occupies, or intends to occupy, as his residence.

In this subsection "dwelling" means a dwelling-house or a flat; and for this purpose—

"dwelling-house" does not include a building containing a flat; and

"flat" means separate and self-contained premises constructed or adapted for use for residential purposes and forming part of a building from some other part of which the premises are divided horizontally.

(3) The Secretary of State may by order amend subsection (2).

(4) No order under this section shall be made unless a draft of it has been laid before and approved by a resolution of each House of Parliament.

DEFINITIONS
"dwelling": subs. (2).
"dwelling-house": subs. (2).
"flat": subs. (2).

GENERAL NOTE

*Subs. (1)*

The Latham Report specifically excluded work on residential premises from the recommendation for legislation on contracts and this was accepted by both Government and the bodies representing the industry. The Act will, however, apply to sub-contracts (e.g. for plumbing, electrical work) sub-let under the main contract with the residential occupier (with regard to subs. (1)(b), see commentary on s.105(3) and 105(4)).

*Subs. (2)*

In the original draft of the Bill this residential exemption applied where the dwelling "the whole or any part of which is the subject of operations to which the [construction] contract relates" (clause 103(1)). The Government recognised that there was some ambiguity in these words since a party could seek to avoid the legislation by making use of the so-called "penthouse loophole". Thus, for example, if the contract is for an office block with a penthouse on the roof it could be exempt from the Act if the client intends to reside in the penthouse (which was "the subject of operations" under the contract). Such loophole would appear to be closed by the requirement that the construction contract must "principally" relate to operations on a dwelling.

But, there remains a difficulty with the wording of subs. (2). It is a matter of fact whether the residential occupier is in occupation of the dwelling but the difficulty arises from the use of the word "intends". This could mean, for example, that a party could contract for building or structure stating that he intends to use it as a dwelling on completion but subsequently changes his mind and uses it for a commercial purpose.

## Provisions applicable only to agreements in writing

**107.**—(1) The provisions of this Part apply only where the construction contract is in writing, and any other agreement between the parties as to any matter is effective for the purposes of this Part only if in writing.

The expressions "agreement", "agree" and "agreed" shall be construed accordingly.

(2) There is an agreement in writing—

(a) if the agreement is made in writing (whether or not it is signed by the parties),

(b) if the agreement is made by exchange of communications in writing, or

(c) if the agreement is evidenced in writing.

(3) Where parties agree otherwise than in writing by reference to terms which are in writing, they make an agreement in writing.

(4) An agreement is evidenced in writing if an agreement made otherwise than in writing is recorded by one of the parties, or by a third party, with the authority of the parties to the agreement.

(5) An exchange of written submissions in adjudication proceedings or in arbitral or legal proceedings in which the existence of an agreement otherwise than in writing is alleged by one party against another party and not denied by the other party in his response constitutes as between those parties an agreement in writing to the effect alleged.

(6) References in this Part to anything being written or in writing include its being recorded by any means.

GENERAL NOTE

*Subs. (1)*

Apart from the words "construction contract" in subs. (1) and "adjudication proceedings" in subs. (5), s.107 is the same as s.5 of the Arbitration Act 1996. Under s.5 of the Arbitration Act 1996, Pt. I of that Act only applies where the arbitration agreement is in writing. However, "writing" is defined extremely widely.

The purpose of this section is rather different to that of s.5 of the Arbitration Act 1996. This Act was not intended to catch the myriad informal arrangements entered into between builders, plumbers, electricians, etc., and individual consumers or householders. By contrast s.5 of the Arbitration Act 1996 provides a liberal definition of writing to ensure that as many arbitration agreements as possible are brought within scope so that they are adequately underpinned by the statutory framework.

It is likely that s.107 may catch transactions for which the Act was not intended but an all-embracing definition of writing was probably required in order to reduce the opportunities for avoidance.

*Prima facie*, contracts partly in writing and partly oral are excluded, since subs. (1) states that the Act applies "only where the construction contract is in writing" (but see notes to subs. (3)).

*Subs. (2)*

Often construction contracts/sub-contracts are executed after the commencement of the work but they may have retrospective effect (see, *e.g. Trollope & Colls v. Atomic Power Constructions* [1963] 1 W.L.R. 333; *City of Box Hill v. E.W. Tauschke* [1974] V.R. 39).

In any event, subs. (2) does not appear to place any temporal limit on when the written agreement must come into existence. The following exchange took place at Committee Stage in the Commons:

"Mr Raynsford: ... where there is a verbal agreement, work has begun on the site and the written confirmation comes 24 hours later—would the written confirmation be within the terms of clause 106(2)(c) [now s.107(2)(c)]?

Mr. Jones: In the interests of brevity, the answer is yes" (House of Commons Official Report, Standing Committee F, June 18, 1996, col. 318).

Initially, there may be some uncertainty about whether the Act will apply pending the issue of the necessary documentation and acceptance of it by the other party. If work has already commenced on the basis of a letter of intent, such letter may not constitute a contract for the works, in which case the Act will not apply at all (see, e.g. *British Steel Corporation v. Cleveland Bridge and Engineering* [1984] 1 All E.R. 504; *Monk Construction v. Norwich Union Life Assurance Society* (1992) 62 B.L.R. 107).

For the most part, subs. (2) will apply to fairly informal arrangements such as an exchange of letters or a written acceptance of a quote.

*Subs. (3)*

Thus, if in an oral agreement the parties refer to, for example, the terms of a written quote or to JCT 80 (the Standard Form of Building Contract published by the Joint Contracts Tribunal), this will be sufficient to satisfy the requirement for writing. There is no requirement that the terms of the oral agreement must be found exclusively in the written terms referred to; therefore, the Act may apply to partly oral and partly written contracts.

Furthermore, the written terms may be found in more than one document.

*Subs. (4)*

Subsection (4) amplifies subs. (2)(c). For example, if the parties reach agreement over the telephone and, with the approval of the other party, the conversation is subsequently noted by one of the parties or by an employee, such note would bring the agreement within the Act. Presumably, if the note did not accurately reflect the agreement, it would not constitute evidence of that agreement but, until this issue is decided, the note would attract the provisions of the Act (provided that the other party had given his authority for the agreement to be recorded).

*Subs. (5)*

This is a rather more controversial extension of s.107. The effect of subs. (5) is that an oral agreement will be converted into a written agreement if one party alleges an oral agreement (which is not denied by the other) in written submissions in adjudication, arbitral and legal proceedings. It is more likely that such result would only arise in arbitral or legal proceedings rather than adjudication proceedings (unless the parties had orally agreed to have their disputes dealt with by an adjudicatory process similar to that provided for in s.108).

In practice, difficulties could arise here. If the oral agreement has not reflected (as is likely) the requirements of the Act, the Scheme will operate retrospectively with the result that one of the parties might have been in breach of his contract. Consequently, it would be in the interests of both parties to avoid disputes if they wish to preserve their oral agreement. Alternatively, the parties would need to ensure that their oral agreement reflects the requirements of the Act even though it was never intended that the Act would apply to such agreements.

*Subs. (6)*
The concept of "writing" is further extended to include, for example, oral communications recorded on audio tape (such as that contained in a telephone answering machine) or video tape.

*Adjudication*

### Right to refer disputes to adjudication

**108.**—(1) A party to a construction contract has the right to refer a dispute arising under the contract for adjudication under a procedure complying with this section.

For this purpose "dispute" includes any difference.

(2) The contract shall—

(a)  enable a party to give notice at any time of his intention to refer a dispute to adjudication;

(b)  provide a timetable with the object of securing the appointment of the adjudicator and referral of the dispute to him within 7 days of such notice;

(c)  require the adjudicator to reach a decision within 28 days of referral or such longer period as is agreed by the parties after the dispute has been referred;

(d)  allow the adjudicator to extend the period of 28 days by up to 14 days, with the consent of the party by whom the dispute was referred;

(e)  impose a duty on the adjudicator to act impartially; and

(f)  enable the adjudicator to take the initiative in ascertaining the facts and the law.

(3) The contract shall provide that the decision of the adjudicator is binding until the dispute is finally determined by legal proceedings, by arbitration (if the contract provides for arbitration or the parties otherwise agree to arbitration) or by agreement.

The parties may agree to accept the decision of the adjudicator as finally determining the dispute.

(4) The contract shall also provide that the adjudicator is not liable for anything done or omitted in the discharge or purported discharge of his functions as adjudicator unless the act or omission is in bad faith, and that any employee or agent of the adjudicator is similarly protected from liability.

(5) If the contract does not comply with the requirements of subsections (1) to (4), the adjudication provisions of the Scheme for Construction Contracts apply.

(6) For England and Wales, the Scheme may apply the provisions of the Arbitration Act 1996 with such adaptations and modifications as appear to the Minister making the scheme to be appropriate.

For Scotland, the Scheme may include provision conferring powers on courts in relation to adjudication and provision relating to the enforcement of the adjudicator's decision.

General Note

*Subs. (1)*
The most significant aspect of this section is that there is not a mandatory requirement for the parties to refer their disputes to adjudication; rather a party has a statutory right to refer disputes to adjudication. The parties are, therefore, free to use alternative methods of dispute resolution. Another possibility is for the parties to resort to adjudication only for certain types of disputes. A difficult question is whether the statutory right can, by contract, be excluded or waived. Reference should be made to the commentary to s.112 but, in any event, s.108(5) would appear to

militate against such exclusion or waiver. If a contract does not conform to the procedure required by s.108(1) (as set out in s.108(2)) or the requirements of ss.108(3) and 108(4), the Scheme will apply. If the statutory right was excluded or waived, the Scheme could not operate and therefore, the implication must be that contracts cannot override the statutory right.

A further difficulty arises when the parties have commenced arbitral or legal proceedings without referring the dispute to adjudication. If one party then decides to exercise his statutory right of adjudication it would appear that the arbitrator or the court would have little choice but to stay the proceedings pending the outcome of the adjudication. The party requesting the adjudication may, however, be penalised in costs for not having made the request before the commencement of the proceedings.

It would have been helpful if s.108 had included a similar provision to s.40 of the Arbitration Act 1996 which requires that: "The parties shall do all things necessary for the proper and expeditious conduct of the arbitral proceedings". Assuming that the adjudication provision in the contract conforms to the requirements of s.108, it may be necessary for contracts to include a similar provision. Without such provision there is a risk that a party could frustrate the procedure by delaying tactics or by simply ignoring it. If there is such a provision, failure by a party to adhere to the procedure would be a breach of contract which could, possibly, be remedied by mandatory injunction to force compliance. But, seeking the aid of the court will have meant that the party practising the non-cooperation will have achieved his aim of delaying matters.

If, on the other hand, an adjudicator decides to act without the involvement of the other party, would that party be bound by his decision? Since adjudication is a statutory right, it would be surprising if a court allowed a party to frustrate the exercise of the right by the simple expedient of pretending that it didn't exist. Again, by way of contrast, s.41(4) of the Arbitration Act 1996 specifically enables the arbitrator to make an award in the absence of any evidence or submissions from one of the parties.

This issue was the subject of an amendment in the House of Lords but the response of the Government spokesman, Lord Lucas, was not entirely convincing:

"If an adjudication procedure is not intended to resolve the disputes which are referred to it and does not require parties to submit to the process and act upon its outcome, it will be defective under the terms of that clause" (*Hansard*, H.L. Vol. 570, col. 1885).

The adjudicator is empowered to deal with disputes "arising under the contract". Therefore, pre-contract matters are likely to be outside his jurisdiction. The following has received judicial consideration within the context of arbitration agreements:

"There is, I suggest, a broad distinction which may be drawn between those clauses which refer to arbitration only, those disputes which may arise regarding the rights and obligations which are created by the contract itself, and other clauses which show an intention to refer some wider class or classes of disputes. This distinction is obviously clear and justified as a matter of law. It may also be one which would be recognised by the parties whose contract it is, for at the very least, by making the contract, they demonstrate their agreement to create a new category of legal rights and obligations, legally enforceable between themselves. Disputes regarding this category may well be described, as a matter of language, as ones arising "under" the contract, and this meaning of that phrase has been authoritatively recognised and established, *e.g.* by the House of Lords in *Heyman v. Darwins* ([1942] 1 All E.R. 337, [1942] A.C. 356) and by the Court of Appeal in *Ashville*. Conversely, if the parties agree to refer disputes arising "in relation to" or "in connection with" their contract, *a fortiori* if the clause covers disputes arising "during the execution of this contract" (*Astro Vencedor Cia Naviera SA v. Mabanaft GmbH, The Damianos* [1971] 2 All E.R. 1301, [1971] 2 Q.B. 588) or in relation to "the work to be carried out hereunder", a common form in construction contracts, then both as a matter of language and of authority, some wider category may be intended". (*per* Evans J. in *Overseas Union Insurance v. A A Mutual International Insurance* [1988] 2 Lloyd's Rep 63 at p.67).

In *Ashville Investments v. Elmer Contractors* (1987) 10 Con L.R. 72, Balcombe L.J. said (at p.93):

"Such a dispute (about mistake leading to rectification) is not as to any matter or thing ... arising *under* the contract ... Similarly, a dispute between the parties as to whether an innocent misrepresentation, or negligent mis-statement, which led Ashville to enter into the contract ... [is not] a dispute as to any matter arising *under* the contract."

In *Fillite (Runcorn) v. Aqua-Lift* (1989) 26 Con L.R. 66, the Court of Appeal held that the words "arising under these heads of agreement" were not wide enough to include claims for negligent mis-statement, negligent misrepresentation under the Misrepresentation Act 1967 (c. 7) or claims arising under a collateral contract. "In my judgment, on the ordinary and natural meaning of words, the phrase 'disputes arising under a contract' is not wide enough to include disputes which do not concern obligations created by or incorporated in that contract" (*per* Slade L.J. at p.76).

It is, of course, up to the parties whether they would wish to extend the adjudicator's jurisdiction to include matters such as mistake, rectification and misrepresentation by expressly including disputes arising in connection with the contract. This was the substance of an Opposition amendment in the House of Commons but it failed to attract the support of the Government. The Government's view was that an extension of the adjudicator's jurisdiction to disputes arising in connection with the contract would cloth the adjudicator with the powers of an arbitrator.

The reference to "difference" in subs. (1) helps to avoid possible delaying tactics by one side, for example, claiming that he is not in dispute because he has not had time to check the veracity or strength of a claim made by the other party. Therefore, to the extent that he has not acceded to the claim, there exists a difference between the parties.

Standard forms of contract in the construction industry generally reserve power to the arbitrator to open up, review and revise architect's or engineer's certificates. It was stated obiter in *Northern Regional Health Authority v. Derek Crouch Construction Co.* [1984] Q.B. 644, that the courts do not have the same power as the arbitrator in this regard (but see *Tarmac Construction v. Esso Petroleum Co.* (1996, (unreported)).

"Despite the fact that the architect is subject to a duty to act fairly, these powers might be regarded as Draconian and unacceptable if they were not subject to review and revision by a more independent individual. That process is provided for by the arbitration clause. It is, however, a rather special clause. Arbitration is usually no more and no less than litigation in the private sector. The arbitrator is called upon to find the facts, apply the law and grant relief to one or other or both of the parties. Under a JCT arbitration clause (cl. 35), the arbitrator has these powers but he also has power to 'open up, review and revise any certificate, opinion, decision, requirement or notice'. This goes far further than merely entitling him to treat the architect's certificates, opinions, decisions, requirements and notices as inconclusive in determining the rights of the parties. It enables, and in appropriate cases requires, him to vary them and so create new rights, obligations and liabilities in the parties. This is not a power which is normally possessed by any court and again it has a strong element of personal judgment by an individual nominated in accordance with the agreement of the parties" (*per* Sir John Donaldson M.R. at p.670).

Section 43A of the Supreme Court Act 1981 (c. 54) (inserted by s.100 of the Courts and Legal Services Act 1990 (c. 41)) allows the courts to take on the powers of the arbitrator under the arbitration agreement provided both parties consent. The issue is whether an adjudicator would also be able to exercise the power to open-up, review and revise certificates. Whilst it is clear that disputes over certificates are disputes arising under the contract, there may be some doubt whether an adjudicator would be able to substitute his own judgment for that of the certifier; it would make the adjudication procedure devoid of substance if the adjudicator was not able to open-up, review and revise certificates. This problem could also arise where one party had reserved to himself those decisions which would otherwise have been the preserve of a third party certifier (see *Balfour Beatty Civil Engineering v. Docklands Light Railway* (1996) C.I.L.L. 1143).

Many disputes in the industry arise because of dissatisfaction with the certified amounts. If the adjudicator was not able to substitute his decision for that of the certifier, his only role would be to examine whether the certifier had acted honestly, fairly and reasonably (see *Balfour Beatty Civil Engineering v. Docklands Light Railway* (1996) C.I.L.L.; 1143; *John Barker Construction v. London Portman Hotel* (1996) C.I.L.L. 1152). For the avoidance of doubt, (and provided that the parties are so agreed) contracts should be expressed to confer upon the adjudicator the power to open-up, review and revise certificates. There may be some resistance to this from certifiers (and, no doubt, their insurers) since their traditional powers will be fettered by adjudicators' decisions.

*Subs. (2)(a)*

Subsection (2) lays down fairly minimal procedural requirements which all contracts must contain. Each party has an unrestricted right to give notice that he intends to refer a dispute to the adjudicator; there is no temporal limitation on the exercise of the right to refer a dispute to adjudication. Thus, such right could be exercised during the progress of the works, after completion or abandonment of the works. But, where a contract has been discharged by breach, the adjudicator is unlikely to have jurisdiction to deal with any disputes since they would not be "arising under the contract"—it is discharged. This would also apply if the contract is discharged following the exercise of any express rights of termination or determination. However, many of the standard forms in use in the industry only provide for the determination of the contractor's 'employment' and, therefore, the contract is preserved.

There is always the danger that one party may "store up" a dispute in order to secure adequate time by which to fully develop his case or to refer it to an adjudicator at a time which is most disadvantageous to the other party. The content of such notice, to whom it must be issued and the means of service are matters for the contract. Where there is no agreement on the "manner of service", ss.115(3) and 115(4) will apply.

*Subs. (2)(b)*
The period of seven days is an extremely short time in which to secure the appointment of the adjudicator and for referral of the dispute to him. Therefore, it would be prudent for the identity of the adjudicator to be agreed upon at the outset of the contract and for the party giving notice of his intention to refer a dispute to the adjudicator (under subs. (2)(a)), to provide with that, notice of the submissions which he intends to rely upon in support of his case. This should allow the party receiving such notice sufficient time in which to forward his own response (see s.116 for how periods of time are reckoned). However, the response time may have to "eat into" the period of 28 days (subs. (2)(c)) to enable the respondent to deal adequately with the case against him which the other party may have prepared over a number of weeks or even months.

Again, in order to streamline the procedure, a copy of the notice in subs. (2)(a) (together with accompanying submissions) could be used for the purpose of referring the dispute to the adjudicator.

It should be noted that the timetable of seven days for appointment of and referral of the dispute to the adjudicator is expressed as an objective and, is not mandatory. Contracts may have to extend the timetable to cater for death, illness or unavailability of the adjudicator or even for delays in securing the appointment of an adjudicator in the first place.

*Subs. (2)(c)*
There is nothing in the Act which forbids the contract from restricting the scope of the decision which the adjudicator might make. Thus, for example, a contractual provision which requires the adjudicator to limit his decision on money claims to £x may not offend the Act. On the other hand, if the limit is extremely low in relation to the contract value, the statutory right to refer disputes to adjudication will have been frustrated. Unfortunately, this could provide some scope for litigation.

Another way in which limits could be placed on the adjudicator's decision making power is by requiring that the adjudicator shall not make a decision which is in excess of that already given by an adjudicator under another contract. For example, an adjudicator under a sub-contract could be restrained from awarding an extension of time which is in excess of that previously awarded by the adjudicator under the main contract (assuming that both the main contract and sub-contract adjudications related to the same factual circumstances).

Given the complexity of disputes that could be referred to the adjudicator, it is understandable that the parties should have the right to extend the 28 day limit. There is no limit on the time by which the statutory period can be extended. There may be an opportunity here for stronger parties to pressurise the weaker into accepting an unreasonable extension.

*Subs. (2)(d)*
If the adjudicator requires an extension of time, it would normally be in the interest of the party referring the dispute to grant it. It should be noted that the period can be extended by any number of days up to the full 14 days.

*Subs. (2)(e)*
All the matters listed in subss. 2(c) to 2(f) should be included in a tripartite agreement between the parties and the adjudicator so that the adjudicator is also contractually bound. Such agreement would require the adjudicator to act impartially which means that, at least, he should apply the rules of natural justice. Therefore, he should declare any interests which could mean that he has a bias towards one of the parties. He should ensure that each party has an adequate opportunity to present his case and deal with that submitted by the other within the time constraints allowed by the statute. Reference should be made to the wealth of precedent concerning the impartiality (or lack of it) of arbitrators stemming from applications to remove them for misconduct (now embodied in s.24 of the Arbitration Act 1996).

*Subs. (2)(f)*
This gives the adjudicator power to seek legal advice and make his own inquiries as to the facts. Thus, for example, he may wish to visit the site to inspect work which is the subject of the dispute and ask questions of relevant personnel. In fact, subject to his duty to act impartially, the adjudicator should be "master in his own house". Procedures which are detailed and prescriptive would undermine the adjudicatory process by providing endless opportunities for jurisdictional disputes arising from procedural lapses by the adjudicator. This was, no doubt, in the mind of Lord Lucas (the Government spokesman) at Committee Stage in the House of Lords.

"An adjudicator should have access to legal or other expert advice and should not have to rely solely on the evidence offered to him by the parties if better evidence is available within the time available to him. There is no need to specify that the adjudicator should restrict himself to the 'relevant' facts. We should leave it to the expert to decide what is relevant and what is not; to do otherwise could be a recipe for wrangling and delays" (*Hansard*, H.L. Vol. 570, col. 1880).

*Subs. (3)*

In the majority of cases, the parties are likely to reserve their right to have disputes considered afresh in arbitration or by the court. In practice, it is likely that the adjudicator's decision will hold sway or, alternatively, the parties will reach a settlement based upon that decision. Indeed, subs. (3) makes clear that the parties may agree to accept the adjudicator's decision as final. It should be noted that there is no requirement that the agreement is to be in writing. There is also the possibility that such agreement could be implied, if it transpires that the parties have conducted their relationship on the assumption that the adjudicator's decision is final.

*Subs. (4)*

Again, this should be included as part of a tripartite agreement between the parties and the adjudicator. If this was only in the contract between the parties to the construction contract, it is possible that one party would not enforce the contract in this regard, if the other decided to sue the adjudicator. It should be noted that the adjudicator does not have statutory immunity as does an arbitrator under s.29 of the Arbitration Act 1996. Therefore, the adjudicator could, for example, face actions in negligence brought by third parties. There may be scope for such actions against the adjudicator under the so-called "reliance cases" (see e.g. *White v. Jones* [1995] 2 W.L.R. 187; *Henderson v. Merrett Syndicates* [1994] 3 W.L.R. 761).

*Subs. (5)*

Contracts draftsmen should faithfully reflect all the requirements in subss. (1) to (4) if they wish to ensure that the Scheme does not apply. The Scheme will, no doubt, have to address the substantive and procedural issues raised in the commentaries on the previous subsections.

*Subs. (6)*

Apart from being a "belt and braces" provision, it is difficult to understand why subs. (6) is required, when s.114(4) states that the Scheme is to take effect as "implied terms of the contract". This would give a sufficient signal to the courts on the extent to which they can intervene in disputes arising out of the application of the Scheme. Nonetheless, the Government has decided to "draw down" the powers of the courts in relation to the Arbitration Act 1996 and extend them to adjudication (in so far as appropriate to adjudication). Since, in Scotland, there is no statutory arbitration law the Scheme will have to give certain powers to the courts. Apart from enforcing decisions of the adjudicator and intervening in jurisdictional issues (preferably substantive rather than procedural), it is difficult to envisage a greater role for the courts in the adjudicatory process. After all, the statutory right of adjudication is designed to obviate the need for litigation. With the very short time span allowed for the adjudication procedure to be completed and, in view of the fact that the adjudicator's decision is only of a temporary nature, the outcome of many applications to the courts is likely to be academic.

Section 24 of the Arbitration Act 1996 gives the courts power to remove an arbitrator on certain grounds such as lack of impartiality, non-possession of qualifications required by the arbitration agreement or failure to conduct the proceedings with all reasonable dispatch. Such powers are required since arbitrators are issuing final awards.

The Scheme will need to provide for an adjudication procedure which "fleshes out" the provisions of s.108. Therefore, the Scheme will have to include matters such as the appointment of the adjudicator, procedures governing the way in which each party is to present its case to the adjudicator, and the time in which the decision is to be implemented. Baring in mind the nature of adjudication and the procedural time limits, there should not be any scope for oral hearings with legal representation.

*Payment*

## Entitlement to stage payments

**109.**—(1) A party to a construction contract is entitled to payment by instalments, stage payments or other periodic payments for any work under the contract unless—

(a) it is specified in the contract that the duration of the work is to be less than 45 days, or

(b) it is agreed between the parties that the duration of the work is estimated to be less than 45 days.

(2) The parties are free to agree the amounts of the payments and the
intervals at which, or circumstances in which, they become due.

(3) In the absence of such agreement, the relevant provisions of the
Scheme for Construction Contracts apply.

(4) References in the following sections to a payment under the contract
include a payment by virtue of this section.

<small>GENERAL NOTE</small>

*Subs. (1)*

Most forms of construction contract (both standard and non-standard forms) either provide
for periodic payments (usually monthly) or stage payments. In the absence of any express provision for interim payments the presumption is that the contract is an entire one—completion of
the works is a condition precedent to payment (see, *e.g. Sumpter v. Hedges* [1898] 1 Q.B. 673;
*Ibmac v. Marshall (Homes)* (1968) 208 E.G. 851). At common law there is some authority which
suggests that interim payments can be implied in construction contracts. In *D.R. Bradley (Cable
Jointing) v. Jefco Mechanical Services* (1989) (6 Construction Law Digest—7–21), Mr Recorder
Rich Q.C., sitting as an Official Referee had to consider a dispute concerning non-payment by a
main contractor under a sub-contract which had no express provisions as to time or method of
payment:

"Having heard their evidence as to the custom of the industry, I concluded that it was an
implied term of a contract that application could be made for payment not more frequently
than monthly. Payment would then be due within a reasonable period of such application, for
the work done and any unused material on site, valued in each case in accordance with the
contract between the parties. I announced in the course of the hearing my intention to hold
that I construed a reasonable time in all the circumstances as 30 days with a period of grace to
allow 42 days in all, and I now hold that 42 days was a reasonable time for payment".

It is not clear what "stage payments" or "periodic payments" in subs. (1) add to the statutory
right to "payment by instalments" other than being illustrative. The industry's standard forms of
contract generally provide for monthly periodic payments based upon the valuation of the total
works carried out to the date of the instant payment less the total of the amounts already
received by way of interim payments and any cash retention. In "Constructing the Team", Sir
Michael Latham recommended that: "The eventual aim should be to phase out the traditional
system of monthly measurement or remeasurement ..." Instead, he recommended: "Express
provision for assessing interim payments by methods other than monthly valuation *i.e.* mile
stones, activity schedules or payment schedules".

Stage payments are different from periodic payments in that completion of a stage is a condition of precedent to payment. Therefore, if, for whatever reason, the stage is not completed,
the obligation to make payment does not arise—this simply reflects the rule relating to "entire
contracts" which has already been referred to above.

The right to payment by instalments extends to "any work under the contract". Thus, it would
seem that off-site work including any design is included in addition to on-site work.

The statutory right to instalment payments will, first, arise if the contract states that the work
will last less than 45 days even if the actual number of days stated is wholly unrealistic. Furthermore, there is no requirement that the figure actually stated must reflect continuous working.
Thus, for example, the work may, in fact, last 30 days in total but those days may be spread over
six months.

Subsection (1)(b) provides an alternative where there is no stipulation in the contract as to the
period for the duration of work. The parties can agree that the work is likely to last less than 45
days; which agreement should be obtained before commencement of the works (although there
is no requirement that this should be so).

*Subs. (2)*

Subsection (2) confirms that, in practice, the effect of s.109 is likely to be minimal. Thus, for
example, a contract lasting 12 months could provide that the bulk of the price will be paid on
completion and that nominal amounts of £5 as advances on the price will be paid at four monthly
intervals.

*Subs. (3)*

It is likely that the Scheme will reflect the norm in the industry which is monthly periodic
payments based upon measurement and valuation of all the work carried out prior to the making
of each interim payment.

**Dates for payment**

**110.**—(1) Every construction contract shall—
(a) provide an adequate mechanism for determining what payments become due under the contract, and when, and
(b) provide for a final date for payment in relation to any sum which becomes due.

The parties are free to agree how long the period is to be between the date on which a sum becomes due and the final date for payment.

(2) Every construction contract shall provide for the giving of notice by a party not later than five days after the date on which a payment becomes due from him under the contract, or would have become due if—
(a) the other party had carried out his obligations under the contract, and
(b) no set-off or abatement was permitted by reference to any sum claimed to be due under one or more other contracts,

specifying the amount (if any) of the payment made or proposed to be made, and the basis on which that amount was calculated.

(3) If or to the extent that a contract does not contain such provision as is mentioned in subsection (1) or (2), the relevant provisions of the Scheme for Construction Contracts apply.

GENERAL NOTE

*Subs. (1)*

There is no definition of "adequate mechanism" in subs. (1)(a). Lord Lucas, on behalf of the Government, sought to justify this omission at Second Reading in the House of Lords:

"The industry covers thousands of different operations and dozens of different types of contract. Payment is already determined in far too many ways for us to come up with a single definition. This legislation requires that payment should be defined in terms of amount and date. That will be a big improvement on what happens at the moment". (*Hansard*, H.L. Vol. 569, col. 1027).

Traditional payment arrangements in the industry (other than at the level of domestic subcontracts) provide for a process of measurement, valuation and certification often by a third party—an architect or engineer. This determines what payments become due. Once a certificate is issued it gives rise to a debt subject to opening-up, review or revision in a subsequent arbitration or, possibly, by a court where the parties are so agreed (see *Lubenham Fidelities and Investment Co. v. South Pembrokeshire D.C.* (1986) 33 B.L.R. 39).

Subject to any contractual provisions to the contrary, it was once assumed that certificated amounts had to be paid in full, irrespective of any set-off or counterclaim (*Dawnays v. M.G. Minter* [1971] 1 W.L.R. 1205). The matter was finally resolved by the House of Lords in *Modern Engineering (Bristol) v. Gilbert Ash (Northern)* [1974] A.C. 689 which held that very clear express terms were required in the contract to deny the right of the payer to set-off or raise a defence to justify a refusal to pay certificated amounts. The sanctity of certificates (if it ever existed) was further undermined in *R.M. Douglas Construction v. Bass Leisure* (1990) 25 Con L.R. 38. The Court held that the payer could resist an application for summary judgment under Ord. 14: "Where ... in good faith and on reasonable material [he] raises an arguable contention that a certificate is open to challenge" (*per* H.H. Judge Bowsher Q.C. at p.48).

The requirement for an "adequate mechanism" is intended, firstly, to identify "what payments become due". The fact that the payer discharges a certificate by paying less than the due amount on account of a set-off or for any other reason is unlikely to offend against subs. (1)(a).

However, the payment machinery in consultants' agreements and in the vast majority of subcontracts (except, for example, the nominated sub-contract documentation published by the Joint Contracts Tribunal) will not involve certification. Nevertheless, excluding work carried out under the various consultants' agreements, the process of measurement and valuation based upon the contract pricing documents (*e.g.* bills of quantities, schedules of rates, contract sum analyses) is likely to suffice for the purposes of subs. (1)(a).

Alternatively, if other methods of payments such as stage payments, activity schedules or payment milestones are used, then as long as there is an apportionment of the contract sum to each stage, milestone or activity this should also suffice. For consultants' agreements, a similar approach may be necessary so that instalments of the consultant's fee is apportioned to the work stages completed.

Where measure and value is the basis of payment, it suggested that contracts should make clear which party has the responsibility for carrying out the valuation in order to produce an authoritative statement of what is due. In some of the industry standard form contracts such as the domestic sub-contracts linked to JCT main forms, it is unclear who has the responsibility for carrying out valuations.

The "adequate mechanism" must also serve to determine when payments become due. To some extent this overlaps with s.109 since it would be expected that on the expiry of the payment period or completion of a stage of work, payment would become due. Nevertheless, subs. (1)(a) would seem to require that contracts clearly identify the event which qualifies as the due date. Thus if interim payments are made dependent upon the issue of certificates, the date of issue of the certificate will need to be identified as the "due date".

Finally, subs. (1)(b) requires the insertion of a further date following the due date by which payment must be discharged. Such requirement tends to be reflected in most of the standard forms of contract use in the industry.

*Subs. (2)*

It should be noted that the requirement for the notice is contractual rather than statutory. The form of notice, how it is to be served and upon whom, are matters for the contract (but if the manner of service is not agreed, ss.115(3) and 115(4) apply). The requirement that the notice shall state the basis upon which the amount was calculated will be of immense help to the payee in deciding whether or not to dispute that amount before the adjudicator. In fact, valuation disputes are likely to provide a substantial slice of an adjudicator's workload.

The contractual notice requirements must apply even if payment would have been due but for:

   (i) Failure by the payee to comply with his contract, *e.g.* the works were not in accordance with the contractual specification (see *Acsim (Southern) v. Dancom Danish Contracting and Development Co.* (1989) 47 B.L.R. 59) and/or;

  (ii) The exercise by the payer of a right of "set-off or abatement (sic) ... under one or more contracts" (subs. (2)(b)).

It is unclear why "set-off" and "abatement" were used in this context. If the payer wishes to exercise set-off rights under another contract they would, in any event, have to be exercised against any sums due under the extant contract since, strictly, set-off negates or reduces the obligation to discharge any *due* payment.

Furthermore, abatement results in the diminution or extinction of the contract price on the ground that it has not been earned because the relevant work has not been carried out or, if it has, it does not comply with the contract. It is generally not possible to abate the price under the extant contract because of deficiencies in the work under another contract. In fact, it would have made for much simpler drafting if the trigger for the giving of the notice had been left at the date on which payment becomes due—which would, in any event, have taken account of any abatement. The fact that payment might not have actually been made between that date and the "final date for payment" because of a set-off is immaterial. (This is further discussed in the commentary on s.111.)

If the "payment made or proposed to be made" is nil because the payer has abated the price or exercised a right of set-off, such notice would be acceptable under s.111(1) provided that it has complied with s.111(2).

*Subs. (3)*

It is unlikely that, the Scheme (in making provision for an "adequate mechanism") would deviate too far from the industry norm of determining payment on a measure and value basis or on the basis of each complete work stage.

## Notice of intention to withhold payment

**111.**—(1) A party to a construction contract may not withhold payment after the final date for payment of a sum due under the contract unless he has given an effective notice of intention to withhold payment.

The notice mentioned in section 110(2) may suffice as a notice of intention to withhold payment if it complies with the requirements of this section.

(2) To be effective such a notice must specify—

  (a) the amount proposed to be withheld and the ground for withholding payment, or

  (b) if there is more than one ground, each ground and the amount attributable to it,

and must be given not later than the prescribed period before the final date for payment.

(3) The parties are free to agree what that prescribed period is to be.

In the absence of such agreement, the period shall be that provided by the Scheme for Construction Contracts.

(4) Where an effective notice of intention to withhold payment is given, but on the matter being referred to adjudication it is decided that the whole or part of the amount should be paid, the decision shall be construed as requiring payment not later than—

(a) seven days from the date of the decision, or

(b) the date which apart from the notice would have been the final date for payment,

whichever is the later.

GENERAL NOTE

*Subs. (1)*

Section 111 is primarily designed to reduce the incidence of set-off abuse by formalising the process by which the payer claims to be entitled to pay less than that expected by the payee. The payer is entitled to refuse to discharge payments on the ground that the payee has failed to comply with his contractual obligations in some respect. In equity such set-off is regarded as a self-help remedy and is a substantive defence to a claim for non-payment. The set-off may be for an unliquidated amount but must arise out of the same or a closely connected transaction.

By contrast, a legal or statutory set-off (compensation in Scotland) can only be raised as a defence in legal proceedings. This avoids the need for a multiplicity of actions where there may be claims and counterclaims arising out of different or unconnected transactions.

Legal or statutory set-off originated in the Statutes of Set-Off in 1729 and 1739 which were repealed by s.2 of the Civil Procedure Acts Repeal 1879 (c. 59) and are now, by virtue of the Supreme Court Act 1981 (c. 54) embodied in rules of court. The Statutes of Set-Off applied to mutual debts but now R.S.C. Ord. 18, r.17 permits a defendant to raise claims in legal proceedings, "whether of an ascertained amount or not".

In *The Nanfri*, Lord Denning M.R. in the Court of Appeal ([1978] 3 All E.R. 1066) explained the nature of equitable set-off in the context of time charters:

"When the ship owner is guilty of a breach of contract which deprives the time charterer of part of the consideration for which the hire has been paid in advance, the charterer can deduct an equivalent amount out of the hire falling due for the next month ... In my opinion, therefore, in a time charter, if the shipowner wrongly and in breach of contract deprives the charterer for a time of the use of the vessel, the charterer can deduct a sum equivalent to the hire for the time so lost".

Furthermore, "when the debtor has a true [equitable] set-off it goes in reduction of the sums owing to the creditor" (at p.1077).

Therefore, unlike legal or statutory set-off, equitable set-off will amount to a discharge of sums due or owing (see also *Laroque v. Beauchemin* [1897] A.C. 358).

Where the contract is silent upon the issue of set-off, "one starts with the presumption that neither party intends to abandon any remedies for its breach arising by operation of law, and clear express words must be used in order to rebut this presumption" (*per* Lord Diplock in *Modern Engineering v. Gilbert-Ash* [1994] A.C. 689 at p.717: see also *Redpath Dorman Long v. Cummins Engine Co.* 1981 S.C. 370). This view has held sway in spite of the statement by Lord Cross in *Mottram Consultants v. Bernard Sunley* [1975] 2 Lloyd's Rep. 197 who said (at p.205): "one should approach each case without any *parti pris* in favour or against the existence of a right of set-off, though one must bear in mind the principle established in *Mondel v. Steel*".

The standard forms of sub-contract for use with the forms of main contract published by the Joint Contracts Tribunal provide the exclusive machinery for the exercise of set-off rights. Non-standard forms of contract/sub-contract tend to extend set-off rights (often expressed—incorrectly—as common law set-off) to include set-off across contracts.

Technically, there is a distinction between set-off and common law abatement which was clearly explained in the classic case of *Mondel v. Steel* [1841] 8 M. & W. 858 where Park B. said at pp.871–2;

"It must however be considered, that in all these cases of goods sold and delivered with a warranty ... the rule which has been found so convenient is established; and that it is competent for the defendant ... not to set-off by a proceeding in the nature of a cross-action, the amount of damages which he has sustained by breach of the contract, but simply to defend himself by showing how much less of the subject-matter of the action is worth, by reason of the breach of contract; and to the extent that he obtains, or is capable of obtaining, an abatement of price on that account, he must be considered as having received satisfaction for the breach of contract, and is precluded from recovering in another action to that extent; but no more".

*Mondel v. Steel* was concerned with defects in a ship delivered under a ship-building contract. For reasons which are not apparently clear, abatement only applies to contracts for the sale of goods and contracts for work and materials. It has the effect, not of discharging payment, but of preventing the obligation to make payment arising in the first place. Since the work is defective (or has not been completed according to the contract) payment has not been earned.

In practice, the distinction between abatement and set-off is of not great consequence—courts sometimes use the terms interchangeably. However, the distinction may be significant where the particular contract expressly excludes rights of set-off or limits the exercise of those rights. This was illustrated by *Acsim (Southern Ltd) v. Dancom Danish Contracting and Development Co.* (1989) 47 B.L.R. 59. The Court of Appeal had to consider the set-off provisions in the "blue" form of domestic sub-contract for use with the 1963 Edition of the Standard Form of Building Contract published by the Joint Contracts Tribunal. The main contractor's entitlement to set-off against sums owing to the sub-contractor were fully set out in the contract. The contractor had failed to give the requisite notice when seeking to exercise his right of set-off on the ground that the work was either not done or it was defective. The Court of Appeal applied *Mondel v. Steel.* The Court held that the contractor had the right to defend a claim for interim payment by showing that the sum claimed had not been earned by reason of the breach of contract. Such defence amounted to common law abatement rather than set-off. (A useful potted history of the evolution of set-off and abatement is given in the judgment by Morris L.J. in *Hanak v. Green* [1958] 2 All E.R. 141 at pp.145–51.)

The Concise Oxford Dictionary (7th Ed.) states that "withhold" means "hold back" but (as has already been discussed), as a matter of strict law, abatement or set-off is not a holding back although, in common parlance it would be regarded as so. Thus, the effect of common law abatement is to deny that monies are due or owing whereas equitable set-off has the effect of discharging monies due or owing.

The question is whether courts will be prepared to approach subs. (1) in a purposive way to deal with the "mischief" which s.111 is seeking to address rather than being too preoccupied with technical considerations. An argument could, of course, be made out that s.111 would otherwise be devoid of any content; it has to refer something. In such a situation the court is able to consider the Parliamentary history of the legislation or *Hansard* to discover the "mischief" (see *Pepper v. Hart* [1993] 1 All E.R. 42). Nonetheless, it is a pity that the parliamentary draftsman did not provide a statutory definition of "withhold" to include "set-off and abatement". However, since the notice in s.110(2) can also serve as a "notice of intention to withhold payment" the draftsman must have contemplated that set-off or abatement was included, since s.110(2) still requires a notice if payment is not made because of failure to perform the contract or a set-off or abatement under other contracts.

*Subs. (2)*

The payer may wish to safeguard his position in the event that the amount(s) stated in the notice or the ground(s) to which it is linked are, subsequently, found to be inaccurate as new information comes to light. There is nothing in s.111 which would prevent the payer from reserving his right to amend the amount(s) withheld and/or the ground(s) for such withholding in the event of any subsequent adjudication, arbitration or litigation.

*Subs. (3)*

Since the s.110(2) notice for specifying payments to be made must be issued within 5 days of the date when payment becomes due, and, since such notice can also qualify as a notice under s.111(1), it would be sensible to relate the "prescribed period" to the 5 days required by s.110(2). In any event, this may be provided by the Scheme.

*Subs. (4)*

If there is a failure to comply with the adjudicator's decision within the stipulated time, the payee could exercise his statutory right of suspension under s.112 or seek to recover the adjudicator's award in debt recovery proceedings.

It should be noted that the obligation to issue an "effective notice" is statutory. The Scheme will not supply such provision where it is not included in the contract. It is unlikely that the obligation can, by contract, be waived or excluded (see commentary on s.108(1) and s.112(1)). In particular the reference in subs. (3) to the Scheme stipulating the "prescribed period" presumes the existence of the statutory obligation.

## Right to suspend performance for non-payment

**112.**—(1) Where a sum due under a construction contract is not paid in full by the final date for payment and no effective notice to withhold payment has been given, the person to whom the sum is due has the right (without prejudice to any other right or remedy) to suspend performance of his obligations under the contract to the party by whom payment ought to have been made ("the party in default").

(2) The right may not be exercised without first giving to the party in default at least seven days' notice of intention to suspend performance, stating the ground or grounds on which it is intended to suspend performance.

(3) The right to suspend performance ceases when the party in default makes payment in full of the amount due.

(4) Any period during which performance is suspended in pursuance of the right conferred by this section shall be disregarded in computing for the purposes of any contractual time limit the time taken, by the party exercising the right or by a third party, to complete any work directly or indirectly affected by the exercise of the right.

Where the contractual time limit is set by reference to a date rather than a period, the date shall be adjusted accordingly.

GENERAL NOTE

*Subs. (1)*

At common law there is no right to suspend the works for non-payment or late payment:
"Apart from suing for interim payments, or requiring arbitration where that is provided for, the remedy—and apparently the only remedy—which the contractor is recognised as having at common law is rescission if a sufficiently serious breach has occurred. If he chooses not to rescind, his own obligations continue. He is bound to go on with the work. All the available English and Commonwealth text books on building contracts state the law consistently with this view ... " (*per* Cooke & Woodhouse JJ. in *Canterbury Pipelines v. Christ Church Drainage* [1979] 2 N.Z.L.R. 347 at p.351).
This view was reinforced by Staughton L.J. in *Eurotunnel v. TML* [1992] C.I.L.L. 754;
"It is well established that if one party is in serious breach, the other can treat the contract as altogether at an end; but there is not yet any established doctrine of English law that the other party may suspend performance, keeping the contract alive".
In fact, apart from making the timing of payment of the essence, it is only in very limited circumstances that the payee can regard late or non-payment as going to the root of the contract allowing him to treat the contract as discharged for breach.
"The case would have been quite different if the defendants' breaches had been such as reasonably to shatter the plaintiffs' confidence in the defendants' ability to pay for the goods with which the plaintiffs supplied them. I think that, in such circumstances, the consequences of the breach could properly have been regarded as most serious, indeed fundamental, and going to the root of the contract so that the plaintiffs would have been entitled to refuse to continue doing business with the defendants." (*per* Salmon L.J. in *Decro-Wall v. Practitioners in Marketing* [1971] 2 All E.R. 216 at p.222; applied in *D.R. Bradley (Cable Jointing) v. Jefco Mechanical Services* (1989) 6-CLD-07-21).
A right of suspension for non-payment is expressly provided in the standard sub-contracts for use with the main contracts published by the Joint Contracts Tribunal.
The right to suspend provided by subs. (1) is a statutory right but there is no bar on contractual waiver or exclusion of such right. Furthermore, s.112 does not provide for the right to be included in the Scheme if it does not appear in the contract.
"Although there is a general principle that a person may waive any right conferred on him by statute (*quilibet protest renunciare juri pro se introducto*) difficulties arise in determining whether the right is exclusively personal or is designed to serve other more broad public purposes. In the latter situation, public policy would require that the right be treated as mandatory and not be waivable by the party for whose benefit it operates. Whether a statutory right is waivable depends on the overall purpose of the statute and whether this purpose would be frustrated by permitting waiver. Thus in *Johnson v. Moreton* [1980] A.C. 37 the House of Lords held that a tenant could not contract out of the protection afforded by s.24 of the Agricultural Holdings Act 1948 (c. 63) as this would undermine the overall purpose of the Act in prompting efficient farming in the national interest" (Chitty on Contracts, 27th Ed. at p.782).

In *Johnson v. Moreton, Lord Simon of Glaisdale* at p.69 said:
"The principle which, in my view, emerges ... is as follows. Where it appears that the mischief which Parliament is seeking to remedy is that a situation exists in which the relations of parties cannot properly be left to private contractual regulation, a party cannot contract out of such statutory regulation (albeit exclusively in its own favour) because so to permit would be to reinstate the mischief which the statute was designed to remedy and to render the statutory provision a dead letter".

The broad public purpose of the Act could be said to be the improvement in the efficiency of the construction industry by stimulating cash flow, improving disputes resolution machinery and reducing the incidence of insolvency. Although, on its own, the exercise of the right of suspension might not be considered as being for the public good, it should be viewed as an integral part of the statutory package.

An Opposition amendment at Report Stage in the House of Commons sought to ensure that all the provisions in the Act would have effect notwithstanding any agreement to set aside the provisions. The amendment was withdrawn after the Government had given an assurance that the parties would not be able to sign away their rights in advance.

Before the right of suspension can be exercised the payee must ensure:
(i) A sum is due; and
(ii) Payment has not been made in *full* by the final date for payment, *i.e.* the expiry of the period of discharge; and
(iii) An effective notice to withhold payment has not been given.

Where the contract provides for certificated payments, the issue of a certificate is a condition precedent to a sum becoming due (see *Lubenham Fidelities and Investment Co. v. South Pembrokeshire D.C.* (1986) 33 B.L.R. 39).

Therefore the exercise of the statutory right of suspension in the absence of a certificate would be rather foolhardy. On the other hand, if a certificate represents a substantial under-valuation the payee may suspend work if he considers that the certifier has not acted honestly, fairly and reasonably (*Northern Regional Health Authority v. Derek Crouch Construction Co.* [1984] Q.B. 644; *Balfour Beatty Civil Engineering v. Docklands Light Railway* (1996) C.I.L.L. 1143).

While doubts remain about whether abatement or set-off rights are, technically, a withholding of payment, there will remain some uncertainty associated with the exercise of the statutory right of suspension which will affect both payer and payee. Thus, for example, if the payer claims that a sum is not due on account of poor workmanship, but has not issued an "effective notice" to withhold payment, he could face severe disruption to the progress of his work. It would not be surprising if this issue was litigated sooner rather than later.

The exercise of the right of suspension is without prejudice to other rights or remedies so that the payee is free to exercise any contractual rights of determination for non-payment or, indeed, to sue for the outstanding sum as a debt.

*Subs. (2)*

A condition precedent to the exercise of the right of suspension is the giving of seven day's notice of intention to suspend but the form and content, manner of service and upon whom it is to be served are matters for the contract (although if manner of service is not agreed, ss.115(3) and 115(4) will apply). It is thought that the ground for exercising the right of suspension would normally be failure by the payer to make payment in accordance with the notice issued under s.110(2) or the balance of the amount stated in such notice after taking into account any sums withheld in any further notice issued under s.111(1).

*Subs. (3)*

It would appear that, in theory, the right of suspension remains even where the parties have compromised the debt since the reference is to "payment in full of the amount due" under the contract. To avoid any ambiguity, contracts should make clear that amounts due include any such amount which has been revised following a compromise or settlement.

*Subs. (4)*

The drafting is tortuous but, in essence, any overrun over the contract period or date for completion will not constitute a breach of contract by the party suspending performance of the works. This protection is also available to a third party such as a sub-contractor who is unable to continue work as a result of suspension by a main contractor.

On the other hand, suspension is not necessarily a convenient excuse for justifying any delay in the works since the delay in question must be traced back to work which was "directly or indirectly" affected by the suspension. If the suspension has occurred on a critical path in the programme, the extent of work indirectly affected by the suspension could be fairly substantial.

It should be noted that there is no express statutory provision for the recovery of any loss or expense incurred by the payee during the period of suspension; this is a matter which should be addressed in the contract.

## Prohibition of conditional payment provisions

**113.**—(1) A provision making payment under a construction contract conditional on the payer receiving payment from a third person is ineffective, unless that third person, or any other person payment by whom is under the contract (directly or indirectly) a condition of payment by that third person, is insolvent.

(2) For the purposes of this section a company becomes insolvent—

(a) on the making of an administration order against it under Part II of the Insolvency Act 1986,

(b) on the appointment of an administrative receiver or a receiver or manager of its property under Chapter I of Part III of that Act, or the appointment of a receiver under Chapter II of that Part,

(c) on the passing of a resolution for voluntary winding-up without a declaration of solvency under section 89 of that Act, or

(d) on the making of a winding-up order under Part IV or V of that Act.

(3) For the purposes of this section a partnership becomes insolvent—

(a) on the making of a winding-up order against it under any provision of the Insolvency Act 1986 as applied by an order under section 420 of that Act, or

(b) when sequestration is awarded on the estate of the partnership under section 12 of the Bankruptcy (Scotland) Act 1985 or the partnership grants a trust deed for its creditors.

(4) For the purposes of this section an individual becomes insolvent—

(a) on the making of a bankruptcy order against him under Part IX of the Insolvency Act 1986, or

(b) on the sequestration of his estate under the Bankruptcy (Scotland) Act 1985 or when he grants a trust deed for his creditors.

(5) A company, partnership or individual shall also be treated as insolvent on the occurrence of any event corresponding to those specified in subsection (2), (3) or (4) under the law of Northern Ireland or of a country outside the United Kingdom.

(6) Where a provision is rendered ineffective by subsection (1), the parties are free to agree other terms for payment.

In the absence of such agreement, the relevant provisions of the Scheme for Construction Contracts apply.

GENERAL NOTE

*Subs. (1)*
Subsection (1) aims to curb the widespread use of pay when paid arrangements which are generally found in bespoke sub-contracts or amended standard forms of sub-contracts. They also tend to spread down the contractual chain to sub-sub-contracts. If the third party (usually the client or building owner) does not make payment, sub-contractors, generally do not have any rights of recourse against the third party for non-payment or late payment.
There is an inherent ambiguity in the term "pay when paid". It can be construed as relating to:

(i) *Timing* so that payment to the payee is made *when* payment is received by the payer from the third party;

(ii) Entitlement to payment so that payment is only made *if* payment has been received by the payer from the third party.

If the pay when paid clause is construed as only relating to the timing of payment, it would seem that, in principle, the courts would enforce such provision. (See, *e.g. Schindler Lifts (Hong Kong) v. Shui On Construction Co.* [1985] HKLR 118; *Brightside Mechanical & Electrical Services Group v. Hyundai Engineering & Construction Co.* (1988) 41 B.L.R. 110).
However, a number of cases decided in the United States, Australia and New Zealand suggest that the courts are reluctant to accept that payment entitlement can be wholly dependent upon receipt of payment from a third party unless very clear words to that effect are used. In effect, a

pay-if-paid clause requires the payee to act as the insurer of the payer following non-payment by the third party. (See, *e.g. Pace Construction Corporation v. OBS Co Inc.* (1988) Fla App 531 So 2d 737 (Florida District Court of Appeal); *Smith & Smith Glass v. Winston Architectural Cladding Systems* [1992] 2 NZLR 473; *Iezzi Constructions Pty v. Currumbin Crest Development Pty* (1994) 10 B.C.L. 408; "*Are 'pay when paid' clauses in construction sub-contracts; conditions precedent or terms of payment?*" by Harold J. Murphy [1989] 61 C.L.R. 196). Furthermore, a pay when paid condition is unlikely to apply if a contract has been brought to an end by some breach on the part of the payer (See, *Scobie & McIntosh v. Clayton Bowmore* (1990) 49 B.L.R. 119).

There is no English precedent on pay when paid clauses but there are probably three fairly slim grounds on which they could be attacked:

(i) If the payer contends that clause in question is a pay if paid arrangement, the courts are likely to construe it *contra proferentum* if there is any ambiguity concerning the purport of the clause.

(ii) Failure by the payer to bring to the payee's notice a particularly onerous requirement; there is some doubt about whether this would apply if the contract in question had been executed by the payee (See *Interfoto Picture Library v. Stiletto Visual Programmes* [1989] 1 Q.B. 433).

(iii) A paid when paid clause could be unreasonable under s.3 of the Unfair Contract Terms Act 1977 (c. 50). Thus, where the payee deals on the payer's "written standard terms of business", the payer cannot "by reference to any contract term [unless such term satisfies the requirement of reasonableness] claim to be entitled in respect of the whole or any part of his contractual obligations to render no performance at all". But, if the pay when paid clause is clearly drafted so that no obligation to make payment arises until and unless payment is received from the third party (*i.e.* receipt of payment from the third party is a condition precedent to payment by the payer), s.3 is unlikely to have any application since there is no contractual obligation to make payment in the first place.

In spite of the note in the margin referring to "Prohibition of conditional payment provisions", such provisions are only ineffective and not all conditional payment arrangements are covered. Thus, for example, it may be possible to re-introduce pay when paid arrangements by the "back door" by inserting other conditions such as making payment dependent upon receipt by the payer of a certificate (which includes the relevant payment) issued by the architect or engineer engaged by the third party—the client or building owner (see *Dunlop & Ranken v. Hendall Steel Structures* [1957] 1 W.L.R. 1102).

At Committee Stage in the Commons, an amendment was passed that "clauses having the effect of pay when paid" should be ineffective. However, this was overturned by the Government at Report Stage ostensibly on the ground that it was too wide and could interfere with the process of issuing certificates for payment which is common in the construction industry.

In the draft of the Bill the word "void" was used instead of "ineffective" which was adopted at Committee Stage in the House of Lords, supposedly to cater for certain, undefined, legal sensitivities in Scotland. "Void" is generally accepted in our legal lexicon as meaning that the contract or clause in question should be regarded as having never existed at all; the change of wording was probably necessary to meet the conceptual difficulty of pronouncing pay-when-paid clauses "void" while resurrecting them again on the insolvency of the third party.

If there exists a pay when paid clause in the sense defined in subs. (1), it may be resurrected where the third person is insolvent. This seems to be the purport of subs. (1) but the drafting is not entirely clear as to *when* the insolvency of the third person must have occurred. Must the third person be insolvent at the time that the payer and payee enter into the contract? The ambiguity seems to stem from the fact that subs. (1) is expressed in the present tense: "*A provision making payment . . . . conditional on the payer receiving payment from a third party is ineffective, unless that third person . . . is insolvent*".

Furthermore subs. (6) enables the parties to agree alternative payment provisions. The effect of any such agreement would be to remove the pay when paid clause from the contract altogether unless its resurrection (on the occurrence of the third person's insolvency) was expressly reserved.

A pay-when-paid arrangement can also be resurrected where the third person was also dependent upon payment (directly or indirectly) by another and that other party has gone into insolvency. However, such further dependency would have to be written into the contract or sub-contract between the payer and payee.

It is unclear what the position is where the contract states that payment will not be made if the third person has set-off monies against the payer with the result that the payer has not received the relevant monies. Arguably, the set-off could mean that payment to the payer has been discharged although he has not actually received the cash (see, commentary on s.111). It would have been better if the condition in subs. (1) was expressed as "discharge of payment" to the payer from the third person rather than "receiving payment". (See *Larocque v. Beauchemin* [1897] A.C. 358; *Brightside Mechanical & Electrical Services Group v. Hyundai Engineering & Construction Co.* (1988) 41 B.L.R. 110).

*Subss. (2)–(5)*
    It would seem that there is no reason why a payee cannot still challenge the validity of a pay if paid arrangement and, if successful, obtain a "*quantum meruit*" for the work executed up to the time the third party became insolvent.
    It would appear that the definition of insolvency as including, for example, administration orders and administrative receivership is rather too wide. In the case of administration, it is contemplated that the insolvent company will carry on business and therefore payments would continue along the contractual chain. This is also the case where the "third person" is in administrative receivership since the receiver may decide to continue the contract in question and continue payment.

*Subs. (6)*
    There may, of course, be resistance to the suggestion that the pay when paid clause is ineffective under the legislation in which case the dispute will have to be referred to the adjudicator as required by s.108. Assuming that this first hurdle is overcome (or does not exist), the agreement must establish a payment procedure which complies with the Act so that:
    (i) payments are made on an instalment basis;
   (ii) there is an adequate mechanism for determining what and when payments are due;
  (iii) the period of grace in which payment has to be made following the due date is stated;
  (iv) there is a requirement that the payer issues a notice within 5 days of the due payment date indicating the amount due and justifying the calculation.
   (v) there is stated the period for the giving of notice for withholding payment under s.111(2).
    In practice, it is likely that some parties will reach agreement by expressly incorporating the provisions of the Scheme or, as is more likely, the Scheme's provisions will apply because of the failure of the parties to reach an agreement.
    If the Scheme applies, there is no provision for what is to happen when a pay when paid clause is resurrected because of the insolvency of the "third person". Presumably, the Scheme would include a provision that it will cease to apply on the insolvency of the third person (provided that there already exists a pay when paid provision in the contract).

## *Supplementary provisions*

## The Scheme for Construction Contracts

    **114.**—(1) The Minister shall by regulations make a scheme ("the Scheme for Construction Contracts") containing provision about the matters referred to in the preceding provisions of this Part.
    (2) Before making any regulations under this section the Minister shall consult such persons as he thinks fit.
    (3) In this section "the Minister" means—
    (a) for England and Wales, the Secretary of State, and
    (b) for Scotland, the Lord Advocate.
    (4) Where any provisions of the Scheme for Construction Contracts apply by virtue of this Part in default of contractual provision agreed by the parties, they have effect as implied terms of the contract concerned.
    (5) Regulations under this section shall not be made unless a draft of them has been approved by resolution of each House of Parliament.

DEFINITIONS
    "Minister; the": subss. (3)(a), 3(b).

GENERAL NOTE
    The Scheme for Construction Contracts—the default scheme—will be introduced as a statutory instrument to be passed by affirmative resolution in both Houses of Parliament. The Government has committed itself to the widest possible consultation.
    The Scheme will provide the following:
  (i) An adjudication procedure.
 (ii) The intervals or circumstances when payments become due.

(iii) An adequate mechanism for determining what and when payments become due; a final date for payment in respect of due sums, and a requirement for a notice setting out the amount which was due to be paid and basis of calculation.

(iv) The period in which notice of withholding payment must be given.

(v) Failure of parties to agree payment terms where a paid when paid clause is "ineffective".

Where the provisions of the Scheme apply, they are to take effect as "implied terms" of the contract. Normally terms are implied (whether under statute or at law) to the extent that there isn't anything expressed in the contract to the contrary. In this context, the function of the Scheme is not only to fill in the gaps when the contract is silent but to override the terms of the contract where it includes provisions which do not reflect the statutory requirements.

### Service of notices, &c.

**115.**—(1) The parties are free to agree on the manner of service of any notice or other document required or authorised to be served in pursuance of the construction contract or for any of the purposes of this Part.

(2) If or to the extent that there is no such agreement the following provisions apply.

(3) A notice or other document may be served on a person by any effective means.

(4) If a notice or other document is addressed, pre-paid and delivered by post—

(a) to the addressee's last known principal residence or, if he is or has been carrying on a trade, profession or business, his last known principal business address, or

(b) where the addressee is a body corporate, to the body's registered or principal office,

it shall be treated as effectively served.

(5) This section does not apply to the service of documents for the purposes of legal proceedings, for which provision is made by rules of court.

(6) References in this Part to a notice or other document include any form of communication in writing and references to service shall be construed accordingly.

GENERAL NOTE

Notice procedures generally underpin most of the requirements in Pt. II and, as already stated in some of the commentaries, contracts will have to determine the form and content of the requisite notices, mode of service and upon whom they are to be served. Section 115 deals with only one aspect of notice procedure—the manner of service. Although service can be carried out by "any effective means", subs. (4) makes clear that where service is carried out in accordance with its provisions, there is effective service whether or not express provisions are included in the contract on this matter.

In subs. (6), as a minimum requirement, notices (and service thereof) can "include any form of communication in writing". It will, no doubt, be in the interests of one of the parties to have more onerous notice requirements in relation to matters such as suspension but, in other matters, where that party is required to issue a notice, it may wish to make the procedure as informal as possible.

### Reckoning periods of time

**116.**—(1) For the purposes of this Part periods of time shall be reckoned as follows.

(2) Where an act is required to be done within a specified period after or from a specified date, the period begins immediately after that date.

(3) Where the period would include Christmas Day, Good Friday or a day which under the Banking and Financial Dealings Act 1971 is a bank holiday in England and Wales or, as the case may be, in Scotland, that day shall be excluded.

GENERAL NOTE

There was an attempt at Committee Stage in the House of Lords to extend subs. (3) to include "days forming part of a customary holiday period within the industry in question". This was rejected by the Government in no uncertain terms. Earl Ferrers, leading for the Government, said: "It seems unreasonable to tell people who are expecting money, and may be expecting some money on, say, 15th August, that everyone has gone on holiday for two weeks and they have to wait for two weeks for their money. After all, this is a case of making payments when payments are known to be expected and payments are due. I should have thought that it is perfectly reasonable to say in those circumstances that only the statutory holidays should be taken into account". (*Hansard*, H.L. Vol. 571, col. 39).

## Crown application

**117.**—(1) This Part applies to a construction contract entered into by or on behalf of the Crown otherwise than by or on behalf of Her Majesty in her private capacity.

(2) This Part applies to a construction contract entered into on behalf of the Duchy of Cornwall notwithstanding any Crown interest.

(3) Where a construction contract is entered into by or on behalf of Her Majesty in right of the Duchy of Lancaster, Her Majesty shall be represented, for the purposes of any adjudication or other proceedings arising out of the contract by virtue of this Part, by the Chancellor of the Duchy or such person as he may appoint.

(4) Where a construction contract is entered into on behalf of the Duchy of Cornwall, the Duke of Cornwall or the possessor for the time being of the Duchy shall be represented, for the purposes of any adjudication or other proceedings arising out of the contract by virtue of this Part, by such person as he may appoint.

GENERAL NOTE
Prior to publication of the Bill there was some doubt about whether contracts entered into with the Crown would be encompassed by the legislation but the Government's acceptance of Sir Michael Latham's recommendation in "Constructing the Team" that it should be a *best practice* client would have "rung" rather hollow if the Crown had been exempted.

## PART III

### ARCHITECTS

INTRODUCTION
This part of the Act revises the law relating to the registration of Architects by amending the Architects (Registration) Act 1931 (c. 33) and the Architects Registration Act 1938 (c. 54) and by repealing the Architects Registration (Amendment) Act 1969 (c. 42). The principle of protecting the use of the word "Architect" is preserved but there are changes to the management of the registration of Architects, the regulation of professional conduct and there is provision for a new code of professional practice. The Board of Architectural Education, the Admission Committee and the Discipline Committee, which were established under the 1931 Act, are abolished and their functions are taken over by the Architects Registration Board and the Register of Architects. The Architects Registration Board also takes over the remaining functions of the Architects Registration Council of the U.K., which was established under the 1931 Act.

COMMENCEMENT
The changes introduced by the Act will come into force in accordance with the provisions of s.150(3) upon such day as may be appointed by the Secretary of State. Different days may be appointed for different areas and different purposes. The Secretary of State also has the power to make transitional provisions and savings as appear to him to be appropriate (s.150(4)).

ABBREVIATIONS
    "1931 Act" : Architects (Registration) Act 1931.
    "Board; the": Architects Registration Board.

*The Architects Registration Board*

## The Board and its committees

**118.**—(1) The Architects' Registration Council of the United Kingdom established under the Architects (Registration) Act 1931 ("the 1931 Act") shall be known as the Architects Registration Board.

(2) The Board of Architectural Education, the Admission Committee and the Discipline Committee constituted under the 1931 Act are abolished.

(3) In section 3 of the 1931 Act (constitution and functions of Architects' Registration Council), after subsection (2) insert—

"(2A) Part I of the First Schedule to this Act makes provision about the constitution and proceedings of the Board.

(2B) There shall be a Professional Conduct Committee of the Board and Part II of that Schedule makes provision about its constitution and proceedings.

(2C) Part III of that Schedule gives to the Board power to establish other committees and makes provision about their constitution and proceedings.

(2D) Part IV of that Schedule makes general provision about the Board and its committees.".

(4) For the First Schedule to the 1931 Act (constitution of Council) substitute the Schedule set out in Part I of Schedule 2.

DEFINITIONS

"Architects Registration Board": s.118(1).

"Board; the": s.118(1), Sched. 2, Pt. II, para. 2(2).

"Professional Conduct Committee": s.118(3) and Sched. 2, Pt. I (new First Schedule as inserted in the 1931 Act at Pt. II).

GENERAL NOTE

This section renames the Architects Registration Council of the U.K. ("ARCUK") as the Architects Registration Board ("ARB"). The Government changed its mind at least twice on this issue, initially taking the view that ARCUK should be abolished and that other arrangements should be made to secure the continued integrity of the architectural profession (see *Hansard*, H.L. Vol. 569, col. 980). The Government ultimately decided that the Council should be reformed in order to make it more efficient. Unfortunately, the Act does not repeal all the earlier legislation but amends by adding sections to previous enactments with consequential amendments and repeals. In consequence, the Act must be read together with the 1931 and 1938 Acts.

Under Sched. 2, Pt. 1, provision is made for the ARB to consist of a total of 15 members, seven of whom shall be elected and eight shall be appointed. The elected members will represent bodies who are deemed to be representative of Architects in accordance with a scheme to be prepared by the ARB and approved by the Privy Council. The appointed members will represent consumer and public interests and will be appointed by the Privy Council. The innovation is that the majority of the members (eight) will be lay members and they will not be Architects. The profession is therefore no longer self-regulating. This is unusual, as in most professions the governing or disciplinary body is constituted of members of the profession itself. The aim of the reforms would seem to be to strike a balance between the interests of Architects generally and those of the general public.

This section also abolishes the Board of Architectural Education, the Admission Committee and the Discipline Committee, which were established under the 1931 Act. The powers and duties of those bodies are conferred upon the ARB (subs. (1)), which is also given power to establish other committees (subs. (3)(2C)), including specifically a Professional Conduct Committee (subs. (3)(2B)). The constitution and regulation of the Professional Conduct Committee is set out in the new 1931 Schedule (see clauses 11–15). The ARB is not expected to spawn several new large or expensive committees. Though Members of any additional committees need not be members of the ARB, the majority must be ARB members (cl. 17 of the new First Schedule and the ARB can only discharge its statutory functions through its own members (cl. 18) (see *Hansard*, H.L. Vol. 571, col. 45). This aim should be ensured by the reduction of members from ARCUK's 73 to ARB's 15 and ensure a minimalist organisation.

**Registrar and staff**

**119.** For section 4 of the 1931 Act substitute—

**"The Registrar**
4.
—(1) The Board shall appoint a person to be known as the Registrar of Architects.
(2) The Board shall determine the period for which, and the terms on which, the Registrar is appointed.
(3) The Registrar shall have the functions provided by or by virtue of this Act and any other functions which the Board directs.
(4) The Board may, in addition to paying to the Registrar a salary or fees—
  (a) pay pensions to or in respect of him or make contributions to the payment of such pensions; and
  (b) pay him allowances, expenses and gratuities.

**Staff**
4A.—(1) The Board may appoint staff.
(2) The Board shall determine the period for which, and the terms on which, its staff are appointed.
(3) Staff appointed by the Board shall have the duties which the Board directs.
(4) The Board may, in addition to paying salaries to its staff—
  (a) pay pensions to or in respect of them or make contributions to the payment of such pensions; and
  (b) pay them allowances, expenses and gratuities.".

DEFINITIONS
  "Board; the": s.118(1) and Sched. 2, Pt. II, para. 2(2).
  "Registrar of Architects": s.119 (new s.4(1) as inserted in the 1931 Act).
  "Registrar; the": Sched. 2, Pt. II, para. 2(b) and s.119.

GENERAL NOTE
  This section creates a new post of Registrar of Architects, who shall be appointed and paid by the ARB and whose function shall be to exercise the responsibilities set out in ss.120 and 121 of the Act, together with such other functions as the ARB may decide. The ARB also has power to appoint other paid staff for such periods and to carry out such duties as the ARB may decide.

*Registration and discipline*

**Registration**

**120.**—(1) Before section 6 of the 1931 Act insert—

**"The Register**
5A.—(1) The Registrar shall maintain the Register of Architects in which there shall be entered the name of every person entitled to be registered under this Act.
(2) The Register shall show the regular business address of each registered person.
(3) The Registrar shall make any necessary alterations to the Register and, in particular, shall remove from the Register the name of any registered person who has died or has applied in the prescribed manner requesting the removal of his name.
(4) The Board shall publish annually the current version of the Register and a copy of the most recently published version of the Register

shall be provided to any person who requests one on payment of a reasonable charge determined by the Board.

(5) A copy of the Register purporting to be published by the Board shall be evidence (and, in Scotland, sufficient evidence) of any matter mentioned in it.

(6) A certificate purporting to be signed by the Registrar which states that a person—

(a) is registered;
(b) is not registered;
(c) was registered on a specified date or during a specified period;
(d) was not registered on a specified date or during a specified period; or
(e) has never been registered,

shall be evidence (and, in Scotland, sufficient evidence) of any matter stated.".

(2) For section 6 of the 1931 Act substitute—

**"Entitlement to registration**

6.—(1) A person who has applied to the Registrar in the prescribed manner for registration in pursuance of this section is entitled to be registered if—

(a) he holds such qualifications and has gained such practical experience as may be prescribed; or
(b) he has a standard of competence which, in the opinion of the Board, is equivalent to that demonstrated by satisfying paragraph (a).

(2) The Board may require a person who applies for registration on the ground that he satisfies subsection (1)(b) to pass a prescribed examination in architecture.

(3) Before prescribing—

(a) qualifications or practical experience for the purposes of subsection (1)(a); or
(b) any examination for the purposes of subsection (2),

the Board shall consult the bodies representative of architects which are incorporated by royal charter and such other professional and educational bodies as it thinks appropriate.

(4) The Board may require—

(a) an applicant for registration in pursuance of this section; and
(b) a candidate for any examination under subsection (2),

to pay a fee of a prescribed amount.

(5) The Board may by rules prescribe the information and evidence to be furnished to the Registrar in connection with an application for registration in pursuance of this section.

(6) Where a person has duly applied for registration in pursuance of this section—

(a) if the Registrar is satisfied that the person is entitled to be registered, he shall enter his name in the Register; but
(b) if the Registrar is not so satisfied, he shall refer the application to the Board.

(7) The Registrar shall not consider an application for registration in pursuance of this section in any case in which it is inappropriate for him to do so (for instance because he is in any way connected with the applicant) but in such a case he shall refer the application to the Board.

(8) Where a person's application is referred to the Board under subsection (6) or (7), the Board shall direct the Registrar to enter the person's name in the Register if the Board is satisfied that the person is entitled to be registered.

(9) The Registrar shall serve on an applicant for registration in pursuance of this section written notice of the decision on his application—

    (a) where the application is made on the ground that he satisfies subsection (1)(a), within three months of his application being duly made; and

    (b) where the application is made on the ground that he satisfies subsection (1)(b), within six months of his application being duly made.".

(3) After section 6A of the 1931 Act insert—

### "Retention of name in Register

6B.—(1) The Board may require a registered person to pay a fee (in this section referred to as a "retention fee") of a prescribed amount if he wishes his name to be retained in the Register in any calendar year after that in which it was entered.

(2) Where, after the Registrar has sent a registered person who is liable to pay a retention fee a written demand for the payment of the fee, the person fails to pay the fee within the prescribed period, the Registrar may remove the person's name from the Register.

(3) Where a person whose name has been removed from the Register under subsection (2) pays the retention fee, together with any further prescribed fee, before the end of the calendar year for which the retention fee is payable or such longer period as the Board may allow—

    (a) his name shall be re-entered in the Register (without his having to make an application under section 6 or 6A); and

    (b) if the Board so directs, it shall be treated as having been re-entered on the date on which it was removed.

### Registration: additional requirements

6C.—(1) Where the Board is not satisfied that a person who—

    (a) applies for registration in pursuance of section 6 or 6A;

    (b) wishes his name to be retained or re-entered in the Register under section 6B; or

    (c) applies for his name to be re-entered in the Register under section 7ZD,

has gained such recent practical experience as rules made by the Board require a person to have gained before he is entitled to have his name entered, retained or re-entered in the Register, his name shall not be so entered or re-entered, or shall be removed, unless he satisfies the Board of his competence to practise.

(2) Where the Board decides that the name of a person to whom paragraph (b) of subsection (1) applies is by virtue of that subsection to be removed from, or not to be re-entered in, the Register, the Registrar shall serve on him written notice of the decision within the prescribed period after the date of the decision.".

DEFINITIONS

    "Board; the": Sched. 2, Pt. II, para. 2(2) and s.118(1).

    "Register of Architects": s.120(1) (new s.5A(1) as inserted into the 1931 Act).

    "Register; the": Sched. 2, Pt. II, para. 2(5) and s.120(1) (new s.5A(1) as inserted into the 1931 Act).

    "registered person": Sched. 2, pt. II, para. 2(3) and s.2 of the 1931 Act.

    "retention fee": subs.(3) (new s.6B(1) as inserted into the 1931 Act).

GENERAL NOTE

    This section adds a new s.5A to the 1931 Act and requires the Registrar of Architects to maintain a Register of Architects, containing the name of every person entitled to be registered and showing the regular business address of each such registered person. The Registrar of Architects is required to make the necessary alterations to the Register in order to keep it up-to-date and also to publish it annually and provide it to anyone requiring a copy, on payment of a reasonable fee which shall be determined by the ARB. A copy of the Register or a Certificate extracted from the Register and purporting to be signed by the Registrar of Architects shall be evidence (Evidence Act 1845 (c. 113), s.1) (or in Scotland, sufficient evidence).

*Subs. (2)*

A new s.6 of the 1931 Act is added and sets out the requirements for registration. An Architect is entitled to be registered, providing he holds such qualifications and practical experience as the ARB shall prescribe, or has satisfied the ARB that he has achieved an equivalent standard of competence. The requirements for either any examination or any alternative qualification will be set by the ARB after consultation with relevant professional and educational bodies. In this context, the Board must now consult the chartered bodies, that is to say the Royal Institute of British Architects and its equivalents in Scotland and Northern Ireland, but may also consult such other professional and educational bodies as it thinks appropriate.

Power is also given to the ARB under a new s.6(4) of the 1931 Act to require an applicant for registration or for examination to pay fees and to provide the information and evidence required in connection with the application for registration. The Registrar himself is entitled to enter the applicant's name on the Register (subs. (6)(a)), if he is properly satisfied that the person is entitled to be registered but otherwise shall refer the application to the ARB (subs. (6)(b)). The Registrar must do so if he is in any way connected with the applicant (subs. 7). All decisions on applications must be made within three months of the application (subs. (9)(a)) and shall be notified to the applicant, save where the applicant is not applying on the grounds of established qualifications and practical experience, when the period shall be six months (subs. 9(b)).

*Subs. (3)*

This sub-section provides a new s.6B to the 1931 Act. Under new 6B(1) a retention fee may be annually charged to any registered person who wishes to retain his name on the Register and provision is made for demands for payment of such fee (s.6B(2)) and for the removal of a registered person's name for failure to pay.

## Discipline

**121.** For section 7 of the 1931 Act substitute—

### "Unacceptable professional conduct and serious professional incompetence

7.—(1) Where an allegation is made that a registered person is guilty of—

(a) unacceptable professional conduct (that is, conduct which falls short of the standard required of a registered person); or

(b) serious professional incompetence,

or it appears to the Registrar that a registered person may be so guilty, the case shall be investigated by persons appointed in accordance with rules made by the Board.

(2) Where persons investigating a case under subsection (1) find that a registered person has a case to answer they shall report their finding to the Professional Conduct Committee.

(3) Where the Professional Conduct Committee receives a report under subsection (2) in relation to a registered person, the Committee shall consider whether he is guilty of unacceptable professional conduct or serious professional incompetence.

(4) Before considering whether a registered person is guilty of unacceptable professional conduct or serious professional incompetence the Professional Conduct Committee shall—

(a) serve on him written notice outlining the case against him; and

(b) give him the opportunity to appear before the Committee to argue his case.

(5) At any such hearing the registered person is entitled to be legally represented.

(6) The Board may make rules as to the procedure to be followed by the Professional Conduct Committee in any proceedings under this section.

(7) If the Board does not make rules for the appointment of persons to investigate whether registered persons have been guilty of unacceptable professional conduct or serious professional incompetence, the Professional Conduct Committee shall consider such questions without any prior investigation.

## Disciplinary orders

7ZA.—(1) The Professional Conduct Committee may make a disciplinary order in relation to a registered person if—

(a) it is satisfied, after considering his case, that he is guilty of unacceptable professional conduct or serious professional incompetence; or

(b) he has been convicted of a criminal offence other than an offence which has no material relevance to his fitness to practise as an architect.

(2) In this Act "disciplinary order" means—

(a) a reprimand;

(b) a penalty order;

(c) a suspension order; or

(d) an erasure order.

(3) Where the Professional Conduct Committee makes a disciplinary order in relation to a person, the Registrar shall serve written notice of the order on the person as soon as is reasonably practicable.

(4) The Professional Conduct Committee shall, at appropriate intervals and in such manner as it considers appropriate, publish—

(a) the names of persons whom it has found guilty of unacceptable professional conduct or serious professional incompetence or in relation to whom it has made a disciplinary order under subsection (1)(b); and

(b) in the case of each person a description of the conduct, incompetence or offence concerned and the nature of any disciplinary order made.

(5) Where, after considering the case of a registered person, the Professional Conduct Committee is not satisfied that he is guilty of unacceptable professional conduct or serious professional incompetence, it shall, if he so requests, publish a statement of that fact in such manner as it considers appropriate.

## Penalty orders

7ZB.—(1) Where a penalty order is made in relation to a registered person, he shall pay to the Board the sum specified in the order.

(2) A penalty order may not specify a sum exceeding the amount which, at the relevant time, is the amount specified as level 4 on the standard scale of fines for summary offences.

In this subsection "the relevant time" means—

(a) in a case within subsection (1)(a) of section 7ZA, the time of the conduct or incompetence of which the registered person is found guilty; and

(b) in a case within subsection (1)(b) of that section, the time when he committed the criminal offence of which he has been convicted.

(3) A penalty order shall specify the period within which the sum specified in it is to be paid.

(4) If the person in relation to whom a penalty order is made does not pay the sum specified in the order within the period so specified, the Professional Conduct Committee may make a suspension order or an erasure order in relation to him.

(5) The Board shall pay into the Consolidated Fund any sum paid under a penalty order.

### Suspension orders

7ZC. Where a suspension order is made in relation to a registered person, the Registrar shall remove his name from the Register but shall re-enter it in the Register at the end of such period not exceeding two years as is specified in the order.

### Erasure orders

7ZD.—(1) Where an erasure order is made in relation to a registered person, the Registrar shall remove his name from the Register and it shall not be re-entered in the Register unless the Board so directs.

(2) No application shall be made for the name of a person in relation to whom an erasure order has been made to be re-entered in the Register—

(a) before the end of the period of two years beginning with the date of the erasure order or such longer period specified in the erasure order as the Professional Conduct Committee considers appropriate in a particular case; or

(b) where he has made a previous application for his name to be re-entered in the Register, before the end of the prescribed period beginning with the date of the decision of the Board on that application.

(3) The Registrar shall serve on a person who applies for his name to be re-entered in the Register under this section written notice of the decision on his application within the prescribed period after the date of the decision.

(4) The Board may require a person whose name is re-entered in the Register under this section to pay a fee of a prescribed amount.".

DEFINITIONS

"Professional Conduct Committee": s.118(3) (new 2B as inserted into the 1931 Act).
"relevant time; the": s.121 (new s.7ZB(2) as inserted into the 1931 Act).

GENERAL NOTE

This section replaces s.7 to the 1931 Act. The powers and obligations of the new Professional Conduct Committee are more extensive than those of the old Discipline Committee which it replaces.

Whereas under the previous law a registered person was liable to be removed from the Register if he had been guilty of disgraceful conduct, the new provisions in this section provide a different basis for disciplinary action which is defined as "unacceptable professional conduct" or "serious professional incompetence".

The provision in old s.7 of the 1931 Act which subjected a registered person to removal from the Register if he had been convicted of a criminal offence is modified. Only those criminal offences which have a material relevance to his fitness to practice as an architect will now be taken into account (new s.7ZA(1)(b)). Concern that professional incompetence alone might lead to some Architects being unjustly penalised, led to a late amendment to the Act requiring that the professional incompetence must be serious. Judicial interpretation of this word may give rise to problems, since it is likely to be wholly a matter of subjective opinion.

The Registrar of Architects is of his own volition entitled to refer a registered person for investigation (new s.7(1)) and, if it is found that a registered Architect has a case to answer, the Professional Conduct Committee must consider the issue. It should be noted that the new s.7(3) requires the Professional Conduct Committee to consider any case where there has been an allegation of either of the two kinds of offences and, since the Committee has no option but to pursue the matter, this may well lead to an increase in its administrative activities and may impair its efficiency.

The Professional Conduct Committee will have a wide range of penalties which it may impose if it is satisfied that a registered person is guilty. The old s.7 only provided for the removal from the Register of a registered person but the Professional Conduct Committee now has discretionary power to make a disciplinary order (s.7ZA(2)) which may be either a reprimand or may impose financial penalties (s.7ZB(5)) or may impose suspension (s.72C) or erasure from the Register of Architects (s.7ZD). The period of suspension which may be imposed by the Professional Conduct Committee may not exceed a period of two years, after which the Registrar must reinstate the architect (s.7ZC) whereas the 1931 Act provided only that there was a discretionary limit upon any period of disqualification from registration. This represents an extension of the equivalent powers provided under the 1931 Act, which were limited to either suspension or erasure. The Professional Conduct Committee is also entitled to publish the names of persons against whom it has made a disciplinary order (s.7ZA(4)), together with a description of the person's conduct giving rise to the offence and the nature of the disciplinary order that may be made. If a person is not found guilty of a disciplinary offence, he may require a statement to be published to that purpose (s.7ZA(5)).

## Code of practice

**122.** After section 7ZD of the 1931 Act insert—

"**Code of practice**
    7ZE.—(1) The Board shall issue a code laying down standards of professional conduct and practice expected of registered persons.
    (2) The Board shall keep the code under review and vary its provisions whenever it considers it appropriate to do so.
    (3) Before issuing or varying the code, the Board shall—
      (a) consult such professional bodies and such other persons with an interest in architecture as it considers appropriate; and
      (b) publish in such manner as it considers appropriate notice that it proposes to issue or vary the code, stating where copies of the proposals can be obtained.
    (4) Failure by a registered person to comply with the provisions of the code—
      (a) shall not be taken of itself to constitute unacceptable professional conduct or serious professional incompetence on his part; but
      (b) shall be taken into account in any proceedings against him under section 7.
    (5) The Board shall provide a copy of the code to any person who requests one on payment of a reasonable charge determined by the Board (and may provide a copy free of charge whenever it considers appropriate).".

GENERAL NOTE
    This section which inserts s.7ZE into the 1931 Act creates a new statutory obligation which is imposed upon the ARB to lay down a code of professional conduct and practice, setting the standards to be expected of registered persons. The code will be kept under continuous review and will be produced after consultation with such professional bodies and such other persons with an interest in architecture as it considers appropriate (s.7ZE(3)). The object of the code appears to be to provide guidelines by which registered persons may avoid unacceptable acts which may lead to disciplinary proceedings under the new s.7 disciplinary provisions. Copies of the code will be available upon request.

### *Miscellaneous*

## Offence of practising while not registered

**123.**—(1) In section 1 (prohibition on practising or carrying on business under title of architect by person who is not registered) of the Architects Registration Act 1938 ("the 1938 Act"), after subsection (1) insert—
    "(1A) In this Act (and in section 17 of the principal Act) "business" includes any undertaking which is carried on for gain or reward or in the course of which services are provided otherwise than free of charge.".
    (2) In section 3 of the 1938 Act (offence of practising while not registered), for the words from "to a fine" to "therefor:" substitute "to a fine not exceeding level 4 on the standard scale:".
    (3) Re-number that section as subsection (1) of that section and after that subsection as so renumbered insert—
    "(2) In relation to an offence under subsection (1)—
      (a) section 127(1) of the Magistrates' Courts Act 1980 (information to be laid within six months of offence);

> (b) Article 19(1) of the Magistrates' Courts (Northern Ireland) Order 1981 (complaint to be made within that time); and
> (c) section 136(1) of the Criminal Procedure (Scotland) Act 1995 (proceedings to be commenced within that time),

shall have effect as if for the references in them to six months there were substituted references to two years.".

(4) Re-number section 17 of the 1931 Act (defence for certain bodies corporate, firms and partnerships) as subsection (1) of that section and after that subsection as so renumbered insert—

> "(2) The Board may by rules provide that subsection (1) shall not apply in relation to a body corporate, firm or partnership unless it has provided to the Board such information necessary for determining whether that subsection applies as may be prescribed.".

DEFINITIONS
"Board; the": Sched. 2, Pt. II, para. 2(2) and s.118(1).

GENERAL NOTE
This clarifies the offence of practising whilst not registered, which was introduced by s.1 of the Architects Registration Act 1938. It is now confirmed that the offence arises also when practising or carrying on the business of an architect under any name, style or title containing the word "architect". As a consequence, since any person using the title "architect" has to be registered, the general public should not be misled by those who might seek to offer themselves as architects in any commercial venture or in any undertaking where architectural services are provided for a consideration and are not free. The maximum penalty for practising whilst not registered is now applicable in Northern Ireland upon the same basis as for the rest of the U.K. The offence is penalised by a fine not exceeding level 4 on the standard scale (currently £2,500, s.143 of the Magistrates' Courts Act 1980 as amended).

### The Education Fund

**124.**—(1) No fees received under the 1931 Act shall be credited to the Architects' Registration Council Education Fund ("the Fund") constituted under the Architects Registration (Amendment) Act 1969 ("the 1969 Act").

(2) The Board may transfer the assets of the Fund to such person and on such terms as may be approved by the Secretary of State.

(3) A person to whom the assets of the Fund are transferred under subsection (2) shall apply the assets, and all income arising from the assets, for the purposes authorised in subsection (4) of section 1 of the 1969 Act (assuming for this purpose that the reference in that subsection to the Council were a reference to the person to whom the assets of the Fund are transferred).

DEFINITIONS
"Board; the": Sched. 2, Pt. II, para. 2(2) and s.118(1).
"Fund; the": ss.(1).

GENERAL NOTE
This provides for the cessation of income to the old Architects Registration Council Education Fund and makes arrangements for it to be wound up and empowers the ARB to transfer the assets of the Fund to such person on such terms as may be approved by the Secretary of State.

### Supplementary

**125.**—(1) The amendments made by Part II of Schedule 2, and the transitional provisions and savings in Part III of that Schedule, shall have effect.

(2) In this Part—

> "the 1931 Act" means the Architects (Registration) Act 1931,
> "the 1938 Act" means the Architects Registration Act 1938, and
> "the 1969 Act" means the Architects Registration (Amendment) Act 1969.

(3) In this Part "the Fund" means the Architects' Registration Council Education Fund.

(4) The 1931 Act, the 1938 Act and this Part may be cited together as the Architects Acts 1931 to 1996.

GENERAL NOTE

This brings into effect the new First Schedule to the 1931 Act and the detailed and consequential amendments required to the 1931 and 1938 Acts and other relevant enactments.

*Subs. (1)*

This subsection brings into effect Pt. I of Sched. 2 to the Act which sets out a replacement first Schedule to the 1931 Act. Part I of this new first Schedule contains the provisions for the constitution of the new ARB, the appointment of its members, its chairmen and their terms of office as well as the filling of casual vacancies on the ARB and its procedures. Part II sets out the provisions governing the appointment of members of the Professional Conduct Committee and that Committee's procedures. Part IV gives power to the Secretary of State after consultation with the ARB and any other persons or bodies which he considers appropriate to amend these provisions though such amendments are subject to annulment by resolution of either House of Parliament.

PART IV

GRANTS &C. FOR REGENERATION, DEVELOPMENT AND RELOCATION

INTRODUCTION

This Part contains two discrete elements: that relating to the single regeneration budget, and that relating to relocation grants.

*Single Regeneration Budget*

The single regeneration budget (SRB) was introduced in April 1994, to combine 20 previously separate programmes, ranging from housing schemes such as Estate Action, through the Urban Programme, to employment schemes such as Business Start-Up and TEC (Training and Enterprise Councils) Challenge. SRB "aims to promote sustainable regeneration, economic development and competitiveness at local level": Environment Committee, First Report, Single Regeneration Budget, Vol. II Memorandum by the Department of Environment, para. 1.

The SRB has built on the experience of City Challenge (which involved urban areas competing for funds) and bids have likewise been allocated on the basis of competitive bidding. During the first round of bids, 469 applications were received of which 201 were successful. Although a budget of £1.4 billion was made available for the year 1995/96, to be used over a timescale of from one to seven years, a large part of it was already committed to the existing projects; accordingly, only £125 million was available for new projects during the 1995–96 first round of bidding. Further bidding took place during 1995 for the second round, for which a further £40 million was made available, and the SRB has now entered into its third round.

Given the wide range of existing funding schemes from which the SRB was drawn, with five different government departments involved, the Government decided that it was more sensible to have one single statutory framework (*per* Lord Lucas (Government Whip), *Hansard*, H.L., Second Reading, February 20, 1996, col. 1029). Sections 126 to 129 constitute this framework, although it may be noted that the SRB is not directly referred to in the legislation, which is drawn broadly enough to be applied to future variations.

*Relocation Grant*

Although major slum clearance programmes are now relatively few, where they do take place they are hugely disruptive of local communities. The new relocation grant, which authorities may introduce in clearance areas, *if* they have adequate resources, "will help people whose homes are in clearance areas and who wish to acquire a replacement home in the same local area. .... This grant will help to keep local communities together by assisting people. It will help to bridge the gap between the cost of a replacement home in the locality and the amount of money which the applicant can reasonably afford, taking into account any compensation which he may receive for the loss of his home" (*per* Lord Ferrers (Minister for the Environment and Countryside), Second Reading, *Hansard*, H.L., February 20, 1996, Vol. 569, cols. 981, 982).

The scheme is based on a pilot project conducted by the DoE and Birmingham City Council in the South Saltley area of Birmingham: The future of Private Housing Renewal Programmes, Explanatory Paper linked to the Housing White Paper, DoE, para. 7.1.

*Financial assistance for regeneration and development*

## Power of Secretary of State to give financial assistance for regeneration and development

**126.**—(1) The Secretary of State may, with the consent of the Treasury, give financial assistance to any person in respect of expenditure incurred in connection with activities which contribute to the regeneration or development of an area.

(2) Activities which contribute to the regeneration or development of an area include, in particular—

(a) securing that land and buildings are brought into effective use;

(b) contributing to, or encouraging, economic development;

(c) creating an attractive and safe environment;

(d) preventing crime or reducing the fear of crime;

(e) providing or improving housing or social and recreational facilities, for the purpose of encouraging people to live or work in the area or of benefiting people who live there;

(f) providing employment for local people;

(g) providing or improving training, educational facilities or health services for local people;

(h) assisting local people to make use of opportunities for education, training or employment;

(i) benefiting local people who have special needs because of disability or because of their sex or the racial group to which they belong.

(3) In subsection (2)—

"local people", in relation to an area, means people who live or work in the area; and

"racial group" has the same meaning as in the Race Relations Act 1976.

DEFINITIONS
"financial assistance": s.127.

GENERAL NOTE
See notes to Introduction, above.

*Subs. (1)*

This subsection contains the broad power for the Secretary of State to give financial assistance (as defined in s.128, below) in connection with activities which contribute to the regeneration or development of an area. The financial assistance may be given to "any person". Thus it is not limited to local authorities: "It could be a person; it could be a company; it could be a non-statutory body" (*per* Lord Ferrers (Minister for the Environment and Countryside), Committee, *Hansard*, H.L., April 1, 1996, Vol. 571, col. 102). Although in the first round of bidding for the Single Regeneration Budget, local authorities were involved in 85 per cent of the bids, and the lead partner in just over half, Training and Enterprise Councils (TECs) also play an important role, being the lead bidder in just under a quarter of bids: Environment Committee, First Report, Single Regeneration Budget, Vol. II, Memorandum by the Department of Environment, para. 15.

*Subs. (2)*

The activities for which assistance may be given is not confined to those listed. They are in any event broadly framed: "We have tried deliberately to propose broad categories of activities so as to ensure that we can accommodate a very wide range of regeneration and development activities" (*per* Lord Ferrers (Minister for the Environment and Countryside), Committee, *Hansard*, H.L., April 1, 1996, Vol. 571, col. 90).

*Subs. (3)*

"Racial group" means "a group of persons defined by reference to colour, race, nationality or ethnic or national origins": Race Relations Act 1976 (c. 74), s.3(1). This has been broadly interpreted to include Sikhs (*Mandla v. Lee* [1983] 2 A.C. 548, H.L.) and gypsies (*Commission for Racial Equality v. Dutton* [1989] 1 All E.R. 306, C.A.) but does not include Rastafarians (*Crown Suppliers (PSA) v. Dawkins* [1993] I.R.L.R. 284, C.A.).

### Regeneration and development: forms of assistance

**127.**—(1) Financial assistance under section 126 (powers of Secretary of State to give financial assistance) may be given in any form.

(2) Assistance may, in particular, be given by way of—

(a) grants,

(b) loans,

(c) guarantees, or

(d) incurring expenditure for the benefit of the person assisted.

(3) The Secretary of State must not, in giving financial assistance under section 126, purchase loan or share capital in a company.

GENERAL NOTE

This section prescribes the forms in which financial assistance may be given by the Secretary of State. Assistance under the Single Regeneration Budget (SRB) has been provided thus far in the form of grants, but under subs. (2) financial assistance may also take the form of loans, guarantees and the incurring of expenditure, but not (subs. (3)) the purchase of loan or share capital in a company. Some of the schemes which were brought into the SRB had been funded by way of credit approvals to local authorities (under Pt. IV of the Local Government and Housing Act 1989 (c. 42)), but the Government has specifically excluded this form of assistance for the SRB, preferring "a form of support that provided maximum flexibility and was of benefit to everyone", and which could fund revenue as well as capital projects (*per* Lord Ferrers (Minister for the Environment and Countryside), Committee, *Hansard*, H.L., April 1, 1996, Vol. 571, col. 106).

### Regeneration and development: terms on which assistance is given

**128.**—(1) Financial assistance under section 126 may be given on such terms as the Secretary of State, with the consent of the Treasury, considers appropriate.

(2) The terms may, in particular, include provision as to—

(a) circumstances in which the assistance is to be repaid, or otherwise made good, to the Secretary of State, and the manner in which that is to be done; or

(b) circumstances in which the Secretary of State is entitled to recover the proceeds or part of the proceeds of any disposal of land or buildings in respect of which assistance was provided.

(3) The person receiving assistance must comply with the terms on which it is given, and compliance may be enforced by the Secretary of State.

DEFINITIONS

"financial assistance": s.127.

GENERAL NOTE

As with all Government funding, it may be given on terms which may be enforced by the Secretary of State.

### Regeneration and development: consequential amendment

**129.** In section 175(2)(b) of the Leasehold Reform, Housing and Urban Development Act 1993, for the words from "sections 27 to 29" to the end, substitute "sections 126 to 128 of the Housing Grants, Construction and Regeneration Act 1996 (financial assistance for regeneration and development)".

GENERAL NOTE

The Urban Regeneration Agency (known as English Partnerships) was created by the Leasehold Reform, Housing and Urban Development Act 1993 (c. 28). By s.175 of that Act, the agency may be appointed to act as agent for the Secretary of State for certain purposes. These included Urban Development Grant (UDG), one of the constituent elements of the SRB, under s.27 of the Housing and Planning Act 1986 (c. 63). As the provisions relating to UDG are now being repealed and superseded (see Sched. 3, Pt. III), this section makes a consequential amendment to the 1993 Act which permits the Secretary of State to appoint English Partnerships as agent for the purposes of the SRB. It should be noted, however, that at the present time the SRB has been administered by the Government Offices for the Regions.

## Regeneration and development: Welsh Development Agency

**130.**—(1) In the Welsh Development Agency Act 1975, after section 10 insert—

### "Financial assistance for regeneration and development

10A.—(1) The Secretary of State may appoint the Agency to act as his agent in connection with such of his functions mentioned in subsection (2) below as he may specify.

(2) The functions are—

(a) functions under sections 126 to 128 of the Housing Grants, Construction and Regeneration Act 1996 (financial assistance for regeneration and development), so far as they relate to—

(i) financial assistance which the Agency has power to give apart from this section; or

(ii) financial assistance given under that Act in pursuance of an agreement entered into by the Secretary of State for Wales before the coming into force of this section, or

(b) functions of the Secretary of State in relation to financial assistance given by the Secretary of State for Wales under sections 27 to 29 of the Housing and Planning Act 1986.

(3) An appointment under this section shall be on such terms as the Secretary of State, with the approval of the Treasury, may specify; and the Agency shall act under the appointment in accordance with those terms.

(4) The Agency's powers in relation to functions under an appointment under this section include the powers it has in relation to functions under subsection (3) of section 1 by virtue of subsections (6) and (7) of that section."

(2) In section 2(8) of that Act, after "declared that" insert ", except as provided by section 10A below,".

GENERAL NOTE

In England, the administration of the SRB has been devolved to the 10 Government Offices for the Regions, providing a single point of contact (although see notes to s.129, above). In Wales, the Secretary of State will have power to delegate the operation of the SRB to the Welsh Development Agency.

*Relocation grants in clearance areas*

## Resolution by local housing authority to pay relocation grants

**131.**—(1) Before deciding whether to declare an area to be a clearance area under section 289 of the Housing Act 1985, a local housing authority shall—

(a) consider whether their resources are sufficient for the purpose of carrying into effect a resolution declaring the power to pay relocation grants to be exercisable as regards that area; and

(b) in deciding that question, have regard to such guidance as may from time to time be given by the Secretary of State.

(2) Where a local housing authority decide that their resources are sufficient for that purpose, they shall—

(a) consider whether to pass such a resolution; and

(b) notify every person on whom notice is required to be served under subsection (2B)(a) of section 289 of the Housing Act 1985 that they are so considering and invite him to make representations.

(3) In deciding whether to pass such a resolution, a local housing authority shall—

(a) have regard to such guidance as may from time to time be given by the Secretary of State; and

(b) take account of any representations made by persons notified under subsection (2)(b).

(4) Where a local housing authority pass such a resolution, they shall transmit a copy of it to the Secretary of State at the same time as they transmit to him a copy of the resolution under section 289 of the Housing Act 1985.

(5) Subsections (2) to (4) of section 604A of the Housing Act 1985 (duty to consider guidance before taking enforcement action) shall apply in relation to guidance under subsection (1)(b) or (3)(a) as they apply in relation to guidance under subsection (1) of that section.

DEFINITIONS
"clearance area": H.A. 1985, s.289.
"local housing authority": s.140; H.A. 1985, s.1.

GENERAL NOTE
A clearance area is "an area which is to be cleared of all buildings ...": Housing Act 1985 (c. 68), s.289(1). By s.289(2) (as amended) a local authority must declare a clearance area if they are satisfied:

"(a) that the buildings in the area which are dwelling-houses or houses in multiple occupation or contain one or more flats (... referred to as 'residential buildings') are unfit for human habitation or are by reason of their bad arrangement, or the narrowness or bad arrangement of the streets, dangerous or injurious to the health of the inhabitants of the area, and

(b) that the other buildings, if any, in the area are for a like reason dangerous or injurious to the health of the inhabitants of the area and

in accordance with section 604A [of the Housing Act 1985] that the most satisfactory course of action is the demolition of all the buildings in the area."

Before deciding to declare such an area, the local housing authority must consider whether they have sufficient resources to pay relocation grants in the area: subs. (1)(a). This requirement to consider sufficiency of resources also arises prior to deciding whether to declare a clearance area at all (H.A. 1985, s.289(4)(b)). In that context, it has been held that the authority are not bound to consider specific figures, but that a general satisfaction may be sufficient: *Goddard v. Minister of Housing and Local Government* [1958] 1 W.L.R. 1151. In reaching the decision as to whether they have sufficient resources, authorities will have to have regard to the guidance issued by the Secretary of State (see further note to subs. (5) below).

*Subss. (2), (3)*
Having made the decision that resources are adequate, the authority must then consider whether to pass a resolution instituting a relocation grant scheme for the clearance area, and must consult prior to making this decision. Under s.289(2B)(a) of the 1985 Act, authorities are required to serve a notice on every person who has an interest in the building (whether as freeholder, lessee or mortgagee), and in the case of a residential building (as defined in s.289(2)(a), see above note), with everyone who has such an interest in any flat within the building. These people must also be consulted regarding the relocation grant scheme: subs. (2)(b).

Having considered the Secretary of State's Guidance and the results of the consultation exercise, the authority may then decide whether or not to implement a relocation grant scheme.

*Subs. (5)*
The Housing Act 1985, s.604A(2) permits the Secretary of State to give guidance generally or to different descriptions of authorities or to authorities in different areas. It also permits him to give guidance in particular in respect of financial and social considerations to be taken into account by authorities. Section 604A(3) and (4) require the draft guidance to be laid on the table in Parliament.

## Relocation grants: applications and payments

**132.**—(1) Where a local housing authority have passed a resolution declaring the power to pay relocation grants to be exercisable as regards a clearance area, they may pay such grants for the purpose of enabling qualifying persons to acquire qualifying dwellings (see section 133).

(2) No relocation grant shall be paid unless—

(a) an application for it is made to the authority by a qualifying person in accordance with the provisions of this section and is approved by them;

(b) the application is accompanied by a certificate falling within subsection (5) in respect of the qualifying dwelling to which the application relates; and

(c) such other conditions (whether as to the dwelling or the interest to be acquired or otherwise) as may be prescribed are fulfilled,

and regulations made under paragraph (c) may provide for particular questions arising under the regulations to be determined by the authority.

(3) An application for a relocation grant shall be in writing and shall specify the qualifying dwelling to which it relates and contain such particulars as may be prescribed.

(4) The Secretary of State may by regulations prescribe a form of application for a relocation grant and an application to which any such regulations apply shall not be validly made unless it is in the prescribed form.

(5) A certificate under this subsection certifies—

(a) that the applicant proposes to acquire an owner's interest in the qualifying dwelling to which the application relates; and

(b) that he, or a member of his family, intends to live in that dwelling as his (or that member's) only or main residence throughout the grant condition period.

(6) A relocation grant shall be paid in such manner and at such time as the authority may determine having regard to the purpose for which it is paid.

(7) Nothing in section 25 of the Local Government Act 1988 (consent required for provision of financial assistance) shall apply in relation to any exercise of the power to pay relocation grants.

DEFINITIONS

"clearance area": H.A. 1985, s.289.
"dwelling": s.140.
"local housing authority": s.140; H.A. 1985, s.1.
"member of family": s.140.
"owner's interest": s.140.
"qualifying dwelling": s.133(2).
"qualifying person": s.133(1).

GENERAL NOTE

*Subs. (1)*

Payment of relocation grants is permitted only to "qualifying persons", to enable them to purchase "qualifying dwellings". Both these terms are defined in s.133, see notes thereto.

*Subss. (2), (3), (4)*

All applications for a relocation grant must be made in writing by a "qualifying person" and be accompanied by the requisite certificate (see notes to subs. (5)). The Secretary of State may also prescribe other conditions for payment of a relocation grant, and these are likely to include conditions as to the size and physical state of the property (*per* Lord Lucas (Government Whip), Report, *Hansard*, H.L., April 22, 1996, Vol. 571, col. 1004). The application must specify the "qualifying dwelling", and the Secretary of State has reserved the power to prescribe the use of a particular application form.

*Subs. (5)*

The certificate required in the case of a relocation grant is the same as the "owner-occupation certificate" for a renovation grant, save that in all cases of a relocation grant the applicant certifies that he is proposing to acquire the interest, rather than that he has already acquired it. See further notes to s.7 ("owner's interest"); s.8 ("only or main residence") and s.98 ("member of the family").

*Subs. (6)*

The manner and timing of payment of the grant is at the discretion of the authority. It is likely that authorities will wish to make the payment at the time of completion of purchase of the qualifying dwelling. They may also make payments directly to the client account of the applicant's solicitors.

*Subs. (7)*

Under s.24 of the Local Government Act 1988 (c. 9), local authorities may provide financial assistance in connection with, *inter alia*, the acquisition of any property which is or is intended to be privately let as housing accommodation. Such assistance is subject to the condition in s.25 of the 1988 Act, that consent is required from the Secretary of State. In so far as relocation grants could be caught by this provision (*e.g.* where the new property is to be part let), the requirements of s.25 are disapplied.

## Relocation grants: qualifying persons and qualifying dwellings

**133.**—(1) A person is a qualifying person for the purposes of section 132 (relocation grants: applications and payments) if—

(a) an interest of his in a dwelling in the clearance area ("the original dwelling") has been, or is to be, acquired by the local housing authority under section 290 of the Housing Act 1985 or section 154 of the Town and Country Planning Act 1990;

(b) that interest on the acquisition date was greater than a tenancy for a year or from year to year; and

(c) the original dwelling was his only or main residence both on the declaration date and throughout the period of 12 months ending with the acquisition date.

(2) A dwelling is a qualifying dwelling for the purposes of section 132 if it is—

(a) in the clearance area; or

(b) in an area designated by the local housing authority as an area for the relocation of persons displaced by the clearance;

and any area so designated may be in or outside the authority's area.

(3) In making a designation under subsection (2) a local housing authority shall have regard to such guidance as may from time to time be given by the Secretary of State.

(4) Subsections (2) to (4) of section 604A of the Housing Act 1985 (duty to consider guidance before taking enforcement action) shall apply in relation to guidance under subsection (3) as they apply in relation to guidance under subsection (1) of that section.

(5) Any reference in the preceding provisions of this section to the clearance area includes a reference to any land surrounded by or adjoining the clearance area which has been, or is to be, acquired by the local housing authority under section 290 of the Housing Act 1985 or section 154 of the Town and Country Planning Act 1990.

(6) In this section—

"the acquisition date", in relation to an acquisition under section 290 of the Housing Act 1985, means the date of—

(a) the notice to treat under section 5 of the Compulsory Purchase Act 1965;

(b) the general vesting declaration under section 4 of the Compulsory Purchase (Vesting Declarations) Act 1981; or

(c) the agreement between the local housing authority and the applicant,

in pursuance of which the interest in the original dwelling was, or is to be, acquired by the authority;

"the acquisition date", in relation to an acquisition under section 154 of the Town and Country Planning Act 1990 (effect of valid blight notice), means the date mentioned in subsection (3) of that section;

"the declaration date" means the date on which the clearance area was declared by the authority.

DEFINITIONS
"clearance area": H.A. 1985, s.289.
"dwelling": s.140.
"local housing authority": s.140; H.A. 1985, s.1.


GENERAL NOTE
This section defines the two key qualifying concepts for relocation grants: "qualifying person" and "qualifying dwelling".


*Qualifying person*
A "qualifying person" must (subss. (1), (5), (6)):
(a) have an interest on the acquisition date (see below) which was greater than a tenancy for a year or from year to year (thus excluding periodic tenants and fixed term tenants of a year or less);
(b) in a dwelling (see s.139, below) that was his only or main residence (see notes to s.8, above) both on the date on which the clearance area was declared and throughout the period of 12 months ending with the acquisition date;
(c) in a clearance area (see notes to s.130, above) or land surrounded or adjoining a clearance area (see below);
(d) which has been or is to be acquired by the local housing authority under the Housing Act 1985, s.290 or the Town and Country Planning Act 1990, s.154.
The interest of the qualifying person may be acquired under either the Housing Act 1985, s.290 or the Town and Country Planning Act 1990 (c. 8), s.154. Under s.290, once a clearance area has been declared, the authority must proceed to "secure the clearance area ... by purchasing the land comprised in the area ...". The authority may also purchase land surrounded by the clearance area where it is reasonably necessary for the purpose of securing a cleared area of convenient shape and dimensions and adjoining land which is reasonably necessary for the satisfactory development or use of the cleared area: s.290(2). The land may be acquired compulsorily or by agreement: s.290(3). Where purchased by agreement, the acquisition date is the date of the agreement to purchase; where compulsorily, it is either the date of the notice to treat under the Compulsory Purchase Act 1965 (c. 56), s.5 or the general vesting declaration under the Compulsory Purchase (Vesting Declarations) Act 1981 (c. 66), s.4: subs. (6).
Where a local authority propose re-development, such as clearance, it may "blight" surrounding properties. In those circumstances the owner of the property may, under the Town and Country Planning Act 1990, s.154 serve a notice on the authority requiring them to purchase the property. The purchase then takes the form of a conventional compulsory purchase, from which the authority are not permitted to withdraw: s.154. In such a case, the acquisition date means two months after the service of the blight notice, unless the notice is appealed to the Lands Tribunal, in which case it is the date specified by the Lands Tribunal in its directions issued following rejection of the appeal: subs. (6), applying 1990 Act, s.154(3).


*"Qualifying dwelling"*
A qualifying dwelling must be either inside the clearance area itself or in an area designated by the authority: subs. (2). For these purposes, "clearance area" includes surrounded or adjoining land acquired under the Housing Act 1985, s.290(2) or the Town and Country Planning Act 1990, s.154: subs. (5). In deciding to designate areas outside the clearance area, authorities must have regard to guidance issued by the Secretary of State under the Housing Act 1985, s.604A: subss. (3), (4) (see notes to s.131(5), above).


## Relocation grants: amount

**134.**—(1) Subject to subsections (2) to (4), the amount of any relocation grant shall be such amount as the local housing authority may determine.
(2) The amount of any relocation grant shall not exceed such amount as may be prescribed.
(3) The amount of any relocation grant shall not exceed the difference between—

(a) the cost of acquiring the qualifying dwelling to which the application relates; and

(b) such part as may be prescribed of the amount which has been, or is to be, paid by the authority in respect of the acquisition of the applicant's interest in the original dwelling.

(4) If the financial resources of the applicant exceed the applicable amount, the amount of any grant which may be paid shall, in accordance with regulations, be reduced from what it would otherwise have been.

(5) For the purposes of subsection (3), the cost of acquiring the qualifying dwelling shall be taken to be whichever of the following is the lesser amount, namely—

(a) the actual cost (including reasonable incidental expenses) of acquiring the dwelling; and

(b) the amount which the authority considers to be the reasonable cost (including such expenses) of acquiring a comparable dwelling in the same area.

(6) Provision may be made by regulations—

(a) for the determination of the amount which is to be taken to be the financial resources of an applicant,

(b) for the determination of the applicable amount referred to in subsection (4), and

(c) as to circumstances in which the financial resources of an applicant are to be assumed (by reason of his receiving a prescribed benefit or otherwise) not to exceed the applicable amount.

(7) Regulations may, in particular—

(a) make provision for account to be taken of the income, assets, needs and outgoings not only of the applicant himself but also of his spouse, any person living with him or intending to live with him and any person on whom he is dependent or who is dependent on him;

(b) make provision for amounts specified in or determined under the regulations to be taken into account for particular purposes.

(8) Regulations may apply, subject to such modifications as may be prescribed by the regulations, any other statutory means-testing regime as it has effect from time to time.

(9) Regulations may make provision requiring any information or evidence needed for the determination of any matter under this section to be furnished by such person as may be prescribed.

(10) In this section—

"the original dwelling" has the same meaning as in section 133;

"regulations" means regulations made by the Secretary of State with the consent of the Treasury.

DEFINITIONS

"local housing authority": s.140; H.A. 1985, s.1.

"qualifying dwelling": s.133(2).

"relocation grant": s.132.

GENERAL NOTE

The amount of grant is to be determined by the authority (subs. (1)) but is subject to two limits:

(a) an amount prescribed by the Secretary of State (subs. (2)); and,

(b) the difference between the cost of acquiring the new dwelling and the prescribed part of the compensation paid to the applicant in respect of acquiring the original dwelling. This requires an applicant to put the compensation he receives for the loss of his old home towards the cost of buying the new one: subs. (3). The cost of acquiring the new dwelling may be limited to the amount that the authority consider to be the reasonable cost of acquiring the dwelling, if this is less than the actual cost: subs. (5).

Payment of grant is also subject to a means test to be carried out by comparison of financial resources and applicable amount, according to a formula or method to be dictated by regulations: subss. (4), (6)–(8).

### Relocation grants: condition for repayment on disposal

**135.**—(1) It is a condition of a relocation grant that, if an owner of the qualifying dwelling makes a relevant disposal (other than an exempt disposal) of the dwelling within the grant condition period, he shall repay to the local housing authority on demand the amount of the grant.

(2) A condition under this section is binding on any person who is for the time being an owner of the qualifying dwelling.

(3) Where the authority have the right to demand repayment of an amount as mentioned in subsection (1), they may—

(a)  if the case falls within subsection (4), or

. (b)  in any other case, with the consent of the Secretary of State,

determine not to demand payment or to demand a lesser amount.

(4) The cases referred to in subsection (3)(a) are where the authority are satisfied that the owner of the dwelling—

(a)  is elderly or infirm and is making the disposal with the intention—

(i) of going to live in a hospital, hospice, sheltered housing, residential care home or similar institution as his only or main residence, or

(ii) of moving to somewhere where care will be provided by any person; or

(b)  is making the disposal with the intention of going to live with and care for an elderly or infirm member of his family or his partner's family.

(5) The consent of the Secretary of State for the purposes of subsection (3)(b) may be given either generally or in relation to any one or more specified authorities or descriptions of authority or in relation to particular cases or descriptions of case.

(6) A condition under this section shall cease to be in force with respect to a dwelling if there is a relevant disposal of the dwelling that is an exempt disposal, other than—

(a)  a disposal within section 54(1)(a) (disposal to associates of person making disposal), or

(b)  a disposal within section 54(1)(b) (vesting under will or on intestacy) to a person who resided with the deceased in the dwelling as his only or main residence throughout the period of twelve months ending with the date of the deceased's death.

(7) Any disposal which—

(a)  by virtue of section 53 (meaning of relevant disposal), is a relevant disposal; or

(b)  by virtue of section 54 (meaning of exempt disposal), is an exempt disposal,

for the purposes of the provisions of Part I of this Act (relating to grant conditions) is also such a disposal for the purposes of this section.

DEFINITIONS
"grant condition period": s.140.
"local housing authority": s.140; H.A. 1985, s.1.
"owner": s.140.
"qualifying dwelling": s.133(2).
"relocation grant": s.131.

GENERAL NOTE
   This section introduces a grant condition similar to that under s.45, above, requiring repayment on a "relevant disposal", which is not otherwise "exempt". The condition applies during the grant condition period, *i.e.* five years from the date of purchase of the dwelling, or such other period as the Secretary of State may prescribe: s.140. See notes to ss.53 and 54 above as to relevant disposal and exempt disposal, which have the same meaning under this section: subs. (7).
   For the definition of "owner", see s.140 and notes to s.45, above.

*Subs. (2)*
Unlike under the equivalent s.45(3), the condition is not a local land charge, since the duty to repay takes effect as a charge on the premises: see s.138 below.

*Subss. (3), (4), (5)*
These subsections contain the only and limited discretion to not recover the grant, in the same terms as are contained in s.45(4), (5), see notes thereto.

*Subs. (6)*
Even though it will not cause repayment, the condition ceases when there is an exempt disposal, other than in the two classes identified, *i.e.* such other disposals keep the condition alive (but, because they are exempt, do not activate repayment).

## Relocation grants: conditions as to owner-occupation

**136.**—(1) It is a condition of a relocation grant that throughout the grant condition period the qualifying dwelling is occupied in accordance with the intention stated in the certificate under section 132(5)(b).

(2) It is also a condition of the grant that if at any time when that condition is in force the local housing authority serve notice on the owner of the qualifying dwelling requiring him to do so, he will within the period of 21 days beginning with the date on which the notice was served furnish to the authority a statement showing how that condition is being fulfilled.

(3) A condition under this section is binding on any person who is for the time being an owner of the dwelling.

(4) In the event of a breach of a condition under this section, the owner for the time being of the dwelling shall on demand repay to the local housing authority the amount of the grant, together with compound interest on that amount as from the beginning of the grant condition period, calculated at such reasonable rate as the authority may determine and with yearly rests.

(5) The local housing authority may determine not to make such a demand or to demand a lesser amount.

(6) Subsections (6) and (7) of section 135 apply for the purposes of this section as they apply for the purposes of that section.

DEFINITIONS
"dwelling": s.140.
"local housing authority": s.140; H.A. 1985, s.1.
"owner": s.140.
"qualifying dwelling": s.133(2).
"relocation grant": s.131.

GENERAL NOTE
This section introduces an "occupation condition" equivalent to that for owner-occupiers in receipt of renovation grant: see notes to s.48, above.

## Relocation grants: cessation of conditions on repayment of grant, &c.

**137.**—(1) If at any time while a condition under section 135 or 136 (a "grant condition") remains in force with respect to a qualifying dwelling—

(a) the owner of the dwelling to which the condition relates pays the amount of the grant to the local housing authority by whom the grant was made, or

(b) a mortgagee of the interest of the owner in that dwelling being a mortgagee entitled to exercise a power of sale, makes such a payment, or

(c) the local housing authority determine not to demand repayment on the breach of a grant condition, or

(d) the authority demand repayment in whole or in part on the breach of a grant condition and that demand is satisfied,

the grant condition and any other grant conditions shall cease to be in force with respect to that dwelling.

(2) An amount paid by a mortgagee under subsection (1)(b) shall be treated as part of the sums secured by the mortgage and may be discharged accordingly.

DEFINITIONS
   "local housing authority": s.140; H.A. 1985, s.1.
   "owner": s.140.
   "qualifying dwelling": s.133(2).

GENERAL NOTE
   This section permits an owner voluntarily to repay a grant in order to free himself from all of the conditions attached to it: see further notes to s.55, above.

### Relocation grants: liability to repay is a charge on dwelling

**138.**—(1) The liability that may arise under a condition under section 135, or under section 136(4), is a charge on the qualifying dwelling, taking effect as if it had been created by deed expressed to be by way of legal mortgage.

(2) The charge has priority immediately after any legal charge securing an amount—
   (a) advanced to the applicant by an approved lending institution for the purpose of enabling him to acquire the dwelling, or
   (b) further advanced to him by that institution;
but the local housing authority may at any time by written notice served on an approved lending institution postpone the charge taking effect by virtue of this section to a legal charge securing an amount advanced or further advanced to the applicant by that institution.

(3) A charge taking effect by virtue of this section is a land charge for the purposes of section 59 of the Land Registration Act 1925 notwithstanding subsection (5) of that section (exclusion of mortgages), and subsection (2) of that section applies accordingly with respect to its protection and realisation.

(4) A condition under section 135 or 136 does not, by virtue of its binding any person who is for the time being an owner of the dwelling, bind a person exercising rights under a charge having priority over the charge taking effect by virtue of this section, or a person deriving title under him.

(5) The approved lending institutions for the purposes of section 156 of the Housing Act 1985 (right to buy: liability to repay discount is a charge on premises) are also approved lending institutions for the purposes of this section.

DEFINITIONS
   "local housing authority": s.140; H.A. 1985, s.1.
   "qualifying dwelling": s.133(2).

GENERAL NOTE
   This section does not have an equivalent in Pt. I, Chap. I. It makes repayment liabilities arising under s.135 and s.136(4) a charge on the dwelling which has been purchased with the relocation grant. The charge is to take effect as if it had been created by deed expressed to be by way of mortgage, and it will have priority immediately following the priority of the mortgage with which the dwelling is itself purchased, or a further advance from the body which gave that initial mortgage (providing that the body is an approved lending institution within subs. (5)). A purchase effected with a loan by someone other than one of the bodies specified, will accordingly mean that the lender's charge on the property takes priority behind the repayment covenant.
   The mortgage is registrable as a land charge under the Land Registration Act 1925 (c. 21), s.59 and thus may be protected against subsequent dealings in the dwelling by entry of a notice or caution.

*Subs. (5)*
   Under the Housing Act 1985, s.156(4), the Housing Corporation, Housing for Wales, building societies, banks, trustee savings banks, insurance companies and friendly societies are all approved lending institutions. The Secretary of State also has power to specify other institutions and has done so in a number of statutory instruments listing institutions similar to those automatically approved. For an up-to-date list see the *Encyclopedia of Housing Law and Practice,* Vol. 1.

## Relocation grants: contributions by the Secretary of State

**139.**—(1) The Secretary of State may pay contributions to local housing authorities towards such expenditure incurred by them under section 132 (payment of relocation grants) as he may determine.

(2) The rate or rates of the contributions, the calculation of the expenditure to which they relate and the manner of their payment shall be such as may be determined by the Secretary of State.

(3) Any determination under subsection (1) or (2) may be made generally, or with respect to a particular local housing authority or description of authority, including a description framed by reference to authorities in a particular area.

(4) Contributions under this section shall be payable subject to such conditions as to repayment, and such conditions as to records, certificates, audit or otherwise, as the Secretary of State may impose.

DEFINITIONS
"local housing authority": s.140; H.A. 1985, s.1.

GENERAL NOTE
This section provides for the subsidy to be provided by the Secretary of State, which may be general, or specific to particular authorities or categories of authorities, including by reference to parts of the country. The government have indicated that they expect to pay subsidy at the same rate as for slum clearance subsidy, *i.e.* 60 per cent (see Annex J, to DoE Circular 6/90, as amended), *per* Lord Lucas (Government Whip), Committee, *Hansard*, H.L., April 1, 1996, Vol. 571, col. 116.

## Minor definitions relating to relocation grants

**140.**—(1) In sections 131 to 139 (provisions as to relocation grants)—
"dwelling" means a building or part of a building occupied or intended to be occupied as a separate dwelling, together with any yard, garden, outhouses and appurtenances belonging to it or usually enjoyed with it;
"grant condition period" means the period of five years, or such other period as the Secretary of State may by order specify, beginning with the date of the acquisition of the owner's interest in the qualifying dwelling;
"local housing authority" has the same meaning as in the Housing Act 1985;
"owner", in relation to a dwelling, means the person who—
(a) is for the time being entitled to receive from a lessee of the dwelling (or would be so entitled if the dwelling were let) a rent of not less than two-thirds of the net annual value of the dwelling; and
(b) is not himself liable as lessee of the dwelling, or of property which includes the dwelling, to pay such a rent to a superior landlord;
"owner's interest", in relation to any premises, means—
(a) an estate in fee simple absolute in possession, or
(b) a term of years absolute of which not less than five years remain unexpired at the date of the application,
whether held by the applicant alone or jointly with others;
"prescribed" means prescribed by regulations made by the Secretary of State;
"qualifying dwelling" has the meaning given by section 133(2);
"qualifying person" has the meaning given by section 133(1);
"relocation grant" means a grant under section 132.

(2) For the purposes of the definition of "owner" in subsection (1), the net annual value of a dwelling means the rent at which the dwelling might reasonably be expected to be let from year to year if the tenant undertook to pay all usual tenant's rates and taxes and to bear the cost of repair and insurance and the other expenses, if any, necessary to maintain the dwelling in a state to command that rent.

(3) Any dispute arising as to the net annual value of a dwelling shall be referred in writing for decision by the district valuer.

In this subsection "district valuer" has the same meaning as in the Housing Act 1985.

(4) Section 113 of the Housing Act 1985 (meaning of "members of a person's family") applies in determining whether a person is a member of another's family for the purposes of sections 132 and 135.

GENERAL NOTE

For the main definitions, see as follows:

Notes to s.1, above—dwelling, local housing authority.

Notes to s.7 above—owner's interest.

Notes to s.45 above—owner.

*Subs. (4)*

See notes to s.98, above.

PART V

MISCELLANEOUS AND GENERAL PROVISIONS

*Miscellaneous provisions*

### Existing housing grants: meaning of exempt disposal

**141.**—(1) Section 124 of the Local Government and Housing Act 1989 (relevant and exempt disposals for purposes of housing grants) is amended as follows.

(2) In subsection (3) (exempt disposals), for paragraph (c) substitute—

"(c) a disposal of the whole of the dwelling in pursuance of any such order as is mentioned in subsection (4A) below;".

(3) After subsection (4) insert—

"(4A) The orders referred to in subsection (3)(c) above are orders under—

(a) section 24 or 24A of the Matrimonial Causes Act 1973 (property adjustment orders or orders for the sale of property in connection with matrimonial proceedings),

(b) section 2 of the Inheritance (Provision for Family and Dependants) Act 1975 (orders as to financial provision to be made from estate),

(c) section 17 of the Matrimonial and Family Proceedings Act 1984 (property adjustment orders or orders for the sale of property after overseas divorce, &c.), or

(d) paragraph 1 of Schedule 1 to the Children Act 1989 (orders for financial relief against parents);".

GENERAL NOTE

This section makes an equivalent extension to the definition of "exempt disposal", to the existing grants regime under the Local Government and Housing Act 1989, as is made under s.54 above (see notes thereto) to overturn the decision in *R. v. Rushmoor B.C., ex p. Barrett* (1988) 20 H.L.R. 366, C.A., and also to add orders under the Matrimonial and Family Proceedings Act 1984 (c. 42) and the Children Act 1989 (c. 41).

**Home energy efficiency schemes**

**142.**—(1) In section 15 of the Social Security Act 1990 (grants for the improvement of energy efficiency in certain dwellings, &c.) for subsection (1) (power to make grants) substitute—

"(1) The Secretary of State may make or arrange for the making of grants—

(a) towards the cost of carrying out work for the purpose of—

(i) improving the thermal insulation of dwellings, or

(ii) otherwise reducing or preventing the wastage of energy in dwellings (whether in connection with space or water heating, lighting, the use of domestic appliances or otherwise), and

(b) where any such work is, or is to be, carried out, towards the cost of providing persons with advice on reducing or preventing the wastage of energy in dwellings;

but no grants shall be made under this section except in accordance with regulations made by the Secretary of State.".

(2) In subsection (10) of that section, after the definition of "functions", insert—

" "materials" includes space and water heating systems;".

GENERAL NOTE

This section makes minor amendments to the home energy grant scheme contained in the Social Security Act 1990 (c. 27), s.15, reflecting the fact that technology has moved on: Robert Jones (Minister for Construction, Planning and Energy Efficiency), *Hansard*, H.C., 11th sitting, Standing Committee F, June 20, 1996, col. 413. In particular, the scheme is extended to include grants for the reduction or prevention of wastage of energy in dwellings, not just through space and water heating but also through lighting, the use of domestic appliances or otherwise.

**Urban development corporations: pre-dissolution transfers**

**143.**—(1) After section 165A of the Local Government, Planning and Land Act 1980 insert—

**"Transfer of property, rights and liabilities to statutory bodies**

165B.—(1) Subject to this section, the Secretary of State may at any time by order transfer to a statutory body, upon such terms as he thinks fit, any property, rights or liabilities which—

(a) are for the time being vested in an urban development corporation, and

(b) are not proposed to be transferred under section 165 or 165A above.

(2) An order under this section may terminate—

(a) any appointment of the corporation under subsection (1) of section 177 of the Leasehold Reform, Housing and Urban Development Act 1993 (power of corporations to act as agents of the Urban Regeneration Agency); and

(b) any arrangements made by the corporation under subsection (2) of that section.

(3) An order under this section may—

(a) establish new bodies corporate to receive any property, rights or liabilities to be transferred by an order under this section;

(b) amend, repeal or otherwise modify any enactment for the purpose of enabling any body established under any enactment to receive such property, rights or liabilities.

(4) An order under this section—

(a) may contain such incidental, consequential, transitional or supplementary provision as the Secretary of State thinks necessary or expedient (including provisions amending, repealing or otherwise modifying any enactment); and

(b) shall be made by statutory instrument which shall be subject to annulment in pursuance of a resolution of either House of Parliament.

(5) Before making an order under this section, the Secretary of State shall consult each local authority in whose area all or part of the urban development area is situated.

(6) In this section—

"enactment" includes any instrument made under any enactment;

"statutory body" means any body established under this section or any other enactment.".

(2) In consequence of the above amendment, the Local Government, Planning and Land Act 1980 is amended as follows.

(3) In section 165(9) (meaning of local authority) for "sections 165A and 166" substitute "sections 165A to 166".

(4) In section 165A(1) (power of Secretary of State to transfer property &c. to himself) for paragraph (b) substitute—

"(b) are not proposed to be transferred under section 165 above or 165B below.".

(5) In section 166(5) (dissolution of corporations) after "section 165A" insert "or 165B".

GENERAL NOTE

This and the following two sections make provision for the transfer of property, rights or liabilities vested in an urban development corporation (this section), a housing action trust (s.144), or the Commission for New Towns (s.145), to a residuary body or bodies. In the case of urban development corporations and housing action trusts, the government intends to create a new body based on a reformed Commission for the New Towns, and in the final case it plans simply to reform that body: Robert Jones (Minister for Construction, Planning and Energy Efficiency), *Hansard*, H.C., 11th sitting, Standing Committee F, June 20, 1996, col. 415.

## Housing action trusts: orders for dissolution

**144.**—(1) Section 88 of the Housing Act 1988 (dissolution of housing action trusts) is amended as follows.

(2) In subsection (4) (contents of dissolution orders) after paragraph (a) insert—

"(aa) where it provides for any such disposal or transfer as is mentioned in subsection (2)(b) above, may contain provisions—

(i) establishing new bodies corporate to receive the disposal or transfer; or

(ii) amending, repealing or otherwise modifying any enactment for the purpose of enabling any body established under any enactment to receive the disposal or transfer;".

(3) In paragraph (b) of that subsection (supplementary and transitional provisions) for the words from "any enactment", where it first appears, to "order" substitute ", repealing or otherwise modifying any enactment".

(4) After that subsection insert—

"(5) In this section "enactment" includes any instrument made under any enactment.".

GENERAL NOTE
See notes to s.143 above.

## The Commission for the New Towns: orders for dissolution

**145.**—(1) In Schedule 9 to the New Towns Act 1981 (additional provisions as to the Commission for the New Towns) paragraph 7 (power to dissolve Commission) is amended as follows.

(2) After sub-paragraph (2) insert—
> "(2A) Any order under this paragraph may—
>> (a) establish new bodies corporate to receive any property, rights, liabilities or obligations vested by an order under this paragraph;
>> (b) amend, repeal or otherwise modify any enactment for the purpose of enabling any body established under any enactment to receive such property, rights, liabilities or obligations.".

(3) In sub-paragraph (3) (incidental, supplemental, consequential or transitional provision) for the words from "amendments" to the end substitute "provisions amending, repealing or otherwise modifying any enactment.".

(4) For sub-paragraph (7) (interpretation) substitute—
> "(7) In this paragraph—
>> "accountable public authority" means a body established under this paragraph or any other enactment;
>> "enactment" includes any instrument made under any enactment.".

GENERAL NOTE
  See notes to s.143 above.

## *General provisions*

### Orders, regulations and directions

**146.**—(1) Orders, regulations and directions under this Act may make different provision for different cases or descriptions of case, including different provision for different areas.

(2) Orders and regulations under this Act may contain such incidental, supplementary or transitional provisions and savings as the Secretary of State considers appropriate.

(3) Orders and regulations under this Act shall be made by statutory instrument which, except for—
(a) orders and regulations subject to affirmative resolution procedure (see sections 104(4), 105(4), 106(4) and 114(5)),
(b) orders under section 150(3), or
(c) regulations which only prescribe forms or particulars to be contained in forms,
shall be subject to annulment in pursuance of a resolution of either House of Parliament.

### Repeals and revocations

**147.** The enactments specified in Schedule 3 are repealed or revoked to the extent specified.

### Extent

**148.**—(1) The provisions of this Act extend to England and Wales.
(2) The following provisions of this Act extend to Scotland—
  Part II (construction contracts),
  Part III (architects),
  sections 126 to 128 (financial assistance for regeneration and development), and
  Part V (miscellaneous and general provisions), except—
>> (i) sections 141, 144 and 145 (which amend provisions which do not extend to Scotland), and
>> (ii) Part I of Schedule 3 (repeals consequential on provisions not extending to Scotland).

(3) The following provisions of this Act extend to Northern Ireland—
  Part III (architects), and

Part V (miscellaneous and general provisions), except—
> (i) sections 142 to 145 (home energy efficiency schemes and residuary bodies), and
> (ii) Parts I and III of Schedule 3 (repeals consequential on provisions not extending to Northern Ireland).

(4) Except as otherwise provided, any amendment or repeal by this Act of an enactment has the same extent as the enactment amended or repealed.

### Corresponding provision for Northern Ireland

**149.** An Order in Council under paragraph 1(1)(b) of Schedule 1 to the Northern Ireland Act 1974 (legislation for Northern Ireland in the interim period) which states that it is made only for purposes corresponding to those of Part II (construction contracts) or section 142 (home energy efficiency schemes)—

(a) shall not be subject to paragraph 1(4) and (5) of that Schedule (affirmative resolution of both Houses of Parliament), but
(b) shall be subject to annulment in pursuance of a resolution of either House of Parliament.

### Commencement

**150.**—(1) The following provisions of this Act come into force on Royal Assent—

section 146 (orders, regulations and directions),
sections 148 to 151 (extent, commencement and other general provisions).

(2) The following provisions of this Act come into force at the end of the period of two months beginning with the date on which this Act is passed—

sections 126 to 130 (financial assistance for regeneration and development),
section 141 (existing housing grants: meaning of exempt disposal),
section 142 (home energy efficiency schemes),
sections 143 to 145 (residuary bodies),
Part III of Schedule 3 (repeals consequential on Part IV) and section 147 so far as relating to that Part.

(3) The other provisions of this Act come into force on a day appointed by order of the Secretary of State, and different days may be appointed for different areas and different purposes.

(4) The Secretary of State may by order under subsection (3) make such transitional provision and savings as appear to him to be appropriate in connection with the coming into force of any provision of this Act.

### Short title

**151.** This Act may be cited as the Housing Grants, Construction and Regeneration Act 1996.

## SCHEDULES

Section 103 SCHEDULE 1

PRIVATE SECTOR RENEWAL: CONSEQUENTIAL AMENDMENTS

*Rent Act 1977 (c.42)*

1.—(1) Section 116 of the Rent Act 1977 (court order where tenant unwilling to consent to works) is amended as follows.

(2) In subsection (2), omit "any of paragraphs (a) to (c) of".

(3) For subsection (3) substitute—

"(3) The condition is that the works were specified in an application for a renovation grant, a common parts grant, a disabled facilities grant or an HMO grant under Chapter I of

Part I of the Housing Grants, Construction and Regeneration Act 1996 and the application has been approved.".

(4) In subsection (5), for the words from "under section 512(2)" to the end, substitute "under section 37 of the Housing Grants, Construction and Regeneration Act 1996.".

### *Housing Act 1985 (c.68)*

2. In section 47(4) of the Housing Act 1985 (limitation of service charges: deduct amount of grant), for the words from "Part XV" to "or conversion)" substitute "section 523 of the Housing Act 1985 (assistance for provision of separate service pipe for water supply) or any provision of Part I of the Housing Grants, Construction and Regeneration Act 1996 (grants, &c. for renewal of private sector housing) or any corresponding earlier enactment".

3. In section 48(3A) of the Housing Act 1985 (information as to relevant costs: grant), for the words from "Part XV" to the end substitute "section 523 of the Housing Act 1985 (assistance for provision of separate service pipe for water supply) or any provision of Chapter I of Part I of the Housing Grants, Construction and Regeneration Act 1996 (grants for renewal of private sector housing) or any corresponding earlier enactment".

4.—(1) In section 100(2) of the Housing Act 1985 (power to reimburse cost of tenant's improvements; grant), for "improvement grant" to "Part XV" substitute "renovation grant or common parts grant under Chapter I of Part I of the Housing Grants, Construction and Regeneration Act 1996 (grants for renewal of private sector housing)".

(2) In that section, omit subsection (2A).

5.—(1) In section 101(1) of the Housing Act 1985 (rent not to be increased on account of tenant's improvements: grant), for "improvement grant" to the end substitute "renovation grant or common parts grant under Chapter I of Part I of the Housing Grants, Construction and Regeneration Act 1996 (grants for renewal of private sector housing).".

(2) In that section, omit subsection (1A).

6. In section 190A of the Housing Act 1985 (repair notices and group repair schemes)—

(a) in subsection (2), for "subsection 130(1)" to the end substitute "subsection 66(1) of the Housing Grants, Construction and Regeneration Act 1996).".

(b) in subsection (5), for "Part VIII" to the end substitute "Chapter II of Part I of the Housing Grants, Construction and Regeneration Act 1996 (group repair schemes).".

7.—(1) In section 244 of the Housing Act 1985 (environmental works: no assistance where grant made), for subsection (3) substitute—

"(3) No such assistance shall be given towards works in respect of which an application for renovation grant or common parts grant under Chapter I of Part I of the Housing Grants, Construction and Regeneration Act 1996 (grants for renewal of private sector housing) has been approved.".

(2) In that section, omit subsection (3A).

8.—(1) In subsection (2)(b) of section 255 of the Housing Act 1985 (general powers of local housing authority not to include making grants), for "an improvement grant" to the end substitute "a renovation grant or common parts grant might be made under Chapter I of Part I of the Housing Grants, Construction and Regeneration Act 1996 (grants for renewal of private sector housing).".

(2) In that section, omit subsection (3).

9. In section 535(1)(a) of the Housing Act 1985 (exclusion of assistance under Part XV of that Act where grant application pending or approved), for the words from "an improvement grant" to "Part XV" substitute "renovation grant or common parts grant under Chapter I of Part I of the Housing Grants, Construction and Regeneration Act 1996 (grants for renewal of private sector housing).".

10. In section 605 of the Housing Act 1985 (consideration by local housing authority of housing conditions in their district), for subsection (1)(e) substitute—

"(e) Part I of the Housing Grants, Construction and Regeneration Act 1996 (grants, &c. for renewal of private sector housing).".

### *Landlord and Tenant Act 1985 (c.70)*

11.—(1) In subsection (1) of section 20A of the Landlord and Tenant Act 1985 (limitation of service charges: grant-aided works), for the words from "Part XV" to "conversion)" substitute "section 523 of the Housing Act 1985 (assistance for provision of separate service pipe for water supply) or any provision of Part I of the Housing Grants, Construction and Regeneration Act 1996 (grants, &c. for renewal of private sector housing) or any corresponding earlier enactment".

(2) In subsection (2) of that section—

(a) for "Part VIII of the Local Government and Housing Act 1989" substitute "Part I of the Housing Grants, Construction and Regeneration Act 1996"; and

(b) for "the outstanding balance determined in accordance with subsections (3) and (4) of section 130 of that Act" substitute "the balance of the cost determined in accordance with section 69(3) of the Housing Grants, Construction and Regeneration Act 1996".

12. In section 21 of the Landlord and Tenant Act 1985 (request for summary of relevant costs)—

(a) in subsection (5), for the words from "Part XV" to "conversion)" substitute "section 523 of the Housing Act 1985 (assistance for provision of separate service pipe for water supply) or any provision of Part I of the Housing Grants, Construction and Regeneration Act 1996 (grants, &c. for renewal of private sector housing) or any corresponding earlier enactment"; and

(b) in subsection (5B) for "Part VIII of the Local Government and Housing Act 1989" substitute "Chapter II of Part I of the Housing Grants, Construction and Regeneration Act 1996 or any corresponding earlier enactment".

### Housing Act 1988 (c.50)

13. In section 121(1) of the Housing Act 1988 (rent officers' functions), for "section 110" to the end substitute "section 31 of the Housing Grants, Construction and Regeneration Act 1996 applies.".

### Local Government and Housing Act 1989 (c.42)

14. In section 93(5) of the Local Government and Housing Act 1989 (general powers of local housing authority: works in renewal area), for "Part VIII of this Act" substitute "Part I of the Housing Grants, Construction and Regeneration Act 1996".

15.—(1) Section 169 of the Local Government and Housing Act 1989 (power of local authority and Secretary of State to provide professional, &c. services in relation to works) is amended as follows.

(2) In subsection (2)(b), for "section 114(3) or (4) above" substitute "section 23 of the Housing Grants, Construction and Regeneration Act 1996 (disabled facilities grants: purposes)".

(3) In subsection (2)(c), for "section 115(3) above" substitute "or under section 12 or 27 of the Housing Grants, Construction and Regeneration Act 1996 (renovation grants or HMO grants: purposes)".

(4) For subsection (2)(d) substitute—

"(d) works in relation to home repair assistance under sections 76 to 79 of the Housing Grants, Construction and Regeneration Act 1996.".

**Sections 118 and 125**                      SCHEDULE 2

Architects

Part I

New First Schedule to the 1931 Act

1. This is the Schedule to be substituted for the First Schedule to the 1931 Act—

**"Section 3**                      FIRST SCHEDULE

The Board and its committees

Part I

The Board

*Membership*

1. The Board shall consist of—
(a) seven elected members; and
(b) eight appointed members.

*Elected members*

2.—(1) The elected members shall be elected in accordance with an electoral scheme made by the Board, with the approval of the Privy Council, after consultation with such bodies as appear to the Board to be representative of architects.

(2) An electoral scheme under sub-paragraph (1) may be amended by the Board with the approval of the Privy Council and after consultation with such bodies as are mentioned in that sub-paragraph.

(3) The persons qualified—

(a)  to elect the elected members; and

(b)  to be elected as elected members,

are all those who are registered persons when the election is held.

### *Appointed members*

3.—(1) The appointed members shall be appointed by the Privy Council, after consultation with the Secretary of State and such other persons or bodies as the Privy Council think fit, to represent the interests of users of architectural services and the general public.

(2) No registered person shall be eligible for appointment as an appointed member.

### *Term of office*

4.—(1) Subject to sub-paragraphs (2) and (3), the term of office of a member of the Board is three years.

(2) A member may resign at any time by notice in writing addressed to the Registrar.

(3) The Board may by rules prescribe grounds (such as repeated absence from meetings or unacceptable professional conduct) on which any member may be removed from office and the procedure for removal.

5. A person who has held office as a member of the Board for a continuous period of six years may not be elected or appointed as a member until at least three years have elapsed since he last held office.

### *Casual vacancies*

6.—(1) Where a vacancy occurs among the members of the Board otherwise than by the expiry of a member's term of office—

(a)  if the vacancy is among the elected members, the Board shall appoint a registered person to fill it; and

(b)  if the vacancy is among the appointed members, the Privy Council shall appoint a person to fill it.

(2) Subject to paragraph 4(2) and (3), a person appointed under sub-paragraph (1) to fill a vacancy holds office until the date on which the term of office of the member whose vacancy he fills would have expired.

(3) A person appointed under sub-paragraph (1)(a) shall be regarded as an elected member and a person appointed under sub-paragraph (1)(b) shall be regarded as an appointed member.

### *Chairman*

7.—(1) The members of the Board shall elect a chairman from among themselves.

(2) The chairman—

(a)  may resign by notice in writing addressed to the Registrar; and

(b)  may be removed by a majority vote of the other members of the Board.

(3) Rules made by the Board may make provision for the appointment of a person to act as chairman in the event of a vacancy in the office of chairman or in such other circumstances as may be prescribed.

8. In the event of a tie in any vote of the Board the chairman shall have an additional casting vote.

### *Procedure*

9. The quorum of the Board shall be nine, of whom at least four shall be elected members and at least four shall be appointed members.

10. The Board may make rules governing its meetings and procedure.

### PART II

### THE PROFESSIONAL CONDUCT COMMITTEE

11. The Professional Conduct Committee shall consist of—

(a)  four elected members of the Board, including at least one whose address in the Register is in Scotland, or (if there is no elected member whose address in the Register is in Scotland or no such elected member who is willing to act) three elected members and one registered person whose address in the Register is in Scotland;

(b) three appointed members of the Board; and

(c) two persons nominated by the President of the Law Society.

12.—(1) The members of the Professional Conduct Committee shall elect a chairman from among themselves.

(2) The chairman—

(a) may resign by notice in writing addressed to the Registrar; and

(b) may be removed by a majority vote of the other members of the Professional Conduct Committee.

(3) Rules made by the Board may make provision for the appointment of a person to act as chairman in the event of a vacancy in the office of chairman or in such other circumstances as may be prescribed.

13.—(1) The quorum of the Professional Conduct Committee shall be one elected member of the Board, one appointed member of the Board and one person nominated by the President of the Law Society.

(2) Where the Committee is considering the case of a person whose address in the Register is in Scotland, the Committee is not quorate unless there is present a member of the Committee who is a registered person and whose address in the Register is in Scotland.

14. In the event of a tie in any vote of the Professional Conduct Committee the chairman shall have an additional casting vote; and in any proceedings relating to a registered person the additional vote shall be cast in favour of that person.

15. The Board may make rules governing the selection and term of office of members of the Professional Conduct Committee (including casual vacancies).

PART III

OTHER COMMITTEES

16. The Board may establish such committees as it considers appropriate to discharge any of its functions under this Act other than—

(a) prescribing fees under section 6(4), 6A(1A), 6B(1) or (3) or 7ZD(4); or

(b) acting under section 6(1), (2) or (5), 6A(1) or (1B), 6C(1) or 7ZE(1), (2) or (3),

or to assist the Board in the discharge by the Board of any of its functions.

17.—(1) Any committee established by the Board may include persons who are not members of the Board; but if a committee is established to discharge any function of the Board, the majority of the members of the committee must be members of the Board.

(2) Subject to that, the membership of any committee established by the Board shall be determined by the Board.

18. No vote of any committee established by the Board for the discharge of any of its functions shall be valid unless the majority of those voting are members of the Board.

19. The Board may make rules governing the term of office of members of any committee established by the Board (including casual vacancies) and the meetings and procedure (including chairmanship and quorum) of any committee established by the Board.

PART IV

GENERAL

20.—(1) The Board, the Professional Conduct Committee and any committee established by the Board may exercise its functions even though there is a vacancy among its members.

(2) No proceedings of the Board, the Professional Conduct Committee or any committee established by the Board are invalidated by any defect in the election or appointment of a member.

21. The Board may by rules provide for the payment to members of the Board, the Professional Conduct Committee or any committee established by the Board of—

(a) fees for attendance at meetings of the Board or committee; and

(b) travelling and subsistence allowances in respect of attendance at such meetings or the conduct of business of the Board or committee.

22.—(1) The Secretary of State may, after consultation with the Board and such other persons or bodies as he thinks fit, by order amend the provisions of this Schedule.

(2) An order under sub-paragraph (1) shall be made by statutory instrument which shall be subject to annulment in pursuance of a resolution of either House of Parliament.".

PART II

OTHER AMENDMENTS

*The 1931 Act*

2.—(1) Section 2 of the 1931 Act (interpretation) is amended as follows.

(2) For the definition of "the Council" substitute—

"The expression "the Board" means the Architects Registration Board.".

(3) In the definition of "registered person", for "registered under this Act" substitute "whose name is in the Register".

(4) In the definition of "prescribed", for "regulations made by the Council" substitute "rules made by the Board".

(5) In the definition of "the Register", for "kept in pursuance of this Act" substitute "of Architects".

(6) After that definition insert—

"The expression "the Registrar" means the Registrar of Architects appointed by the Board under section 4.

The expressions "penalty order", "suspension order" and "erasure order" shall be construed in accordance with sections 7ZB, 7ZC and 7ZD.

The expression "disciplinary order" has the meaning given by section 7ZA.".

3.—(1) Section 3 of the 1931 Act (constitution and functions of Architects' Registration Council) is amended as follows.

(2) In subsection (1), for the words from the beginning to "name," substitute "The Architects Registration Board shall be a body corporate".

(3) In subsection (2)—

(a) omit the first sentence, and

(b) in the second sentence, for "Council" (in both places) substitute "Board".

(4) For the sidenote substitute "The Board and its committees.".

4.—(1) Section 6A of the 1931 Act (European qualifications) is amended as follows.

(2) In subsection (1), for the words from "shall" to the end substitute "and has applied to the Registrar in the prescribed manner for registration in pursuance of this section is entitled to be registered.".

(3) After that subsection insert—

"(1A) The Board may require an applicant for registration in pursuance of this section to pay a fee of a prescribed amount.

(1B) The Board may by rules prescribe the information and evidence to be furnished to the Registrar in connection with an application for registration in pursuance of this section.".

(4) In subsection (7), for the words from "The Council" to "aware that" substitute "An application by a person for registration in pursuance of this section may be refused if".

(5) In subsection (8), for the words from "Council" to "applicant" substitute "Registrar shall serve on an applicant for registration in pursuance of this section written notice of the decision on his application".

(6) In subsection (9)—

(a) for "Council consult" substitute "Board consults", and

(b) for "Council of" substitute "Board of".

5.—(1) Section 7A of the 1931 Act (removal of name from Register: disqualification in another member State) is amended as follows.

(2) In subsection (1)—

(a) for "Council were" substitute "Board was",

(b) for "Council, on" substitute "Board, on", and

(c) for "cause his name to be removed" substitute "order the Registrar to remove his name".

(3) In subsection (2), for "7 of this Act" substitute "7ZA(1)".

(4) After that subsection insert—

"(3) Where the Board orders the Registrar to remove a person's name from the Register under this section, the Registrar shall serve written notice of the removal on the person as soon as is reasonably practicable.".

6.—(1) Section 9 of the 1931 Act (right of appeal against removal from Register) is amended as follows.

(2) For the words "by the removal" onwards substitute "by—

(a) his name not being re-entered in, or being removed from, the Register by virtue of section 6C(1);

(b) the making of a disciplinary order in relation to him; or

    (c) the Board ordering the Registrar to remove his name from the Register under section 7A,

may appeal to the High Court or the Court of Session within three months from the date on which notice of the decision or order concerned is served on him; and on an appeal under this section the Court may make any order which appears appropriate, and no appeal shall lie from any decision of the Court on such an appeal.".

(3) For the sidenote substitute "Appeals.".

7. In section 11 of the 1931 Act (removal of name from Register for failure to notify change of address), for "Council" (in each place) substitute "Registrar".

8. In section 12 of the 1931 Act (penalty for obtaining registration by false representation), for "wilfully" substitute "intentionally".

9. For section 13 of the 1931 Act (regulations) substitute—

**"Rules**

13.—(1) The Board may make rules generally for carrying out or facilitating the purposes of this Act.

(2) The Board shall, before making any rules under this Act, publish a draft of the rules and give those to whom the rules would be applicable an opportunity of making representations to the Board.".

10.—(1) Section 15 of the 1931 Act (supply of regulations and forms) is amended as follows.

(2) For "Council" substitute "Registrar".

(3) For "regulations" (in each place, including the sidenote) substitute "rules".

11.—(1) Section 16 of the 1931 Act (service of documents) is amended as follows.

(2) In subsection (1), for "to be sent" substitute "to be served".

(3) In subsection (2), for "to the removal from the Register of the name of any registered person" substitute "required to be served by section 6C(2), 7(4)(a), 7ZA(3) or 7A(3)".

12.—(1) Section 17 of the 1931 Act (defence for certain bodies corporate, firms and partnerships) is amended as follows.

(2) In paragraph (a), for "superintendent who is a registered person and" substitute "registered person".

(3) In paragraph (b), for the words from "and" to "who is" substitute "it is carried on by or under the supervision of".

(4) For the sidenote substitute "Defence for business under control and management of registered person.".

13. For section 18(2) of the 1931 Act (application to Northern Ireland) substitute—

"(2) This Act extends to Northern Ireland.".

*The 1938 Act*

14.—(1) Section 1A of the 1938 Act (visiting EC architects) is amended as follows.

(2) In subsections (2), (3) and (4), for "Council" (in each place) substitute "Registrar".

(3) In subsection (3), for "they consider" substitute "the Registrar considers".

(4) In subsection (6), for the words from "when" to the end substitute "when—

    (a) he is subject to a disqualifying decision in another member State;

    (b) his name has been removed from the Register pursuant to a suspension order or an erasure order and has not been re-entered; or

    (c) he is required under section 6C(1) of the principal Act to satisfy the Board of his competence to practise but has not done so.".

(5) In subsection (8), for the words from the beginning to "the regulation of" substitute "The provisions of, and of rules under, the principal Act relating to".

15. In section 3 of the 1938 Act (offence of practising while not registered), in the proviso—

(a) in paragraph (a), omit "of the Council" and "subsection (2) of section six of", and

(b) for paragraphs (b) and (c) substitute—

    "(b) in a case where the contravention is occasioned by the removal of the defendant's name from the Register in circumstances in which notice is required to be served on him—

        (i) that the notice had not been duly served before that date,

        (ii) that the time for bringing an appeal against the removal had not expired at that date, or

        (iii) that such an appeal had been duly brought, but had not been determined, before that date.".

16. In section 5 of the 1938 Act (construction and citation), in subsection (2), for the words from "Acts 1931 and" to the end substitute "Act 1931".

17. For section 6(1) of the 1938 Act (application to Northern Ireland) substitute—

"(1) This Act extends to Northern Ireland.".

*Other enactments*

18. In section 6 of the Inspection of Churches Measure 1955 (interpretation), in the definition of "qualified person", for "Architects Registration Acts 1931 to 1969" substitute "Architects Acts 1931 to 1996".

19. In section 52(1) of the Cathedrals Measure 1963 (interpretation), in the definition of "architect", for "Architects (Registration) Acts 1931 to 1938" substitute "Architects Acts 1931 to 1996".

20. In section 20(1) of the Care of Cathedrals Measure 1990 (interpretation), in the definition of "architect", for "Architects Registration Acts 1931 to 1969" substitute "Architects Acts 1931 to 1996".

PART III

TRANSITIONAL PROVISIONS AND SAVINGS

*First elections and appointments to the Board*

21.—(1) Part I of the First Schedule to the 1931 Act as substituted by Part I of this Schedule shall have effect before the appointed day so far as is necessary to enable the election and appointment of members of the Board to take office on that day.

(2) Until the appointed day references to the Board in paragraph 2 of that Schedule shall have effect as references to the Council.

(3) Where persons elected or appointed as members of the Board by virtue of this paragraph attend meetings before the appointed day in preparation for the conduct of business of the Board on or after that day, the Council may pay to them any such fees or travelling or subsistence allowances in respect of their attendance as appear appropriate.

(4) The term of office of the members of the Board appointed by the Privy Council (by virtue of this paragraph) to take office on the appointed day—

(a) is one year beginning with that day in the case of three of those members,

(b) is two years beginning with that day in the case of another three of those members, and

(c) is three years beginning with that day in the case of the remaining two members.

*Registration*

22. Where before the appointed day a person has duly applied for registration under the 1931 Act but no decision on the application has been made, the application shall be dealt with on and after the appointed day in the same way as an application duly made on or after that day (except that no further fee may be required to be paid).

23. Examinations in architecture which immediately before the appointed day were recognised by the Council for the purposes of subsection (1)(c) of section 6 of the 1931 Act (as it has effect before the substitution made by section 120 of this Act) shall (subject to rules made by the Board) be treated on and after that day as qualifications prescribed under subsection (1)(a) of that section (as it has effect after that substitution).

24. Section 6B of the 1931 Act shall have effect as if the reference in subsection (3) of that section to a person whose name has been removed from the Register under subsection (2) of that section included a reference to a person whose name was removed from the Register under section 13(5) of the 1931 Act before the appointed day.

25. The first reference to the Board in section 7A(1) of the 1931 Act shall be construed, in relation to the entry of a name in the Register at a time before the appointed day, as a reference to the Council.

*Discipline*

26. Where before the appointed day—

(a) the Discipline Committee has begun an inquiry into a case in which it is alleged that a registered person has been guilty of conduct disgraceful to him in his capacity as an architect, but

(b) the Council has not decided whether to remove his name from the Register,

the case shall be referred to the Professional Conduct Committee which shall consider whether he is guilty of unacceptable professional conduct or serious professional incompetence.

27.—(1) Subject to sub-paragraph (2), the provisions substituted by section 121 of this Act for section 7 of the 1931 Act have effect in relation to anything done or omitted to be done before the appointed day as in relation to anything done or omitted to be done after that day.

(2) The Professional Conduct Committee—

(a) may only make a disciplinary order in respect of anything done, or omitted to be done, by a person before the appointed day if the Council could have removed his name from the

Register under section 7 of the 1931 Act (as it had effect before the substitution made by section 121 of this Act), and

(b) may not make a reprimand or penalty order in respect of anything so done or omitted to be so done.

#### Pre-commencement removals and disqualifications

28.—(1) Where a person's name has been removed from the Register under section 7 of the 1931 Act before the appointed day, he may at any time on or after that day apply to the Board for his name to be re-entered in the Register.

(2) If he does so, the Board may direct that his name shall be re-entered in the Register.

(3) The Registrar shall serve on a person who applies for his name to be re-entered in the Register under this paragraph written notice of the decision on his application within the pre-scribed period after the date of the decision.

(4) The Board may require a person whose name is re-entered in the Register under this paragraph to pay a fee of such amount, not exceeding the fee then payable by an applicant for registration in pursuance of section 6 of the 1931 Act, as may be prescribed.

29. A person may appeal under section 9 of the 1931 Act against—

(a) the removal of his name from the Register before the appointed day, or

(b) a determination of the Council before the appointed day that he be disqualified for regis-tration during any period,

within three months from the date on which notice of the removal or determination was served on him.

30. Section 1A(6)(b) of the 1938 Act shall have effect as if it included a reference to a period of disqualification imposed by the Council.

#### Offence of practising while not registered

31. The amendments made in sections 1 and 3 of the 1938 Act and section 17 of the 1931 Act by section 123(1), (3) and (4) of this Act do not apply in relation to an offence committed before the appointed day.

32. The repeal made in section 3 of the 1938 Act by section 123(2) of this Act applies in relation to an offence committed before the appointed day (as well as in relation to one committed on or after that day).

#### Transfer of Fund

33. If the transfer of the assets of the Fund takes place after the appointed day, the repeal by this Act of sections 1(1) and (4) to (6), 3 and 4 of the 1969 Act shall not come into force until the transfer is made; and during the period beginning with the appointed day and ending with the transfer references in those provisions to the Council shall have effect as references to the Board.

#### Supplementary

34.—(1) In this Part of this Schedule—

(a) "the Board" means the Architects Registration Board, and

(b) other expressions used in the 1931 Act have the same meanings as in that Act.

(2) In this Part of this Schedule "appointed day" means the day appointed by the Secretary of State for the coming into force of this Part of this Act.

35. Nothing in this Schedule prejudices the operation of section 16 or 17 (effect of repeals) of the Interpretation Act 1978.

**Section 147**               SCHEDULE 3

REPEALS AND REVOCATIONS

PART I

GRANTS, &C FOR RENEWAL OF PRIVATE SECTOR HOUSING

| Chapter | Short title | Extent of repeal |
|---------|-------------|------------------|
| 1977 c. 42. | Rent Act 1977. | In section 116(2), the words "any of paragraphs (a) to (c) of". |
| 1985 c. 68. | Housing Act 1985. | Section 100(2A). <br> Section 101(1A). <br> Section 244(3A). <br> Section 255(3). |
| 1989 c. 42. | Local Government and Housing Act 1989. | Part VIII. <br> In Schedule 11, paragraph 52, paragraph 63, and paragraphs 66 to 69. |
| 1993 c. 10. | Charities Act 1993. | In Schedule 6, paragraph 30, the words "The Local Government and Housing Act 1989 section 138(1)". |
| 1994 c. 19. | Local Government (Wales) Act 1994. | In Schedule 8, paragraph 10(1) and (2). |
| 1994 c. 29. | Police and Magistrates' Courts Act 1994. | In Schedule 4, paragraph 40. |

PART II

ARCHITECTS

| Chapter | Short title | Extent of repeal |
|---------|-------------|------------------|
| 21 & 22 Geo. 5 c. 33. | Architects (Registration) Act 1931. | In section 3, in subsection (2), the first sentence and subsections (3) and (4). <br> Section 5. <br> In section 6A(1), the words "Subject to the provisions of this Act,". <br> In section 7A(1), the words "of this Act". <br> Section 8. <br> The Second Schedule. <br> The Third Schedule. |
| 1 & 2 Geo. 6 c. 54. | Architects Registration Act 1938. | In section 1(3), the words "the words "Registered Architects" in subsection (3) of section three of the principal Act, and for", "respectively" and "the word "Architects" and". <br> In section 3, the words "of the Council" and "subsection (2) of section six of". |
| 1969 c. 42. | Architects Registration (Amendment) Act 1969. | The whole Act. |
| 1977 c. 45. | Criminal Law Act 1977. | In Schedule 6, the entry relating to the Architects Registration Act 1938. |
| S.I. 1987/1824. | Architects' Qualifications (EEC Recognition) Order 1987. | Article 4. |
| 1995 c. 40. | Criminal Procedure (Consequential Provisions) (Scotland) Act 1995. | In Schedule 2, in Part II, the entry relating to the Architects Registration Act 1938. |

PART III

FINANCIAL ASSISTANCE FOR REGENERATION AND DEVELOPMENT

| Chapter | Short title | Extent of repeal |
|---------|-------------|------------------|
| 1986 c. 63. | Housing and Planning Act 1986. | Part III. <br> In section 58(1) and (2), the words "Part III (financial assistance for urban regeneration);". |
| 1993 c. 28. | Leasehold Reform, Housing and Urban Development Act 1993. | Section 174. <br> In section 188(6), the words "174,". |

# INDEX

Generally, references are to the relevant section or Schedule number of the Act. References to the commentary to the section or Schedule are denoted by the letter 'N'. Thus the reference s.35N is to the commentary to section 35 of the Act.

[3]

[4]